OCR HISTORY B

Race and American Society, 1865–1970s

Andrew Pickering | Series Editors: Martin D W Jones

www.heinemann.co.uk

✓ Free online support
✓ Useful weblinks
✓ 24 hour online ordering

0845 630 33 33

Heinemann

Part of Pearson

Heinemann is an imprint of Pearson Education Limited, a company incorporated in
England and Wales, having its registered office at Edinburgh Gate, Harlow, Essex, CM20 2JE.
Registered company number: 872828. www.heinemann.co.uk. Heinemann is a registered
trademark of Pearson Education Limited

Text © Andrew Pickering

First published 2009

13
10 9 8 7 6 5 4 3 2

British Library Cataloguing in Publication Data is available from the British Library on request.

ISBN 978-0435312312

Edited by Charonne Prosser
Original illustrations © Pearson Oxford
Cover photo/illustration © British Library
Typeset by Saxon Graphics Limited
Printed in the UK by Ashford Colour Press Ltd., Gosport, Hampshire.

The author and publisher would like to thank the following individuals and organisations for permission to
reproduce photographs:

Chapter 2 Source 3 © Library of Congress, Source 10 © Getty/Hulton Archive, Source 12 © Corbis/Bettmann;
Chapter 3 Source 9 © Smithsonian Institute; Chapter 4 Source 5 © New York Public Library;
Chapter 5 Source 7 © Getty/Hulton Archive; Chapter 6 © Corbis/Bettmann;
Chapter 7 Source 23 © Getty/Hulton Archive/David Fenton

Every effort has been made to contact copyright holders of material reproduced in this book. Any omissions
will be rectified in subsequent printings if notice is given to the publishers.

Websites
There are links to relevant websites in this book. In order to ensure that the links are up-to-date,
that the links work, and that the sites are not inadvertently linked to sites that could be
considered offensive, we have made the links available on the Heinemann website at
www.heinemann.co.uk/hotlinks. When you access the site, the express code is **2312P**

Contents

Notes for teachers

This book, *Race and American Society 1865–1970s* is designed to support OCR's History B specification. It is relevant to the following unit: Using Historical Evidence (F984), Topic 4.

Each chapter uses activities, sources and the Exam Café to consolidate learning and help students develop a sound understanding of the topic.

How to use this book

Each unit in OCR GCE History B is designed to be introduced through a consideration of the historical concepts. The modes of historical thinking should preface the start of every new topic, and might also make valuable conclusions too. Teaching programmes might adopt a dynamic pattern of alternating between theory and topic content, the one buttressing, developing and reinforcing the other.

In line with the Unit F983 specification this book covers approximately one hundred years of the relevant period and encourages students to develop an understanding of the issues connected with the use of historical sources and their interpretation.

It encourages students to:

- Understand the differing and changing attitudes towards racial minorities and why these changed over time
- Understand the role of individuals and organisations in the history of race and American society
- Use a range of historical evidence to evaluate interpretations
- Consider why historical sources are useful but also raise problems and issues for an historian using them.

Methods of assessment

The AS GCE is made up of two units that are externally assessed. There are four units at AS of which candidates do two, either:

- Historical Explanation – British History, with Using Historical Evidence – Non-British History
- Historical Explanation – Non-British History, with Using Historical Evidence – British History.

Historical Explanation is assessed by a written paper, 1.5 hours for 50 marks. Candidates answer **one** question from a choice of two questions for their chosen period. Questions are structured in two parts; two out of the three historical explanations (explaining events, explaining ideas, attitudes and beliefs, explaining actions) will be examined in each two-part question.

Using Historical Evidence is assessed by a written paper, 1.5 hours for 50 marks. Candidates answer **two** questions for their chosen period. The first question is worth a maximum of 35 marks, the second question a maximum of 15 marks. Questions are source based with five to seven sources per option. The first question requires students to use the sources and their own knowledge to evaluate and possibly amend an interpretation. The second question will require candidates to analyse the sources for their usefulness and their problems.

Race and American Society 1865–1970s is a Using Historical Evidence topic – and thus will be examined by two source based questions.

Notes for students

How to use this book

This book has been specifically written to support you through Unit F983, Topic 2 of the OCR B GCE History course: *Race and American Society 1865–1970s*. You should also refer back to this book during your revision. The Exam Café section at the end of the book will be particularly helpful as you prepare for your exam; you should refer to it regularly throughout the course.

The book includes the following features:

■ Sources
A wide variety of sources throughout the book will allow you to practise your historical skills.

> Source 9 Uncle Thomas
>
> *Today's Uncle Tom doesn't wear a handkerchief on his head. This modern, twentieth-century Uncle Thomas now often wears a top hat. He's usually well-dressed and well-educated. He's often the personification of culture and refinement. The twentieth-century Uncle Thomas sometimes speaks with a Yale or Harvard [top American universities] accent. Sometimes he is known as Professor, Doctor, Judge, and Reverend, even Right Reverend Doctor. This twentieth-century Uncle Thomas is a professional Negro… by that I mean his profession is being a Negro for the white man.*
>
> From Malcolm X and Alex Haley, *The Autobiography of Malcolm X*, published in 1965.

■ Activities
These have been designed to help you understand the specification content and develop your historical skills.

> **ACTIVITY**
>
> 1 What does Source 9 reveal of the extent to which racial equality had been achieved by the middle of the 20th century?
>
> 2 Who do you think Malcolm X was thinking of when he referred to the 'Right Reverend Doctor'? Why did he consider this person an 'Uncle Tom'?

■ Think like an historian
You should be thinking like an historian throughout your history course. Questions are asked about the content to encourage you to think like this; sometimes you really should just think through these ideas!

> **THINK LIKE AN HISTORIAN**
>
> To what extent and why did the world wars change race relations in the USA?

■ Exam tips
These highlight common errors and give you advice about exam preparation to help you achieve the best grade you can.

> **EXAM TIP**
>
> Look for evidence in the selection of sources provided in the exam for ways in which things changed across the period. A quick comparison of Sources 8 and 9, for example, reveals how the phrase 'Uncle Tom' had different connotations at the start and at the end of the period.

■ Definitions
Definitions of new words can be found in the margin close to where the word appears in the text to help put the word in context.

> **Civil Rights Movement**
>
> Term usually used to describe the struggle for equality in post-Second World War America.

■ Key Questions
These feature at the start of each chapter and encourage you to think about key issues and questions.

> **Key Questions:**
>
> 1 What were the attitudes of Americans towards racial minorities?
>
> 2 How did these change over time?
>
> 3 Why did these attitudes change?

■ Exam Café
In our unique Exam Café you'll find lots of ideas to help you prepare for your exams. You'll see the Exam Café at the end of the book. You can **Relax** because there's handy revision advice

from fellow students, **Refresh your memory** with summaries and checklists of the key ideas you need to revise and **Get the result!** through practising exam-style questions, accompanied by hints and tips on getting the very best grades.

Introduction

Congratulations! You are studying the most exciting and useful of the six AS/A2 History specifications. OCR's History B gets to grips with what History actually is. Famously, the author of *The Go-Between* said "The past is a foreign country; they do things differently there." Spec B will teach you how to understand that other world: how to judge the surviving evidence; how to make sense of the past by putting that evidence together; how and why that evidence generates rival interpretations of the past; and how to measure the significance of people and their actions. Through Spec B, you will see why History is alive with argument and debate, always being rethought and revised. Along the way, you will also learn to assess the motives of our ancestors and the consequences of their actions. That matters, for their decisions shaped our world; their tomorrows are our yesterdays.

Heinemann's series of books are tailored to meet the requirements of Spec B. Whichever topics you are studying, you have to learn how to think like a historian. *Historical Explanation and Using Historical Evidence (AS)* and *Historical Significance and Historical Controversies (A2)* will teach you the skills that you need for success. This book covers all the issues underpinning the eight AS topics of Units F981/F982 Historical Explanation and the eight topics of F983/F984 Using Historical Evidence; and the eight A2 topics in Units F985/F986 Historical Controversies and your personal study (F987).

Using this book will develop your thinking and understanding. Ideas and issues are highlighted throughout. Case studies with sources and activities set you problems to consider. 'Think like an historian' questions encourage you to see the bigger picture. Exam Tips work on your question skills. All will help you when you are starting to study a topic as well keeping you on course during the term – and remember to refer back to them when revising for mocks and then the real thing.

Don't overlook the Exam Café section, which is not just for revision – its focused advice and help are always on hand. The tips, revision checklists and advice show you how to write better essays. 'Get the result!' offers student answers with feedback and advice which should help you to improve your own answers.

Using historical evidence

History is not the story of everything that happened. The past is not a one way street. Events might have turned out differently. Equally, the surviving evidence can generate alternative accounts of the past. History starts when comparisons and connections are made. History really comes to life when those comparisons and connections are analysed and their relative importance is established. So, focus on understanding the patterns. The past has to be given meaning.

Chapter 2 of this book introduces you to the range of sources available for the study of race and American society. All offer the historian opportunities to find out about the past but often they present problems when the historian tries to interpret them. Sources, as the chapter explains, are, by definition, singular and each is just a piece of a vast historical jigsaw. If you spend some time working through Chapter 2 you will be in a better position to reflect upon the range and relative value of the sources you will have to analyse in the exam. The activities labelled Using Historical Evidence will give you useful practice in working with groups of sources.

Be alert to what the sources can offer you. The first step is to mine them for information, but that is using them at the most basic level. The next step is to use them for reference: to illustrate a point or start a discussion. But even at this point, you are still hardly *using* the sources. You will also need to evaluate them both singly and as a set. You will need to interpret what is in them. The most effective approach is to use sources as an evidence bank from which to build argument and counter-argument. So interrogate sources carefully. Be forensic and sceptical when you examine, verify and compare sources – but always treat evidence with respect. Evidence is partial in both senses of the word, that is, incomplete and one-sided. The obvious temptation is to reject such evidence. You may have done that at GCSE, dismissing a source as biased, but look again. If it is one-sided, its very subjectivity is of great value because of the attitudes and prejudices it reveals. These help us 'get under the skin' of the past.

Understanding the civil rights movement

The civil rights movement is the most important upheaval in recent American history. How is it to be understood and its meaning interpreted? The most common versions explain the process as only really starting with the Supreme Court's decision in *Brown v. Board of Education* (1954) and ending with the assassination of Martin Luther King (1968). Such explanations pivot on a charismatic leader who led a non-violent movement of African Americans and supportive whites against the legal and social barriers to equality. This book will show you that the evidence reveals a more complicated picture. Through the sources, you will hear radical voices that mainstream interpretations play down: deep divisions with the African-American cause; eloquent leaders preaching violent struggle; campaigns aimed at removing economic barriers to equality. The history of oppressed peoples is especially liable to being used politically. The historian's job is to keep questioning the assumptions embedded in all interpretations. Can they be supported by the evidence?

You will read here the words of many people explaining passionately-held beliefs. To us now, some are repugnant. Vicious prejudice does not belong just in the past, a phenomenon of the era of the Atlantic slave trade or of Nazi Germany. It divides nations and peoples in our world, as Bosnia, Tibet and Burma demonstrate. So listen carefully to these voices as they speak to you. Your task is to understand them and their world in their context.

Acknowledgements

The Publishers and authors wish to thank the following copyright holders for the extracts from:

Graph: 'Number and Percent of African Americans' by Michael Siegel, used by courtesy of The Schomburg Center for Research in Black Culture, The New York Public Library; 'Black population, urban and rural, 1960' from *Economic Geography* Volume 48, issue 1, used by permission of John Wiley and Sons, Inc.; 'The Southern Manifesto' Congressional Record, 84th Congress Second Session, vol. 102, part 4 (March 12, 1956); 'Will join rights aides in Mississippi' by Lillian McLaughlin © 1964, printed with permission by The Des Moines Register; 'The Migration Numbers' used by courtesy of The Schomburg Center for Research in Black Culture, The New York Public Library; *The Autobiography of Malcolm X* by Malcolm X and Alex Haley © 1964 by Alex Haley and Malcolm X © 1965 by Alex Haley and Betty Shabazz, used by permission of Random House, Inc.; extracts from *The Civil Rights Movement* by B. J. Dierenfield © 2004 used by permission of Pearson Education; extracts from *Race Relations in the USA, 1863–1980* by Vivienne Saunders © 2006 reproduced by permission of Hodder & Stoughton Ltd; 'Black Leaders of the Nineteenth Century' © 1988 by the Board of Trustees of the University of Illinois used with permission of the University of Illinois Press; *Lifting as we Climb* by Dulcie Straughan from Media History Monographs, 2005–2006 used by permission of the author; 'The Niagara Movement Speech' from *The Autobiography* by W.E.B. Dubois © 1968 used by permission of International Publishers; Platform adopted by the National Negro Committee, 1909 used by permission of the NAACP; '*The History and Rhetoric of the NAACP*' by Stephen Collins and Katherine Scott Sturdevant published by *Black History Bulletin*, 22 June 2008, used by permission; extracts from *Black Civil Rights in America* by K. Verney © 2000 used by permission of Taylor and Francis Books Ltd; *Prejudice and Your Child* by Kenneth B. Clark © 1955 by Beacon Press, 1963 by Beacon Press, renewed 1983 by Kenneth B. Clark, reprinted by permission of Beacon Press, Boston; Daisy Bates, excerpts from *The Long Shadow of Little Rock* © 1962, 1986 by Daisy Bates reprinted with the permission of the University of Arkansas Press; Interview with Melba Pattilo from *Eyes on the Prize* used by permission of Washington University Film and Media Archive; Martin Luther King, reprinted by arrangement with The Heirs to the Estate of Martin Luther King Jr., c/o Writers House as agent for the proprietor New York, NY © 1963 Dr Martin Luther King Jr, copyright renewed 1991 Coretta Scott King; extract from *Cesar Chavez: Autobiography of La Causa* by J. Levy published by Minnesota University Press; extract from 'The Problem of American Conservation' by Alan Brinkley from *American Historical Review* used by permission of University of Chicago Press; extract from *The Civil Rights Movement* by J.E. Davis © 2001 published by Wiley-Blackwell; extract from *Death of Rhythm and Blues* by Nelson George © 1988 used by permission of Sarah Lazin Books; 'Message to the Grassroots' by Malcolm X © 1965, 1989 by Betty Shabass and Pathfinder Press reprinted with permission; 'The Black Panther Party's 10 Point Platform' by Bobby Seale and Huey Newton from *Seize the Time* by Bobby Seale © 1970 published by Random House used by kind permission of the author; extract from *Revolutionary Suicide* by Huey P. Newton © 1973 by Stronghold Consolidated Productions, Inc., reprinted by permission of Houghton Mifflin Harcourt Publishing Company; extracts by Vernon Bellecourt from *American Civil Rights: Primary Sources* by Phillis Engelbert; *The Day the Police Rioted* by Herman Baca © 2005 used by permission of La Prensa, San Diego; 'Verdict of Booker T. Washington' from *The Souls of Black Folk* by W.E.B. Dubois © 1994 used by permission of Dover Publications

Race and American Society: change and continuity

Overview

The history of race and American society between 1865 and the 1970s is the complex story of people and their organisations, changing views and the clash of beliefs, and the impact of events and circumstances both within America and abroad. These include the following:

Individuals and groups:

- Activists such as Booker T. Washington and Rosa Parks
- Racial groups such as the NAACP and the Ku Klux Klan
- Politicians such as President Roosevelt and President Eisenhower
- Institutions such as Congress and the Supreme Court

Ideas and beliefs:

- Democracy
- Segregation
- Supremacy
- Pan-Africanism

Events and circumstances:

- Migrations
- The World Wars
- The Great Depression
- Assassinations

Sometimes these acted as forces of change and sometimes they prevented it. We need look no further than the fact that Americans elected their first black president in 2008 to see that huge changes have occurred in this history, but the processes by which change was achieved are sometimes very hard to unravel, and they demand the rigorous and critical examination of the available evidence. This chapter introduces, in outline, the story of those changes and many of the reasons for how they occurred as they did and when they did.

EXAM TIP

Change and development across the period studied is a key element of the assessment criteria for this unit. In the exam you will need to be able to show, through your own knowledge, that you can place sources in their historical context and that you can use this in your evaluation.

Key Questions:

1   What were the attitudes of Americans towards racial minorities?

2   How did these change over time?

3   Why did these attitudes change?

Racial groups: patterns of growth and change 1865–1970s

Modern America is a multicultural society comprising a population that is as ethnically diverse as any on the planet. With increasing difficulty, as the proportion of 'mixed race' Americans rises, individuals continue to be defined by their apparent ethnicity and are categorised in groups such as:

White Americans

Black Americans

Hispanic Americans

Native Americans

European Americans

African Americans

Asian Americans

Such terms are immensely problematic. For example, the term 'Native Americans' is now used to describe the aboriginals of the northern part of the continent (once known as 'Red Indians'), but in the first half of the 20th century denoted those of descent from the first British settlers. These Native Americans have been vastly outnumbered by those descended from immigrants from other parts of the world.

Although all of these groups have an important place in the history of race and American society, and several are addressed in this book, for the period 1865 to 1970 the subject is dominated by the relationship of the majority white population to the largest of the ethnic minorities, the African-American population. At the time of the American Civil War (1861–65) African Americans comprised almost 15 per cent of the total population; most in the South were slaves; and virtually all, North and South, were the children or grandchildren of slaves. This then, in some respects, is the continuation of America's African slavery story and its impact upon the world in which we live today.

Population growth in America was spectacular between 1860 and 1970.

Census year	Population in millions	Percentage of population comprising African Americans
1860	31.5	14.1%
1870	40	12.7%
1880	50	13.1%
1890	63	11.9%
1900	76	11.6%
1910	93.5	10.7%
1920	106	9.9%
1930	123	9.7%
1940	131.5	9.8%
1950	150.5	10%
1960	179	10.6%
1970	205	11.1%

■ **Table 1.1** Population growth in the USA 1860–1970

Hispanic Americans

American citizens with Spanish American origins.

Native Americans

Term now used to describe the aboriginals of the northern part of the American continent, once known as 'Red Indians'. In the first half of the 20th century it denoted those of descent from the first British settlers.

African Americans

Formerly known by such problematic terms as 'Negro Americans' or 'Black Americans', this term is accepted, presently, as the best way to describe American citizens who are identified as, or identify themselves as, having ancestors who originated in the African continent.

In demographic terms the most important development regarding African Americans in the period 1865 to 1970 was that of internal migration, notably the '**Great Migration**' of the inter-war years. A combination of three factors helps explain why so many people in this period moved from the rural South to industrial cities, particularly in the North:

- Discriminatory treatment in the South
- Rural poverty
- Industrial and urban growth and labour shortages in northern cities, especially during wartime.

the 'Great Migration'

Internal migration, particularly in the inter-war years, in which large numbers of people, including a high proportion of African Americans, moved from the rural South to industrial cities, particularly in the North.

THINK LIKE AN HISTORIAN

Look at Figures 1.1 and 1.2.

1 How are tables like this collated?

2 What are the problems with such methods in producing accurate results?

3 What are the problems in trying to define individuals in multiracial societies by such terms as 'Black' or 'African American'?

4 What are the limitations of these statistics for understanding the demographic history (i.e. population history) of modern America?

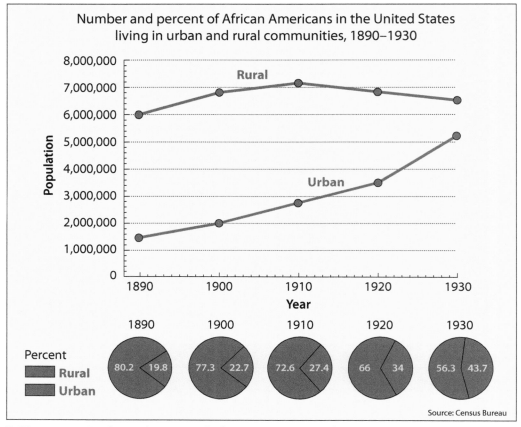

Source: Census Bureau

▌ **Figure 1.1** Number and percent of African Americans in the United States living in urban and rural communities, 1890–1930
Source: *The Schomburg Centre for Research in Black Culture, The New York Public Library*

ACTIVITY

Test your understanding of the key concepts of **change** and **continuity** by reviewing the ways in which the pattern of African-American population history developed between the 1860s and 1970. Use the evidence of Table 1.1 and Figures 1.1 and 1.2 in forming your answer. Try to find elements of continuity as well as change by asking yourself 'What changed? What stayed much the same?' On the basis of the available evidence do you agree with the interpretation that 'Continuity outweighed change in the pattern of African-American population history between 1860 and 1970'? If you disagree, suggest an amended interpretation. Think carefully about what changed most and try to identify periods in which changes were particularly evident.

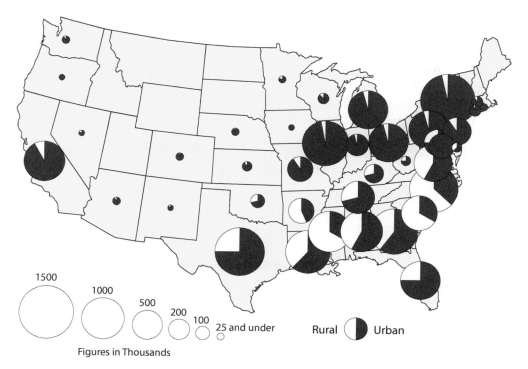

Figure 1.2 Black population, urban and rural, 1960
Source: *STOR, Economic Geography, Vol. 48, No. 1*

THINK LIKE AN HISTORIAN

1   Of what value are these diagrams as evidence for historians interested in the migration of African Americans in modern times?

2   What are their limitations?

3   What can the historian infer from this data regarding the issues of change and continuity in America's population history in the period 1860–1970?

Immigration

Much of America's population growth in the period can be explained by continuing high levels of immigration. In three decades, 1890 to 1920, 18 million immigrants arrived from all over the world, including Europe, Mexico, China and Japan. Like the presence of African Americans in the Southern states, they made a bigger impact in some places, the Irish in New York for example, than others; immigrant populations were not distributed evenly and urban environments fostered 'ghetto' communities based upon common ethnic backgrounds and cultures. Many immigrants became potential targets of the **KKK** because they did not conform to the white, Christian-Protestant ideal of the European-American supremacists.

From the middle years of the 19th century waves of Chinese immigrants had settled in America, providing cheap and reliable labour for such projects as the building of the railroads. These Chinese Americans, typically, were treated very badly by the white majority, paid miserable wages for the least desirable jobs and sometimes victimised in the **ghettoes**, the '**Chinatowns**' in which they lived, by white mobs. Furthermore they were excluded from the citizenship rights in the 15th Amendment of the Constitution (see Chapter 3). Like African Americans in the '**Jim Crow**' years, Chinese and Japanese children were prevented from attending white schools.

KKK (The Ku Klux Klan)

A white-supremacist organisation founded in the South in the late 1860s.

Ghettoes

Communities living close together based upon common ethnic backgrounds and cultures.

Chinatowns

Ghettoes in American cities inhabited mainly by people of Chinese origin.

'Jim Crow'

Laws passed in the southern states of America from the late 19th century legalising the segregation of African Americans and white Americans.

**THINK LIKE
AN HISTORIAN**

In what ways, if at all, do you think changing patterns of immigration into America might have changed the attitudes of the white majority to other races?

The Chinese Exclusion Act of 1882 prevented further Chinese immigration for ten years. The National Origins Act of 1924 was designed, in part, to prevent the immigration of anyone of Asian origin. When the Second World War broke out the Japanese community was further subjected to institutionalised racial intolerance when over 100,000 Japanese Americans were interned in overcrowded camps that were little more than temporary prisons. Despite all this many Japanese Americans, like thousands of African Americans, fought in the American armed forces during the war. The American-Japanese community received some recompense after the war when President Truman drew up the American Evacuation Claims Act to help those who had had property confiscated as part of the internment process.

Conditions and opportunities for these American-Asian communities improved in the aftermath of the Second World War as such things as segregation in educational establishments were successfully challenged and the attitude of white society generally towards racial minorities softened.

The racist immigration rules, that favoured white Europeans, were finally dismantled in 1968 when the 1965 Immigration Act came into effect. This massively increased the size of the Mexican-American population which was also subjected to the racial intolerance of the white majority.

The situation in 1865 – differing attitudes towards slavery

A common misconception is the assumption that the Northern States went to war between 1861 and 1865 in order to eradicate slavery in the Southern States. Nevertheless, despite widespread hostility in the North as well as the South to the concept of emancipation, this is what was achieved when the conflict came to an end. Crucially the attitude of President Lincoln, leading loyal states against the rebels in the South, seems to have hardened against slavery as the war progressed, not least because around 10 per cent of his army by the end of the war comprised men of African descent. Despite personal beliefs that white people were superior to black, Lincoln agreed with abolitionists that slavery contravened the principles of America's Declaration of Independence. In so doing he occupied the middle ground between **white supremacists** and ardent abolitionists and, largely for political reasons, such as the need to dissuade Britain from shipping out further arms to the South, he became identified with emancipation within months of war breaking out. For Southerners this represented the threat of a ruined slave-dependent economy. In the North too there were concerns that the emancipation of slaves would upset the economy with the arrival of thousands of ex-slaves looking for employment in Northern towns. For racists everywhere the cause of racial equality was intolerable.

White supremacists

Those who believe that people of Caucasian ethnic origin are superior, for example, intellectually, to the other races.

The era of reform and reconstruction

The period of reform and **reconstruction** after the American Civil War promoted racial equality, primarily, through three amendments to the Constitution:

the Reconstruction

The period of reform and reconstruction after the American Civil War promoted racial equality, primarily, through three amendments to the Constitution.

- The 13th Amendment: outlawing slavery
- The 14th Amendment: guaranteeing full citizenship for all Americans
- The 15th Amendment: providing universal suffrage for all men.

In addition a Republican-dominated Congress (see Chapter 3) pushed through the Civil Rights Acts of 1866 and 1875 which promoted political equality (1866) and the ending of segregation in all public areas except schools (1875). In retaliation to this 'reconstruction' white supremacists organised the Ku Klux Klan (KKK) which appeared in the late 1860s.

Timeline

1852	Publication of Harriet Beecher Stowe's anti-slavery novel *Uncle Tom's Cabin*. Her passive 'Uncle Tom' would be used in the 1960s as a term of derision for African Americans prepared to make compromises in the struggle for equal rights.
1859	John Brown raided the federal arsenal at Harpers Ferry, Virginia, to gain weapons and ammunition for a slave revolt. Brown was hanged but became a martyr to the cause of emancipation and a role model for those supporting a more 'physical' approach in the struggle for equal rights.
1865	End of the American Civil War. Ratification of the 13th Amendment outlawing slavery.
1866	The Civil Rights Act of 1866 gave African Americans full citizenship and equal rights. The Memphis Massacre in which 46 African Americans were killed and many homes, schools and churches were burned to the ground by a white mob and police. Founding of the Ku Klux Klan.
1867	Start of the 'Reconstruction' with acts passed granting the vote to freed slaves in the Southern states.
1868	Ratification of the 14th Amendment giving full citizenship to all born or naturalised Americans. Massacre in Louisiana in which around 250 African Americans were killed.
1870	Ratification of the 15th Amendment enfranchising African Americans.
1875	The Clinton Massacre in which over 200 African Americans were killed in Mississippi. The 1875 Civil Rights Act which prohibited segregation in all public areas except schools.

The age of 'Jim Crow'

Following the period of 'Reconstruction', the United States entered a phase of unprecedented industrial growth. Although the average income per capita rose substantially, the new wealth was unevenly distributed. Small farmers struggled to keep going, and industrial workers combined together in trade unions to combat the oppressive practices of their employers. This '**Gilded Age**', as it was nicknamed, came to an end with a period of depression known as '**the Panic**' lasting from 1893 until 1896 as banks collapsed following excessive investment in failed railway building schemes. In this period unemployment soared to a level of around 18%.

In this economic context hostility towards the newly emancipated Black community in the South developed. The 1875 Civil Rights Act was nullified by the Supreme Court (see Chapter 3) in 1883, and the 'Jim Crow' laws in the Southern states of America legalised segregation of blacks and whites; these extended to housing, school and public facilities; they kept whites and blacks separate on trains and buses, and in cemeteries, schools, parks, theatres, restaurants, etc. Thousands of newly enfranchised African-American voters were prohibited by various means from exercising their right to vote.

Gilded Age

A phrase used to describe unprecedented industrial growth in late 19th century America.

The Panic

A period of economic depression lasting from 1893 until 1896.

Timeline

1877 — End of the 'Reconstruction' with the election as president of the Republican Rutherford B. Hayes, and the withdrawal from the South of federal troops who had safeguarded African-American civil rights.

1881 — First 'Jim Crow' law to segregate railroad carriages in Tennessee – an example copied over the next three decades in many Southern states.

1882 — The Chinese Exclusion Act is passed by Congress to prevent further Chinese immigration for ten years.

1883 — The 1875 Civil Rights Act is nullified by the Supreme Court.

1887 — The Dawes Act undermines Native-American culture by breaking up tribal reservation lands.

1890 — 'Jim Crow' legislation in Mississippi uses literacy and 'understanding' rules to disenfranchise African Americans – an example followed in several Southern states over the next two decades.

1895 — The Atlanta Compromise. Booker T. Washington's 'Atlanta Compromise' speech advocating the principle of the gradual accommodation (integration) of African Americans into white-dominated American society.

1896 — *Plessy v. Ferguson* case heard by the Supreme Court validates 'Jim Crow' segregation laws as being true to the spirit of the 14th Amendment. Formation of the National Association of Colored Women (NACW).

1898 — Formation of the National Afro-American Council.

1899 — National day of fasting in protest against lynching, organised by the National Afro-American Council.

1905 — Formation of the Niagara Movement.

1909 — Formation of the NAACP.

1910 — 'Jim Crow' laws start to be introduced in Southern states legitimising segregation of white and non-white neighbourhoods.

The impact of the First World War

America did not formally enter the First World War (1914–18) until 1917. However it had been involved, not least as a supplier to Europe of all manner of manufactured goods, from the start. The boom in America's armaments industry, together with the need to replace white workers who enlisted as soldiers, increased the migration of African Americans from the agrarian southern states to the industrial northern cities. Here they settled in formerly white areas, such as New York's Harlem, where thousands lived in poverty in virtually all-black 'ghettoes'. Here too they acquired the vote and began to elect African Americans to local councils. White citizens, who had felt distant from the race issue, now confronted it, some with compassion, but many with resentment and fear. Meanwhile thousands of African-American servicemen were exposed to different attitudes towards race in Europe and returned home with a deeper loathing for the racial intolerance of their own society. With the ending of the war competition for jobs increased. All of this combined to increase the tension that erupted into violent race riots in urban areas with large black populations.

Several organisations, such as Marcus Garvey's Universal Negro Improvement Association were formed to promote civil rights, to combat 'Jim Crow', and to counter the reformed KKK and other white supremacist organisations. The later 1920s and the 1930s proved to be less turbulent but little significant progress along the path to racial equality was made.

Timeline

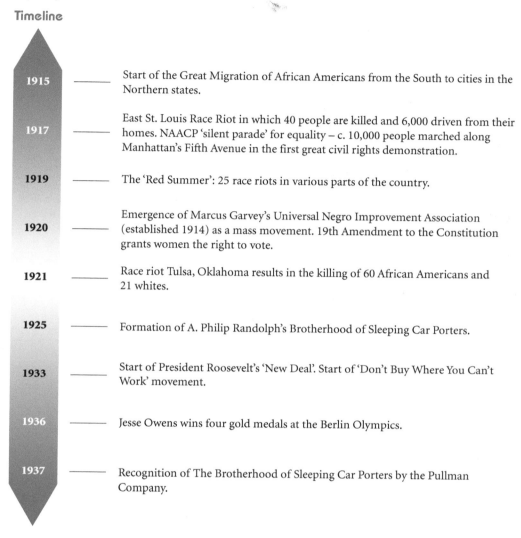

1915	Start of the Great Migration of African Americans from the South to cities in the Northern states.
1917	East St. Louis Race Riot in which 40 people are killed and 6,000 driven from their homes. NAACP 'silent parade' for equality – c. 10,000 people marched along Manhattan's Fifth Avenue in the first great civil rights demonstration.
1919	The 'Red Summer': 25 race riots in various parts of the country.
1920	Emergence of Marcus Garvey's Universal Negro Improvement Association (established 1914) as a mass movement. 19th Amendment to the Constitution grants women the right to vote.
1921	Race riot Tulsa, Oklahoma results in the killing of 60 African Americans and 21 whites.
1925	Formation of A. Philip Randolph's Brotherhood of Sleeping Car Porters.
1933	Start of President Roosevelt's 'New Deal'. Start of 'Don't Buy Where You Can't Work' movement.
1936	Jesse Owens wins four gold medals at the Berlin Olympics.
1937	Recognition of The Brotherhood of Sleeping Car Porters by the Pullman Company.

The impact of the Second World War

As in the era of the First World War, the economic opportunities provided by the Second World War (1939–45) led to a second great wave of migration of African Americans from the South to the North and West. It also encouraged the immigration of Mexicans, also in search of work. Once again the settlement by blacks in former white areas led to violence and riots, notably in Detroit in 1943. Meanwhile the hypocrisy of a white American government fighting a war against fascism while tolerating racism at home provided a powerful tool for civil rights propagandists. The reliance on African-American workers in the armaments industry was a further stimulus to President Roosevelt to begin addressing racial inequality in the workplace. A new civil rights organisation, the Congress of Racial Equality (**CORE**), was established in 1942 by James Farmer. Farmer, inspired by Mahatma Gandhi, the Indian leader, advocated non-violent but assertive methods and pioneered the tactics of sit-ins and boycotts to challenge segregation. Meanwhile some Native Americans who refused to fight in this white man's war were imprisoned.

CORE

Congress of Racial Equality established in 1942 by James Farmer.

Timeline

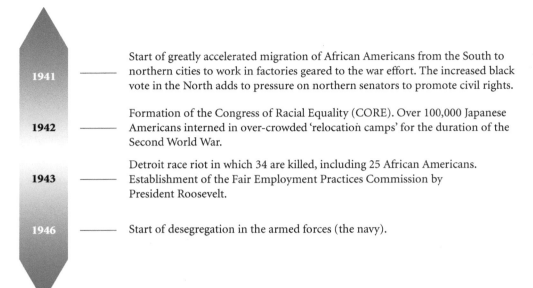

1941 ——— Start of greatly accelerated migration of African Americans from the South to northern cities to work in factories geared to the war effort. The increased black vote in the North adds to pressure on northern senators to promote civil rights.

1942 ——— Formation of the Congress of Racial Equality (CORE). Over 100,000 Japanese Americans interned in over-crowded 'relocation camps' for the duration of the Second World War.

1943 ——— Detroit race riot in which 34 are killed, including 25 African Americans. Establishment of the Fair Employment Practices Commission by President Roosevelt.

1946 ——— Start of desegregation in the armed forces (the navy).

THINK LIKE AN HISTORIAN

To what extent and why did the world wars change race relations in the USA?

Lynch mob

A crowd of people intent on punishing without a trial, usually by hanging, an individual accused of a serious misdemeanour.

Lynchings

During the 'Jim Crow' era the old American tradition of 'street justice' at the end of a **lynch-mob**'s rope continued but, as the figures in the table below reveal, these increasingly targeted African Americans.

Year	Whites	Blacks	Total	Year	Whites	Blacks	Total
1882	64	49	113	1901	25	105	130
1883	77	53	130	1902	7	85	92
1884	160	51	211	1903	15	84	99
1885	110	74	184	1904	7	76	83
1886	64	74	138	1905	5	57	62
1887	50	70	120	1906	3	62	65
1888	68	69	137	1907	3	58	61
1889	76	94	170	1908	8	89	97
1890	11	85	96	1909	13	69	82
1891	71	113	184	1910	9	67	76
1892	69	161	230	1911	7	60	67
1893	34	118	152	1912	2	62	64
1894	58	134	192	1913	1	51	52
1895	66	113	179	1914	4	51	55
1896	45	78	123	1915	13	56	69
1897	35	123	158	1916	4	50	54
1898	19	101	120	1917	2	36	38
1899	21	85	106	1918	4	60	64
1900	9	106	115	1919	7	76	83

Year	Whites	Blacks	Total
1920	8	53	61
1921	5	59	64
1922	6	51	57
1923	4	29	33
1924	0	16	16
1925	0	17	17
1926	7	23	30
1927	0	16	16
1928	1	10	11
1929	3	7	10
1930	1	20	21
1931	1	12	13
1932	2	6	8

Year	Whites	Blacks	Total
1933	2	24	26
1934	0	15	15
1935	2	18	20
1936	0	8	8
1937	0	8	8
1938	0	6	6
1939	1	2	3
1940	1	4	5
1941	0	4	4
1942	0	6	6
1943	0	3	3
1944	0	2	2
1945	0	1	1

▌ **Table 1.2** Lynchings: by year and race (statistics provided by the Archives at Tuskegee Institute)

ACTIVITY

1 Plot these figures from Table 1.2 on a graph.
2 What questions does it raise for the historian regarding the lynching phenomenon in America in the late 19th century and first half of the 20th century?
3 How might an historian set about finding the answers to some of these questions?
4 What difficulties might he/she encounter along the way?

THINK LIKE AN HISTORIAN

Table 1.2 gives you plenty of opportunities to reflect upon the key concepts of **change** and **continuity** throughout the period. These will become even more apparent if you plot the data on a graph. As you study this evidence you need to think carefully about how things appear to have changed and when these changes were most evident. You should also look for evidence of consistency – times within the period when, in some respects, there was very little change at all.

The Civil Rights Movement

The first major triumph of the post-war **civil rights movement** was the Supreme Court decision outlawing segregation in schools in the *Brown v. Board of Education* case of 1954. In 1955, in Montgomery, Alabama, Rosa Parks refused to change seats on a bus because of a city ruling that forbade African-American passengers from sitting in the same section as white passengers. Her action and subsequent arrest prompted a boycott of buses to draw attention to discrimination while at the same time undermining the business interests of white-owned bus companies. Subsequently, two acts (1957 and 1960), passed under the Eisenhower administration, established an agency to investigate and address further claims of racial discrimination.

In the early 1960s, activists employed various forms of direct action such as 'sit-ins' at places such as cinemas, libraries and lunch-counters to speed up the process of

Civil Rights Movement

Term usually used to describe the struggle for equality in post-Second World War America.

desegregation. In August 1963, leading civil rights activist, Martin Luther King, led 200,000 '**Freedom Marchers**' to Washington DC. Racial discrimination in areas such as education, employment and politics became illegal with the Civil Rights Act (1964) and the Voting Rights Act (1965) under the Johnson Administration. Although on a personal level President Johnson had shared the racist convictions common among white Americans at that time, he became publicly committed to desegregation in his pursuit of what he termed his '**Great Society**'.

Freedom Marchers

Civil rights activists who joined protest marches.

the 'Great Society'

President Johnson's vision for a better and fairer America.

Timeline

1946	Segregated interstate bus travel found to be unconstitutional by the US Supreme Court in the *Morgan v. Virginia* case.
1948	President Truman desegregates the armed forces. Inter-racial marriages permitted in California. The American Evacuation Claims Act helps those Japanese who had property confiscated as part of the wartime internment process.
1953	Boycott by African Americans of segregated buses in Baton Rouge, Louisiana.
1954	Segregation in schools is found unconstitutional by the Supreme Court in the *Brown v. Board of Education* case.
1955	Rosa Parks' action launches the Montgomery Bus Boycott, soon led by Martin Luther King.
1956	Segregated intrastate bus travel found to be unconstitutional by the US Supreme Court in the *Gayle v. Browder* case.
1957	The Civil Rights Act of 1957 (see page 54). The Little Rock crisis (see page 100).
1958	Formation of Dr Martin Luther King's Southern Christian Leadership Conference (SCLC).
1960	Student sit-in at Woolworth's in Greensboro, North Carolina. Formation of the Student Nonviolent Coordinating Committee (SNCC). The Civil Rights Act of 1960 (see page 55). American Indian Movement (AIM) established in Minneapolis
1961	Freedom Rides organised by CORE (see page 114).
1962	Enrolment of James Meredith, the first African-American student to attend the University of Mississippi; federal troops sent in to suppress rioting.
1963	Martin Luther King's 'Letter from a Birmingham Jail' (see page 106). Assassination of Medgar Evers (see page 37). 200,000 join the March on Washington; Martin Luther King gives his 'I have a dream' speech. Malcolm X dubs it 'The Farce on Washington'.
1964	The Civil Rights Act of 1964 (see page 57).
1965	The Immigration Act ends preferential consideration for immigrants of European origin (comes into effect in 1968). This results in a dramatic increase in the size of the Mexican-American population.

THINK LIKE AN HISTORIAN

On the basis of this evidence why do you think historians have identified the emergence of the post-war civil rights movement as a major change in the history of race and American society? In what respects was the era of the post-war civil rights movement a continuation of earlier history?

Black Panthers

Paramilitary Black Power movement formed in 1966.

Brown Berets

Paramilitary Brown Power movement formed in the later 1960s.

Black, Red and Brown Power

The civil rights movement split in the 1960s with the growth of a more radical and militant wing. This was led by individuals like the Black nationalist and Muslim, Malcolm X, and armed groups like the **Black Panthers** and **Brown Berets**. In April 1968, Martin Luther King was assassinated. Although some parts of his 'dream' had been realised by the time of his death, a great deal more needed to be done, not least in closing the rifts within the movement, advancing the political representation of ethnic minorities, and further improving the social and economic conditions in which ordinary African-American citizens lived.

Timeline

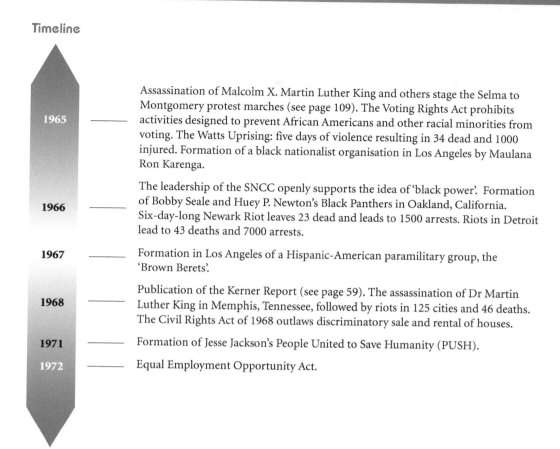

1965	Assassination of Malcolm X. Martin Luther King and others stage the Selma to Montgomery protest marches (see page 109). The Voting Rights Act prohibits activities designed to prevent African Americans and other racial minorities from voting. The Watts Uprising: five days of violence resulting in 34 dead and 1000 injured. Formation of a black nationalist organisation in Los Angeles by Maulana Ron Karenga.
1966	The leadership of the SNCC openly supports the idea of 'black power'. Formation of Bobby Seale and Huey P. Newton's Black Panthers in Oakland, California. Six-day-long Newark Riot leaves 23 dead and leads to 1500 arrests. Riots in Detroit lead to 43 deaths and 7000 arrests.
1967	Formation in Los Angeles of a Hispanic-American paramilitary group, the 'Brown Berets'.
1968	Publication of the Kerner Report (see page 59). The assassination of Dr Martin Luther King in Memphis, Tennessee, followed by riots in 125 cities and 46 deaths. The Civil Rights Act of 1968 outlaws discriminatory sale and rental of houses.
1971	Formation of Jesse Jackson's People United to Save Humanity (PUSH).
1972	Equal Employment Opportunity Act.

THINK LIKE AN HISTORIAN

To what extent and in what ways did the civil rights movement develop and change in the 1960s? To what extent and in what ways had both racial issues and American society changed between 1865 and the 1970s?

Summary – what you have learned in Chapter 1

This chapter has introduced you to the multi-racial character of modern America and the range of strategies employed by civil rights activists of many racial backgrounds to promote the pursuit of racial equality. These include:

- Federal legislation
- State legislation
- Violent forms of protest
- Peaceful forms of protest.

You have learned how the pace of change was very uneven: a period of reform and reconstruction, in the aftermath of the American Civil War, was followed by one of reaction which endured until well after the Second World War.

You have discovered, in outline, the significance of a number of individuals and several important organisations in the struggle against inequality in this period, but also how they did not always work together and, perhaps, sometimes themselves slowed the pace of reform.

You have learned that **change and continuity** are key concepts and that success in the exam, in part, depends upon your ability to evaluate sources in the context of your own general knowledge and understanding of how the history of race and American society developed between 1865 and the 1970s.

The various activities in this chapter have encouraged you to start thinking analytically about historical evidence and to draw your own conclusions on the basis of this evidence and the historical context in which it is set. These key skills are the focus of the remaining chapters in this book.

Race and American Society: examining the evidence

2

Overview

There is a great range of material available to be used by historians of race and American society. Historians of the subject have a large literature of all kinds that they can draw on, such as:

- official documents
- newspaper articles
- personal correspondence
- works of fiction
- memoirs and autobiographies.

In addition, there exists a wealth of statistics and images, including political cartoons, film, and photographs. Every historical source has value, but the historian must handle every source with care in order to assess its historical worth. Each source makes a unique contribution to the historical record, but it is also likely to bring with it a particular set of problems in its interpretation. Different types of evidence need to be approached in different ways.

The evidence the historian uses is not merely a *record* of the history in the form of such things as photographs and memoirs. The evidence *is* the history and, as the examples here show, much of this material, speeches and suchlike, had a profound effect upon the shaping of that history.

Every piece of evidence needs to be rigorously interrogated by the historian. The historian needs to find out about its '**provenance**' – Who produced it? When? Where? Why? – in order to assess its full historical significance. This chapter is designed to introduce you to the range of evidence available and to help you to hone your skills of analysis.

In the exam you will be required to analyse several sources, usually six or seven, in order to evaluate an interpretation. This involves the very careful reading of the sources and having an awareness of any problems they might pose to the historian in terms of such things as incompleteness or the danger of taking them at face value. You will also need to demonstrate your skills in the comparison of sources and the evaluation of a range of sources as a set. The development of these skills is at the heart of this and all of the subsequent chapters. As you work through them you should pay particular attention to the 'Using Historical Evidence' boxes.

Provenance

Where something, e.g. a piece of historical evidence, comes from.

Key Questions:

1   What is the range of historical evidence available to the historian of race and American society?

2   What different issues (e.g. problems) do they raise for the historian using them?

3   What different uses do they have?

4   Why can they be interpreted in different ways?

The evidence of official documents

In a world that demands accountability, governments and other public institutions in modern democracies are pressured into recording and making available information that can be deemed to be in 'the public interest'. State papers relating to the civil rights struggle are numerous and, mostly, available. A great many presidential speeches and congressional acts can now be found on the Internet. So too can some of the records of the organisations involved in this struggle, such as the Ku Klux Klan and the **NAACP**.

The single most important official document in this context is the American Constitution. The civil rights battles were fought largely over how this might be interpreted, amended, and enforced. In 1956 the crucial *Brown v. Board of Education* verdict promised an end to segregation in schools. This provoked an uproar in the South and a document known as 'The Southern Manifesto' was drawn up by 101 Southern politicians, comprising 99 Democrats and two Republicans and including 19 senators, which contested the legitimacy of the verdict on constitutional grounds.

NAACP

the National Association for the Advancement of Colored People formed in 1909.

Source (1) The Southern Manifesto

… *The unwarranted decision of the Supreme Court in the public school cases is now bearing the fruit always produced when men substitute naked power for established law.*

The Founding Fathers gave us a Constitution of checks and balances because they realized the inescapable lesson of history that no man or group of men can be safely entrusted with unlimited power. They framed this Constitution with its provisions for change by amendment in order to secure the fundamentals of government against the dangers of temporary popular passion or the personal predilections of public officeholders.

We regard the decisions of the Supreme Court in the school cases as a clear abuse of judicial power. It climaxes a trend in the Federal Judiciary undertaking to legislate, in derogation of the authority of Congress, and to encroach upon the reserved rights of the States and the people.

The original Constitution does not mention education. Neither does the 14th Amendment nor any other amendment. The debates preceding the submission of the 14th Amendment clearly show that there was no intent that it should affect the system of education maintained by the States.

… *In the case of Plessy v. Ferguson in 1896 the Supreme Court expressly declared that under the 14th Amendment no person was denied any of his rights if the States provided separate but equal facilities. This decision has been followed in many other cases. It is notable that the Supreme Court, speaking through Chief Justice Taft, a former President of the United States, unanimously declared in 1927 in Lum v. Rice that the "separate but equal" principle is "within the discretion of the State in regulating its public schools and does not conflict with the 14th Amendment."*

This interpretation, restated time and again, became a part of the life of the people of many of the States and confirmed their habits, traditions, and way of life. It is founded on elemental humanity and commonsense, for parents should not be deprived by Government of the right to direct the lives and education of their own children.

Though there has been no constitutional amendment or act of Congress changing this established legal principle almost a century old, the Supreme Court of the United States, with no legal basis for such action, undertook to exercise their naked judicial power and substituted their personal political and social ideas for the established law of the land.

This unwarranted exercise of power by the Court, contrary to the Constitution, is creating chaos and confusion in the States principally affected. It is destroying the amicable relations between the white and Negro races that have been created through 90 years of patient effort by the good people of both races. It has planted hatred and suspicion where there has been heretofore friendship and understanding.

Without regard to the consent of the governed, outside mediators are threatening immediate and revolutionary changes in our public schools systems. If done, this is certain to destroy the system of public education in some of the States.

With the gravest concern for the explosive and dangerous condition created by this decision and inflamed by outside meddlers:

We reaffirm our reliance on the Constitution as the fundamental law of the land.

We decry the Supreme Court's encroachment on the rights reserved to the States and to the people, contrary to established law, and to the Constitution.

We commend the motives of those States which have declared the intention to resist forced integration by any lawful means.

We appeal to the States and people who are not directly affected by these decisions to consider the constitutional principles involved against the time when they too, on issues vital to them may be the victims of judicial encroachment.

Even though we constitute a minority in the present Congress, we have full faith that a majority of the American people believe in the dual system of government which has enabled us to achieve our greatness and will in time demand that the reserved rights of the States and of the people be made secure against judicial usurpation.

We pledge ourselves to use all lawful means to bring about a reversal of this decision which is contrary to the Constitution and to prevent the use of force in its implementation.

In this trying period, as we all seek to right this wrong, we appeal to our people not to be provoked by the agitators and troublemakers invading our States and to scrupulously refrain from disorder and lawless acts.

The Southern Manifesto from *Congressional Record*, 84th Congress Second Session. Vol. 102, part 4 (March 12, 1956).

ACTIVITY

1   What methods did the writers of The Southern Manifesto employ to argue their case?

2   What was the purpose of this document?

3   What does it reveal regarding the place of political structures in the struggle for civil rights?

4   What, in addition to the segregation issue, appears to have been of such concern to the senators who signed this petition?

5   Would the worries and motives of 101 individuals be identical?

When organisations release 'official' statements it is very important to recognise that these are not necessarily the views of all members of that organisation. Even in non-democratic organisations there are likely to be those who challenge the 'official' line of the organisation itself. In the case of The Southern Manifesto it appears that some southern senators were more temperate than others. The final version of this controversial document was actually less extreme than the original version that had been largely the work of South Carolina's Senator Strom Thurmond. Even so, many of those who signed the more liberal version soon regretted doing so because of the way in which it divided the Democrat party. It was widely criticised by northern Democrats on its release. So, this official statement neither represented the views of all elected members of the political party that engineered it, nor did it accurately reflect the views of the extremists who initiated it. For their political opponents, however, it provided useful propaganda with which to rubbish the views of the Democrats as a whole.

THINK LIKE AN HISTORIAN

Why is it important for historians to avoid taking official documents at face value?

EXAM TIP

Whenever you are presented with a piece of evidence that claims to represent the views of a large group of people, always consider whether or not they were likely to agree on all points. Consider how the document might have been produced and whether, in fact, you are simply reading the views of the individual or individuals who created it in on behalf of the group.

The evidence of newspapers

When read with care and with a keen eye for bias and an understanding of an article's purpose, newspapers are an invaluable source for the historian of race and American society. Newspaper articles do not always mirror public opinion and it would be naïve to assume that everything stated in a newspaper would meet the approval of its readership. However, the weekly newspapers of civil rights organisations (and most had at least one) are a mine of information for the history of the movement. At the same time, the regular dailies, such as the *New York Herald Tribune*, provide the broader picture of changing attitudes in the wider world.

The following source is an article from the *Des Moines Tribune* in 1964. It profiles a young white student preparing to work as a volunteer civil rights activist in Mississippi.

Source (2) Patti Miller, civil rights activist

An Audubon… who never had known a Negro "as a person" before she entered Drake University three years ago is planning to join other student civil rights volunteers in Mississippi next month. She is Patti Miller, 21, a junior majoring in music education, the daughter of Mr. And Mrs. Donald B. Miller. Her father is principal of Audubon High School.

Miss Miller's application has been accepted by the Council of Federated Organizations (COFO), but she has not yet received an assignment.

Orientation

A summer student at Drake, she was unable to attend the orientation program at Oxford, Ohio, but will get this training at Edwards, Miss. (near Jackson), where she will report first, probably in mid-July. She has volunteered, Miss Miller said, because it is something she "has to do."

"I have to live what I've been saying," she said. "I hope to become involved as a Christian, become part of a movement, part of a Christian concern."

She is apprehensive about what awaits her and other volunteers in Mississippi, she admits. She produced newspaper clippings telling of warnings given volunteers in training at Oxford about what they might expect.

Sincerity

A petite blonde, Miss Miller has a kitten-like charm in appearance. She speaks with sincerity and humility. She had read books recommended by COC, acknowledge the influence "of persons on the campus whose view I respect." But she has obviously gone beyond these views and searched for her own answers.

The disappearance of three civil rights workers in Mississippi has added to her apprehension, she says. "I have to admit I am afraid," she said. "I hope I won't go to pieces when I get down there. But my principal worry is for my parents. I can imagine what they will be going through, and I must make every effort to keep in touch with them. I have been

unusually fortunate in my parents. Their reaction, when I first asked them if I could volunteer, was that if it was what I felt I had to do, then I should go ahead. A few days after I first talked to them about it, I received a letter from my father, repeating this."

Studying

Awaiting her assignment, Miss Miller is avidly studying the instruction sheets sent her. These include two typewritten pages suggesting materials that volunteers who will work in proposed community centers or freedom schools should bring if possible. These range from paper clips and rolls of butcher paper, to tape recorders, phonographs, typewriters.

"Many people who want to help can provide these needed items," Miss Miller said. (Her personal concern is how she'll "manage that butcher paper roll on a bus.")

No Shorts

Women volunteers are advised to bring light, cool clothing – no slacks, shorts, etc. Men are advised not to bring Bermuda shorts. Each volunteer is asked to bring a sleeping bag. Volunteers must have $500 for bond money. "I told my parents that if I got jailed several times, there'd go my tuition next fall," Miss Miller said. Volunteers also are told to bring about $60 over their bus fare, and are advised they should receive $10 or $15 a week from home (her parents will send this, Miss Miller said).

Choir Director

Some of the money for the expedition Miss Miller has earned by directing the choir at Forest Avenue Baptist Church. Her family has been active in the Methodist Church throughout her life, and when she came to Drake she moved into the Methodist student life of the campus, Miss Miller said.

During her sophomore year she went through "the usual stage" of doubt and rejection of religion, which to some students, she said, "doesn't seem relevant any more, doesn't speak to Now." But she remained active in the Wesley Foundation, Methodist campus organization, was its president last year. Her period of doubts passed, she said.

She has made trips with the Wesley group to study conditions in the south, also to Washington, D. C. During her first year at Drake, Miss Miller began to make friends with various Negro students, the first of their race she had ever known. (She said she knows of no Negroes who ever have lived in Audubon.) She worked with Des Moines Youth for Betterment of Human Relations, next year will be the Student-Faculty Council's human relations chairman.

"Average Student"
She describes herself as "an average student" with something of an activity bug. She laughs as she counts the "elections I've lost," in part, she suspects, because of her interracial friendships. She has volunteered for one month's duty in Mississippi, in community centers, freedom schools or voter registration, listed on her application in that order of preference. When she returns she will go to South Dakota for a leadership training conference of young Methodists. She plans after graduation to apply to the Methodist Board of Missions for duty as a short-term missionary and would like to spend two years teaching in Africa, she said.

From Will Join Rights Aides in Mississippi, Lillian McLaughlin, published in the *Des Moines Tribune*, June 26, 1964.

THINK LIKE AN HISTORIAN

What are the strengths and limitations of Source 2 as historical evidence for the civil rights struggle in America?

How does Source 2 compare with Source 1 as historical evidence? Think about the purpose of each source and how far this might affect its reliability.

ACTIVITY

1   What kind of civil rights activities might Patti have become involved in Mississippi?

2   Why Mississippi?

3   Why was 1964 a significant time in the civil rights struggle in the USA?

4   What does this source reveal about the structure of the civil rights movement in 1964?

5   What is the tone of the piece? Does the journalist reveal a point of view on the subject?

6   How and why, according to this source, was the Methodist Church involved in the civil rights movement?

7   Would all black equal rights campaigners have approved of Patti Miller's participation in 1964? Explain your answer.

The evidence of political cartoons

Political cartoons in newspapers concerning the issue of racial equality can usually be relied upon to reflect the attitude of the readership the newspaper catered for. Unlike the work of the modern historian, the work of the cartoonist is openly opinionated and designed to provoke an emotional, rather than an intellectual, response. A cartoon that works is one that angers the reader or makes the reader laugh. Cartoons rarely provide a literal truth, but the most useful ones give a direct and succinct insight into the concerns of a time and place regarding some contentious issue. It is their very subjectivity, their bias, that makes them such important sources of evidence. The fact that they tend to use metaphors to make points, that they can grossly exaggerate the truth, and that they sometimes rely on irony, however, can make them problematic sources for historians; without a good knowledge of the historical context in which they appeared, the historian is likely to miss the cartoon's point entirely. All need to be treated with the same care since they are essentially propagandist – their object is to provoke the viewer into thinking about a subject and to persuade the viewer into a particular line of thinking. As such, they are an immensely useful type of evidence; even propaganda that lies is of use in illuminating a particular set of values current in a particular place and time.

Source ③ One Vote Less

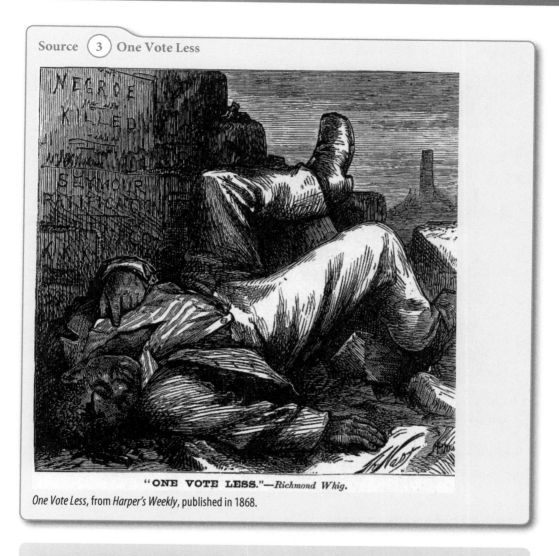

"ONE VOTE LESS."—*Richmond Whig.*

One Vote Less, from *Harper's Weekly*, published in 1868.

THINK LIKE AN HISTORIAN

1 What is the historical context in which Source 3 is set?

2 What is the tone set by this cartoon?

3 What is its purpose?

4 For what reasons can it be described as a 'political cartoon'?

5 With whom do the cartoonist's sympathies seem to lie? Explain your answer.

6 How might a cartoonist sympathetic to the Ku Klux Klan have chosen to depict the dead man?

ACTIVITY

Compare the **provenance** of Sources 2 and 3. Make a list of all of the similarities and differences you can identify between them in terms of source type, purpose and period. Do the similarities outweigh the differences? How far do they differ in terms of content? Which, if either, is the most reliable as historical evidence? Explain your answers.

The evidence of statistics and distribution maps

Statistics have a central role in historical enquiries. However, they need to be handled with care since the results are only as reliable as the methods by which the statistics were gathered. Even when the results can be considered trustworthy, it is easy for historians to misinterpret them.

In Source 4 below, statistics for African Americans living in America by 1921 have been plotted on a distribution map. It was published by the Tuskegee Institute in Alabama, the premier southern educational institution for African-American students. Its Principal in 1881 was the early civil rights leader and ex-slave, Booker T. Washington.

Source (4) Population distribution map

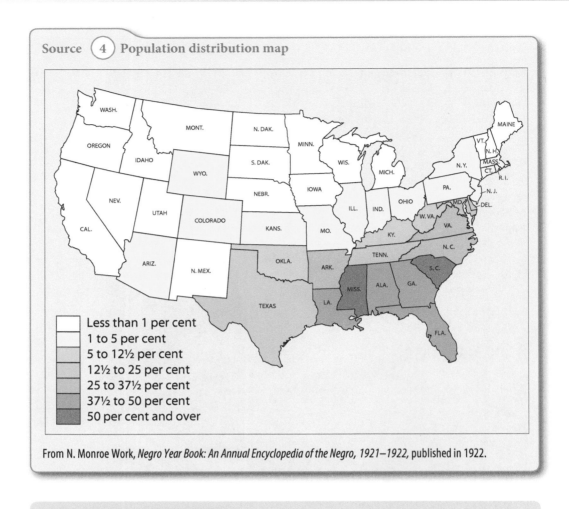

Less than 1 per cent
1 to 5 per cent
5 to 12½ per cent
12½ to 25 per cent
25 to 37½ per cent
37½ to 50 per cent
50 per cent and over

From N. Monroe Work, *Negro Year Book: An Annual Encyclopedia of the Negro, 1921–1922,* published in 1922.

THINK LIKE AN HISTORIAN

1   What was the historical context regarding the race issue in which this map was produced?

2   Consider the provenance of this source. What do you think was the main reason this map was produced?

3   What general conclusions regarding the distribution of African Americans can be drawn from this map?

4   What are the limitations of this map? What does it *not* tell you about the African-American population and its distribution?

5   How do you think this data might have been collected?

6   How reliable is this data likely to be? Explain your answer.

7   How might an historian of the struggle for civil rights be able to use this map as evidence?

In the next source statistics for African-American migration from the start of the 20th century up until the 1970s are provided.

Source ⑤ The great migration

Between 1910 and 1940, roughly 1.5 million African Americans left the South for Northern cities; however, during the decade that followed the stock market crash of 1929, this emigration slowed to a trickle. But with America's entry into World War II looming on the horizon, the exodus of blacks from their Southern homeland resumed. Between 1940 and 1950, another 1.5 million African Americans left the South. The migration continued at roughly the same pace over the next twenty years. By 1970, about five million African Americans had made the journey, and the geographic map of black America had fundamentally changed. Roughly one of every seven black Southerners pulled up stakes and headed north or west. Both their places of origin and destination shifted from earlier patterns.

They drove, or boarded trains straight north or west. They went from Alabama to Detroit. They left the Carolinas and Georgia for New York, Philadelphia, and Boston. The migrants from Mississippi and Arkansas headed up Highway 61 or took the Illinois Central railroad to Chicago as their predecessors had done during the Great Migration. What was new was that many moved west to California.

The Western states, especially California, witnessed an explosive growth of their African-American populations. In 1930, some 50,200 African Americans lived in Los Angeles, San Francisco, and Oakland; twenty years later, the three cities' combined black population had soared to 254,120. Altogether, 339,000 African Americans moved to the Western half of the country during the 1940s, in contrast to a mere 49,000 in the previous decade.

Most of the migrants to California came from Southwestern and Central states like Louisiana, Texas, Arkansas, and Oklahoma. Almost three times as many African Americans left this region between 1940 and 1950 as had done so during the previous thirty years. The South Atlantic states, however, remained the most frequent point of origin for migrants, accounting for some 30 to 40 percent of those leaving the South in each decade. This is particularly striking given that Delaware, Maryland, the District of Columbia, and Florida usually had net gains in their black population during this period. Thus, the combined totals for the region mask the fact that the two Carolinas and Georgia experienced a virtual hemorrhage of their black citizenry. Well over half a million African Americans left those three states in each of the three postwar decades.

Over the thirty-year course of the migration, arrivals to the West remained constant; those to the Northeast steadily increased, while those to the North Central region decreased considerably. The centuries-long era during which black Americans had lived mostly in the rural South and worked primarily in agriculture was over. By 1950, most African Americans no longer worked in agriculture or as domestic labor - the occupations that had always characterized their existence in America - and the population was more evenly distributed throughout the nation.

From The Migration Numbers at *In Motion – the African-American migration experience.*

THINK LIKE AN HISTORIAN

1   How do you think the data in Source 5 might have been collected?

2   How reliable is the data in this source? Explain your answer.

3   In what alternative ways might the data in this source have been presented?

4   Choose some of this data and represent it in an appropriate graphic format.

5   What patterns in the story of African-American migration can be identified from this passage?

6   How can these patterns be explained?

7   Why is it important for the historian of the civil rights movement to understand the pattern of African-American migration between 1865 and the 1970s?

Stretch and challenge

To find out more about the fascinating story of the migration experience of African Americans, browse through a selection of the thousands of sources at 'In Motion – the African-American migration experience'.

The evidence of personal accounts

You will discover in this book that many civil rights leaders wrote memoirs of their lives and contributions to the movement. In some cases, notably the autobiography of Malcolm X, dictated to Alex Haley, their work was written down, edited and compiled into a book by someone else. It was effectively a piece of 'oral history'. Oral history is fallible on two counts: it is determined by what the subject tells the interviewer and what the interviewer asks the subject. Memories are imperfect and people can unintentionally, sometimes intentionally, distort past truths. Interviewers may have an agenda that shapes the interview and they cannot be relied upon to be entirely objective when making the results of the interview available to a wider audience. Recollections, arguably, are less reliable than contemporaneous sources of evidence since people's memories are not infallible. Furthermore, eyewitness accounts of the past are not necessarily any more truthful than the statements of witnesses in courts of law.

An oral historian, Paul Thompson, has commented on the importance of personal accounts as historical evidence in the study of race relations in modern America (Source 6).

Malcolm X's autobiography makes fascinating reading. Unlike some other eminent race leaders, Malcolm X came from a severely deprived background. Before his self-education and conversion to Islam in prison, he spent his formative years as a 'hustler' dealing drugs on the streets of Harlem, New York. His was a very different life experience to that of the relatively privileged Martin Luther King. His city-ghetto world helped shape his politics and his aggressive black nationalism. The analysis of this one life sheds a great deal of light upon the reasons why the civil rights movement tore itself apart in the early and mid-1960s, just as it seemed to be achieving its principal goals.

Source 7 provides a good example of the value of oral history. Malcolm X came from a class of people that rarely left a personal record of their lives. In this passage, an ex-hustler explains the meaning of another hustler's 'street-talk' to the African-American writer, Alex Haley, most famous for his book on slavery, *Roots*.

ACTIVITY

Using Historical Evidence

Comparing sources. In the exam you will need to compare a range of source types and show how they illuminate a particular theme. Practise this skill by comparing and contrasting Sources 5 and 6. How far do they support each other in terms of their content? How far do they provide the historian with different kinds of evidence? Do they in any way seem to contradict each other? These are the kind of questions you will need to come up with when you interrogate the sources you are given in the exam.

Source 6) Oral history

What do they do, which could not otherwise have been done? Three things. First, they penetrate the otherwise inaccessible. Two come from the great city ghettoes of urban America. Paul Bullock's 'Watts, the Aftermath' is an account of a mass confrontation in Los Angeles; while Alex Haley's 'Autobiography of Malcolm X' has few equals for conveying the bitter richness of city life or as a powerful portrait of an individual leader. Nor did the illiterate rural Black communities leave records for future historians. William Montell's 'The Saga of Coe Ridge' is the leading American example of a serious fully documented community study by its subject largely dependent on oral evidence: an account of a Black colony, settled on a remote hill spur after emancipation from slavery, surviving at first through subsistence farming and lumbering, but degenerating through lethal fights with neighbouring Whites… Secondly, where records do exist, oral history provides an essential corrective to them. This is especially true of the old rural South – where history matters, as nowhere else in America,

because it is employed to justify or deny the claims of White supremacy. It was thus no mere accident that the rich interview material which had been collected in the 1920s and 1930s from former plantation slaves and their dependants remained unused by historians for more than three decades…

… Finally, oral evidence can achieve something more pervasive, and more fundamental to history… Oral history, by transforming the 'objects' of study into 'subjects', makes for a history which is not just richer, more vivid and heart-rending, but truer… Theodore Rosengarten's 'All God's Dangers', the autobiography of Nate Shaw, an illiterate Alabama sharecropper born in the 1880s, based on 120 hours of recorded conversations: [is] one of the most moving, and certainly the fullest, life story of an 'insignificant' person yet to come from oral history.

From P. Thompson, *The Voice of the Past*, published in 1988.

Source (7) The memoirs of Malcolm X

… *time and time again when I spoke at street rallies [c. 1963], I would draw ten and twelve times as many people as most other so-called 'Negro leaders'… I knew the great lack of most of the big-named 'Negro leaders' was their lack of any true rapport with the ghetto Negroes. How could they have rapport when they spent their time 'integrating' with white people? I know that the ghetto people knew that I never left the ghetto in spirit, and I never left it physically any more than I had to.*

… *After a Harlem street rally, one of these downtown 'leaders' and I were talking when we were approached by a Harlem hustler. To my knowledge I'd never seen this hustler before; he said to me, approximately: 'Hey, baby! I dig you holding this all-originals scene at the track… I'm going to lay a vine under the Jew's balls for a dime – got to give you a play… Got the*

shorts out here trying to scuffle up on some bread… Well, my man, I'll get on, got to go peck a little, and cop me some z's' And the hustler went on up Seventh Avenue.

I would never have given it another thought, except that this downtown 'leader' was standing, staring after that hustler, looking as if he had just heard Sanskrit. He asked me what had been said, and I told him. The hustler had said he was aware that the Muslims were holding an all-black bazaar at Rockland Palace, which is primarily a dancehall. The hustler intended to pawn a suit for ten dollars to attend and patronize the bazaar. He had very little money but he was trying hard to make some. He was going to eat, then he would get some sleep.

From Malcolm X and Alex Haley, *The Autobiography of Malcolm X*, published in 1965.

THINK LIKE AN HISTORIAN

1   How does Source 7 reveal the importance of oral accounts as historical evidence?

2   What does it reveal regarding the reasons for divisions within the civil rights movement in the 1960s?

3   What are its limitations as historical evidence?

The evidence of novels

To a greater or lesser degree, a novel is a work of fiction; it tells a story and, ultimately it is designed to 'entertain', in the broadest sense of the term, in order to sell copies. Often it distorts or oversimplifies the truth to make a point or perhaps simply 'for effect'. As such, it can be a particularly problematic source of evidence for the historian in search of 'facts'.

The most influential novel in the history of race relations in America is *Uncle Tom's Cabin* by Harriet Beecher Stowe, written in 1852. With a storyline exposing the grim reality of slavery and the nobility of its African-American characters, it is thought to have contributed to the divisions that provoked the Civil War. On meeting Stowe in 1862, President Lincoln is believed to have said "So this is the little lady who made this big war." The book was massively popular and the biggest seller of the 19th century after the Bible, selling many hundreds of thousands of copies and inspiring numerous staged adaptations ('Tom Shows') and, throughout the 20th century, films.

It was abhorred by Southern slave-owners and white supremacists in the 19th century who challenged both its historical accuracy and its political message. Ironically, however, it came to be regarded as racist itself, perceived by many as a template for the negative stereotypes imposed by the white majority upon African Americans in the 20th century. By the 1960s militant black civil rights campaigners were using the terms '**Uncle Toms**', or simply 'Toms' to describe African Americans who adopted the character's gentle, passive stance and worked with and for, rather than against, their white oppressors.

ACTIVITY

Compare Sources 2 and 7. In what ways are these source types similar? What are their main differences? How far does the **provenance** of each source make it more or less reliable than the other as historical evidence? Explain your answer.

Uncle Toms

Term used in the 1960s as a term of derision for African Americans prepared to make compromises in the struggle for equal rights.

The following source is an extract from the opening scene of *Uncle Tom's Cabin* in which Tom's owner, Mr Shelby, is negotiating his sale to Mr Hayley, a slave-trader.

Source ⑧ Uncle Tom

"Why, the fact is, Haley, Tom is an uncommon fellow; he is certainly worth that sum anywhere,--steady, honest, capable, manages my whole farm like a clock."

"You mean honest, as niggers go," said Haley, helping himself to a glass of brandy.

"No; I mean, really, Tom is a good, steady, sensible, pious fellow. He got religion at a camp-meeting, four years ago; and I believe he really did get it. I've trusted him, since then, with everything I have,--money, house, horses,--and let him come and go round the country; and I always found him true and square in everything."

"Some folks don't believe there is pious niggers Shelby," said Haley, with a candid flourish of his hand, "but I do. I had a fellow, now, in this yer last lot I took to Orleans--'t was as good as a meetin, now, really, to hear that critter pray; and he was quite gentle and quiet like. He fetched me a good

sum, too, for I bought him cheap of a man that was 'bliged to sell out; so I realized six hundred on him. Yes, I consider religion a valeyable thing in a nigger, when it's the genuine article, and no mistake."

"Well, Tom's got the real article, if ever a fellow had," rejoined the other. "Why, last fall, I let him go to Cincinnati alone, to do business for me, and bring home five hundred dollars. 'Tom,' says I to him, 'I trust you, because I think you're a Christian--I know you wouldn't cheat.' Tom comes back, sure enough; I knew he would. Some low fellows, they say, said to him--Tom, why don't you make tracks for Canada?' 'Ah, master trusted me, and I couldn't,'--they told me about it. I am sorry to part with Tom, I must say. You ought to let him cover the whole balance of the debt; and you would, Haley, if you had any conscience."

From H.B. Stowe, *Uncle Tom's Cabin*, published in 1852.

ACTIVITY

1   What does the tone and content of this source reveal about its author?

2   Why, on the evidence of this source, did African-American activists, such as the Black Muslims' leader, Malcolm X, regard Stowe as a racist?

ACTIVITY   Using Historical Evidence

Considering the value of sources. In part **b** of the exam you will be required to comment on the value of the sources you have been presented with. Since you will have to comment on several sources and time will be short it will be sensible to group them into the 3 or 4 main source types represented by the selection. In your analysis you will need to recognise that the value of each source depends upon the historian's purpose and the questions the historian asks. Have another look at Sources 3, 7 and 8 and try to summarise the particular value and limitations of these three distinct types of source.

Stretch and challenge

Read the whole of *Uncle Tom's Cabin* (see: www.heinemann.co.uk/hotlinks)

As you read it consider how the novel tries to

■ show the destructive impact of slavery on the families of slaves

■ show the reader how slavery harms each individual slave

■ use religion to undermine the justification for slavery

■ persuade the reader that slavery is a particular evil.

In the following source, the legacy of *Uncle Tom's Cabin* is identifiable in Malcolm X's recollection of the things he said in a 1960 speech after his conversion to Islam in the 1950s.

Source (9) Uncle Thomas

Today's Uncle Tom doesn't wear a handkerchief on his head. This modern, twentieth-century Uncle Thomas now often wears a top hat. He's usually well-dressed and well-educated. He's often the personification of culture and refinement. The twentieth-century Uncle Thomas sometimes speaks with a Yale or Harvard [top American universities] accent. Sometimes he is known as Professor, Doctor, Judge, and Reverend, even Right Reverend Doctor. This twentieth-century Uncle Thomas is a professional Negro… by that I mean his profession is being a Negro for the white man.

From Malcolm X and Alex Haley, *The Autobiography of Malcolm X*, published in 1965.

ACTIVITY

1   What does Source 9 reveal of the extent to which racial equality had been achieved by the middle of the 20th century?

2   Who do you think Malcolm X was thinking of when he referred to the 'Right Reverend Doctor'? Why did he consider this person an 'Uncle Tom'?

EXAM TIP

Look for evidence in the selection of sources provided in the exam for ways in which things changed across the period. A quick comparison of Sources 8 and 9, for example, reveals how the phrase 'Uncle Tom' had different connotations at the start and at the end of the period.

The evidence of films

The early 20th century marked the start of the movie industry which, through a single film, played an important role in the development of the civil rights movement. This pioneering feature-length film was D.W. Griffith's *The Birth of a Nation*, first screened in 1915. The film, set in the South, concerns the end of the Civil War and the Reconstruction era. Hugely popular in its day, it is now notorious for its negative portrayal of the consequences of slave emancipation and its celebration of the original Ku Klux Klan as a heroic organisation seeking to protect the white population in the Southern states. The storyline, based on a play, *The Clansman*, by Thomas Dixon, involves the sexual advances by an ex-slave, Gus, on a white girl called Flora. In trying to escape him she jumps to her death from a cliff top. Gus, subsequently, is lynched by the Klan. The part of Gus was played, in 'blackface', by a white actor named Walter Long.

The film created a furore: the NAACP launched a campaign against it and published articles that highlighted its historical inaccuracies. Riots in various cities, including Chicago, Boston and Denver, prevented showings, and attacks on black people, including one murder in Lafayette, Indiana, have been attributed to its inflammatory impact. Furthermore, it is likely to have contributed to the rebirth of the Ku Klux Klan in the 1920s.

ACTIVITY

Using Historical Evidence

Discussing change and continuity in the historical record. In both part **a** and part **b** of the exam you should look for opportunities to comment on how the sources reveal change and/or continuity in the historical record. Practise this skill by comparing the content of Sources 8 and 9. What are the problems presented by these sources as evidence for the changing position of African Americans in America?

Stretch and challenge

View the film online (see: www.heinemann. co.uk/hotlinks) and draw your own conclusions regarding its message.

ACTIVITY

1 Why did this scene from the film *The Birth of a Nation* cause such controversy?

2 Do you think this film probably did more to help or hinder the campaign for racial equality? Explain your answer.

THINK LIKE AN HISTORIAN

1 What problems does an historian face in trying to assess the impact of this film on the struggle for racial equality?

2 How might an historian attempt to measure its impact?

Source (10) Still from *The Birth of a Nation*, 1915

Even films, like *The Birth of a Nation*, that aim to be historical, tell us most about the time in which they were written. As the 20th century and the civil rights movement developed, the racial attitudes of the Hollywood film-makers, like those of society at large, changed. In early westerns, for example, the Native-American 'Indians' were depicted as hostile, ignorant aliens, devoid of personality. By the 1970s, however, they were being depicted in much more sympathetic and empathetic ways. For example, one ground-breaking movie from 1970 was Arthur Penn's *Little Big Man* in which Dustin Hoffman played the part of a white man adopted by a loving Cheyenne family. In the following source, an historian writing about that film, 13 years after its release, reflects upon the political climate in which it was created.

Source (11) Westerns

[The] understanding that historical transition can mean irreparable loss underlies the 'Indian' films of the Vietnam era, most notably Arthur Penn's 'Little Big Man' and Ralph Nelson's 'Soldier Blue' (both 1970). The one can be faulted for its unhappy mixture of sentiment towards the Indians and self-contempt towards white culture, the other for the gratuitous violence with which it closes. Nonetheless, each tries to show that the triumph of white America was built on the bloody defeat of native Americans, and that the people who were beaten had been human beings, with their own societies, cultures, and ways of living and loving. Both films are captivity narratives, telling of the transformations undergone by whites who are forced into close contact with Indian ways.

From Edward Countryman, 'Westerns and United States' History', in *History Today*, published in 1983.

ACTIVITY

1 How does the language of this historian (Source 11) reveal changed attitudes in the 20th century towards America's ethnic minorities?

2 What do the criticisms of these films have in common with criticisms of the novel *Uncle Tom's Cabin*? Answer with reference to both this source and Source 8.

For discussion

1 What are the limitations of films as historical sources?

2 Should historians use films as evidence?

The evidence of photographs

The most 'immediate' form of evidence for the history of the struggle for civil rights is the photograph. As with other sources of evidence, the historian needs to consider the provenance of an historic photograph in evaluating it as historical evidence. The principle question to ask is what motivated the photographer to take that particular photograph in the first place. 20th century history is littered with photographs that served a purely propagandist purpose. Of course, this does not make a photograph less valuable, but it does highlight how important it is to avoid falling into the trap of taking a photograph at face value.

The photograph in Source 12 was taken by a professional photographer, Lawrence Beitler, who went on to make thousands of copies of it which he sold for 50 cents each. It shows the bodies of two men, Thomas Shipp and Abram Smith, hanging from a tree, lynched by a mob that broke into the jail in which they were being kept on a charge of murdering a young white man and raping his girlfriend.

ACTIVITY

Using Historical Evidence

Comparing images. At first sight, Sources 10 and 12 seem to have a great deal in common. However, as with all sources, their relative value is determined by their provenance. In what ways do the sources have different value as evidence? Is either source any more valuable as historical evidence than the other? What do these sources reveal about the danger of taking sources at face value?

Source (12) Thomas Shipp and Abram Smith, lynched in Marion, Indiana, August 1930

Lawrence Beitler, 1930.

ACTIVITY

1　Why was this scene (Source 12) photographed?

2　Why did the photograph become so well-known?

3　What sort of people would want to buy such a photograph?

4　Who are the people in the foreground: sightseers or murderers? Explain your answer.

5　What does the photograph reveal about race relations in 1930?

6　What are the strengths and limitations of this photograph as historical evidence?

An American-Jewish writer, Abel Meeropol ('Lewis Allan'), was inspired by the photograph, when he first saw it in 1937, to write a poem about the subject of lynching which he later turned into a song, *Strange Fruit*. This was subsequently made famous by the African-American jazz and blues singer, Billie Holiday, who first performed it in 1939. It is widely considered one of the greatest and most influential songs of the 20th century.

Source **Strange Fruit**

Southern trees bear strange fruit,
Blood on the leaves and blood at the root,
Black bodies swinging in the southern breeze,
Strange fruit hanging from the poplar trees.

Pastoral scene of the gallant south,
The bulging eyes and the twisted mouth,
Scent of magnolias, sweet and fresh,
Then the sudden smell of burning flesh.

Here is fruit for the crows to pluck,
For the rain to gather, for the wind to suck,
For the sun to rot, for the trees to drop,
Here is a strange and bitter crop.

From Lewis Allan, *Strange Fruit*, published in 1937.

ACTIVITY

Using Historical Evidence

Identifying continuity in the historical record. Practise this important skill by comparing the provenance and content of Sources 10, 12 and 13. Use the sources and your own knowledge (look back at Chapter 1) to comment on the ways in which the information provided is incomplete. What questions might an historian ask of the history of lynching that these sources alone cannot answer?

THINK LIKE AN HISTORIAN

1　What does Source 13 reveal about the possible impact of photographs and the extent to which they can raise public awareness?

2　How might the impact of this photograph on the civil rights struggle have been different in the 1960s from the impact it had in the 1930s?

Stretch and challenge

View Billie Holiday performing 'Strange Fruit' on YouTube.

The evidence of popular music

By the early 1960s a new genre of popular music had emerged: protest songs. Led by the charismatic young Jewish-American singer, Bob Dylan (Robert Zimmerman), this music built on the tradition of an earlier left-wing singer-songwriter, Woody Guthrie; the Blues; white folk music; and the social conscience literature of writers like John Steinbeck. On August 28, 1963, Dylan, and other folk music stars, sang to the 250,000 people who had joined Martin Luther King's historic March on Washington. Dylan opened his short set with a song about the killing of a prominent African American, Medgar Evers, the NAACP's 'field secretary' in Mississippi. This source from a modern history book relates the details of his assassination.

> **Source (14) The murder of Medgar Evans**
>
> *Racists tried to shut down the voter drive by eliminating [Mississippi's] most visible civil rights leader. Not only did Medgar Evers register black voters, he encouraged sit-ins and organized boycotts… After a read-in at a whites-only library, a spectator pistol-whipped Evers, and the police clubbed him from behind. Anonymous death threats came over the telephone, and his house was bombed. Facing his own mortality, Evers remarked prophetically, 'You can kill a man, but you can't kill an idea.' After a lengthy strategy meeting that ended past midnight on 12 June 1963, the 37-year-old Evers returned to his home. A sniper waited for him, crouching in the honeysuckle bushes behind the brightly lit carport. As Evers got out of his station wagon carrying 'Jim Crow Must Go' T-shirts, he was shot in the back with a deer-hunting rifle. With blood soaking his white shirt, a dying Evers crawled up the stairs where his three children screamed, 'Get up, Daddy, get up!' After 25,000 mourners viewed his remains, Evers was buried with full military honors in Virginia's Arlington National Cemetery.*
>
> From B.J. Dierenfield, *The Civil Rights Movement*, published in 2004.

Stretch and challenge

Use the Internet or a Bob Dylan songbook to compare this account of Evers' death with the lyrics of Dylan's song, 'Only a Pawn in their Game'.

Despite common knowledge that he was the killer, Byron de la Beckwith, a fertiliser salesman and a member of the Ku Klux Klan, was not tried until 1994. In later years he even ran for the lieutenant governorship, boasting to his supporters that he was a 'straight shooter'.

ACTIVITY

1   How 'accurate' is Dylan's version of the killing of Medgar Evers?

2   What explanation does Dylan provide for Beckwith's action?

3   In who's 'game' is Evers a 'pawn'?

4   Why do you think Bob Dylan wrote this song?

5   Is Dylan's American-Jewish heritage of any relevance in evaluating this song and his involvement in the civil rights movement? Explain your answer.

6   What is the value and what are the limitations of this song as historical evidence for the civil rights movement of the early 1960s?

Stretch and challenge

View Dylan's performance of 'Only a Pawn in their Game' at the end of the March on Washington (August 1963) on YouTube. Dylan sang shortly before King made his 'I have a dream' speech.

ACTIVITY

For discussion

Do protest-singers, typically, 'preach to the converted'? Do protest songs actually change peoples' attitudes?

The most famous civil rights song of the period, 'We Shall Overcome', was based upon an old gospel song. It became the 'anthem' of the movement co-ordinated by Martin Luther King, and was sung by Dylan's girlfriend, Joan Baez, during the March on Washington. It is also associated with the work of another white civil rights activist, Pete Seeger, whose adaptation was, and remains, the best known.

Source (15) **We Shall Overcome**

1. We shall overcome,
We shall overcome,
We shall overcome some day.

Chorus:
Oh, deep in my heart
I do believe
We shall overcome some day.

2. We'll walk hand in hand,
We'll walk hand in hand,
We'll walk hand in hand some day.

Chorus

3. We shall live in peace…

4. We shall all be free…

5. We are not afraid… (Today!)

6. The whole wide world around…

7. Black and white together… (Now!)

8. WE SHALL OVERCOME…

From Pete Seeger and Bob Reiser, *Carry It On*, Blandford Press, published in 1985. (new words and arrangement by Zilphia Horton, Frank Hamilton, Guy Carawan and Pete Seeger)

THINK LIKE AN HISTORIAN

1   What problems do historians encounter in trying to assess the historical significance of this kind of evidence?

2   What does it reveal about the ways in which the civil rights movement had developed since the end of the Second World War?

Summary – what you have learned in Chapter 2

This chapter has introduced you to something of the range of historical evidence available to historians of race and American society from 1865 to the 1970s. It has encouraged you to think about the value and limitations of different types of historical sources. You have developed your understanding of the importance of not taking evidence at face value and, in analysing evidence critically, the importance of considering its provenances.

By working through the various *Activity* and *Think like an historian* tasks, you have practised and developed your skills in the critical analysis and evaluation of sources, and in the forming and testing of hypotheses. In particular, you have practised your skill in considering the provenance of sources. You have considered the different problems posed by different types of evidence and how these can be addressed. Furthermore, you have been encouraged to consider how different people might respond differently to the same piece of historical evidence.

You have also practised the following skills:

- considering the value of sources
- discussing change and continuity in the historical record
- comparing images
- identifying continuity in the historical record
- appreciating the value of a range of sources
- comparing and contrasting a group of sources.

Now take a look at the Exam Café at the back of the book for more advice and practice.

Change from above: evidence concerning the role of state and federal authorities

Overview

It goes without saying that America is a big country. It is a **federation** of states and these states, united by the outcome of the American Civil War (1861–65), fiercely guard their independence. The civil rights struggle was set in the context of a once relatively weak central 'federal' government trying to impose its will on the semi-autonomous and independently-minded states.

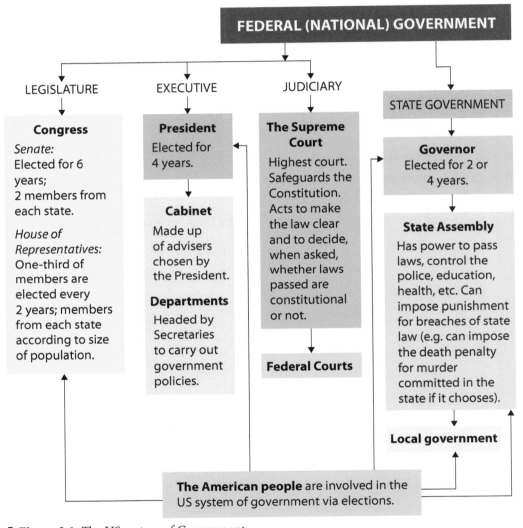

FEDERAL (NATIONAL) GOVERNMENT

LEGISLATURE

Congress

Senate:
Elected for 6 years;
2 members from each state.

House of Representatives:
One-third of members are elected every 2 years; members from each state according to size of population.

EXECUTIVE

President
Elected for 4 years.

Cabinet
Made up of advisers chosen by the President.

Departments
Headed by Secretaries to carry out government policies.

JUDICIARY

The Supreme Court
Highest court. Safeguards the Constitution. Acts to make the law clear and to decide, when asked, whether laws passed are constitutional or not.

Federal Courts

STATE GOVERNMENT

Governor
Elected for 2 or 4 years.

State Assembly
Has power to pass laws, control the police, education, health, etc. Can impose punishment for breaches of state law (e.g. can impose the death penalty for murder committed in the state if it chooses).

Local government

The American people are involved in the US system of government via elections.

▌ **Figure 3.1** The US system of Government

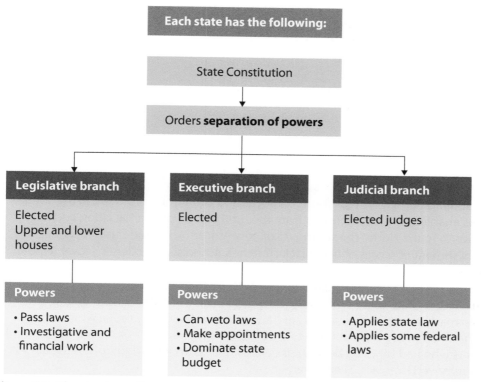

Figure 3.2 The structure of state government in the US

Although the system of 'checks and balances' in the US political system was designed to prevent any one institution becoming too powerful, for example, the ability of the Supreme Court to override Congressional legislation, presidents were very powerful and their attitude to racial and civil rights issues was of considerable importance. President Johnson in the Reconstruction era objected to the reformism of a Republican-led Congress whereas turn of the century presidents, such as Cleveland and McKinley, were more sympathetic to black concerns. McKinley, for example, gave many government posts to African Americans. This chapter first explores the role of state and federal authorities and then the racial views and contributions to the race issue of seven of the most influential 20th century presidents.

Separation of powers

Federal government in America is divided into three areas, the Presidency (the executive branch), the Congress (the legislative branch), and the Courts (the judicial branch). Each has specific powers and responsibilities. This 'separation of powers' is replicated in each state. This system is based on the principle of 'checks and balances' and is designed to prevent any one part from having a monopoly on power.

Key Questions:

1. In what ways did Congress influence the history of race and American society after 1865?
2. What was the influence of the Supreme Court?
3. What was the contribution of US Presidents in the struggle for civil rights?

Congress, the Constitution and Reconstruction

Enshrined in the **American Constitution** were the principles for which civil rights activists fought. The most relevant elements to the race issue were Amendments 13, 14 and 15. Their objective was not to change the Constitution but to ensure that the principles of tolerance and equality upon which it was founded were fully implemented.

American Constitution

This is the list of 'rules' according to which America is governed.

41

The 13th Amendment, **ratified** in December 1865, abolished slavery:

Ratify

Ratification is the process by which proposed constitutional changes receive approval from the peoples' representatives in Congress and become law.

Black Codes

Legislation in the southern states, evolving into the 'Jim Crow' laws, that undermined endeavours in the post-Civil War 'Reconstruction' era to promote racial equality.

Source (1) Amendment 13

1   Neither slavery nor involuntary servitude, except as a punishment for crime whereof the party shall have been duly convicted, shall exist within the United States, or any place subject to their jurisdiction.

2   Congress shall have power to enforce this article by appropriate legislation.

ACTIVITY

To what extent, if at all, does the 13th Amendment challenge the principle of segregation? Explain your answer.

The abolition of slavery represented a social and economic revolution in the southern states enabling a mass migration from the rural plantations to the cities; and later from the South to the North; the setting up of new African-American businesses; and the establishment of scores of new black churches, schools and colleges. However, the southern former slave states resisted any further concessions to equality by imposing through their own state legislatures the so-called **Black Codes**. Although they varied from state to state these effectively prevented most freed slaves from voting, sitting on juries, marrying whites, carrying guns, and giving evidence against a white person. Furthermore many were obliged to agree to binding new contracts with the plantation owners who had formerly been their owners, the terms and conditions of which were little removed from actual enslavement.

Source (2) Amendment 14

1   All persons born or naturalized in the United States, and subject to the jurisdiction thereof, are citizens of the United States and of the State wherein they reside. No State shall make or enforce any law which shall abridge the privileges or immunities of citizens of the United States; nor shall any State deprive any person of life, liberty, or property, without due process of law; nor deny to any person within its jurisdiction the equal protection of the laws.

2   Representatives shall be apportioned among the several States according to their respective numbers, counting the whole number of persons in each State, excluding Indians not taxed. But when the right to vote at any election for the choice of electors for President and Vice-President of the United States, Representatives in Congress, the Executive and Judicial officers of a State, or the members of the Legislature thereof, is denied to any of the male inhabitants of such State, being twenty-one years of age, and citizens of the United States, or in any way abridged, except for participation in rebellion, or other crime, the basis of representation therein shall be reduced in the proportion which the number of such male citizens shall bear to the whole number of male citizens twenty-one years of age in such State.

3   No person shall be a Senator or Representative in Congress, or elector of President and Vice-President, or hold any office, civil or military, under the United States, or under any State, who, having previously taken an oath, as a member of Congress, or as an officer of the United States, or as a member of any State legislature, or as an executive or judicial officer of any State, to support the Constitution of the United States, shall have engaged in insurrection or rebellion against the same, or given aid or comfort to the enemies thereof. But Congress may by a vote of two-thirds of each House, remove such disability.

4. The validity of the public debt of the United States, authorized by law, including debts incurred for payment of pensions and bounties for services in suppressing insurrection or rebellion, shall not be questioned. But neither the United States nor any State shall assume or pay any debt or obligation incurred in aid of insurrection or rebellion against the United States, or any claim for the loss or emancipation of any slave; but all such debts, obligations and claims shall be held illegal and void.

5. The Congress shall have power to enforce, by appropriate legislation, the provisions of this article.

In retaliation northern Republicans in Congress, without the support of President Johnson who was sympathetic to southern interests, passed a Civil Rights Act in 1866 and demanded a 14th Amendment that would make the Black Codes illegal. This Amendment was ratified in 1868.

ACTIVITY

1. To what extent, if at all, does the 14th Amendment challenge the principle of segregation? Explain your answer.

2. To what extent are documents like the 14th and 15th Amendments useful evidence for assessing (a) the intentions of politicians and (b) the impact of reforms?

The third and last of these 'Reconstruction' Amendments was the 15th Amendment. This theoretically guaranteed the voting rights of African Americans although, in practice, intimidation and other strategies **disenfranchised** many for a long time afterwards. The 15th Amendment was ratified in 1870.

> Source (3) Amendment 15
>
> 1. *The right of citizens of the United States to vote shall not be denied or abridged by the United States or by any State on account of race, color, or previous condition of servitude.*
>
> 2. *The Congress shall have power to enforce this article by appropriate legislation.*

ACTIVITY

The 15th Amendment did not specify who was qualified to vote. What voting qualifications were states likely to impose in order to reduce the black vote?

Theoretically at least, the 15th Amendment enfranchised 700,000 southern black people and gave them a majority over the 600,000 white voters. Despite this, although many African Americans were elected to lesser posts, none during the Reconstruction era were elected governors, and white politicians continued to dominate all of the state senates. Vivienne Sanders has identified several possible reasons why this was the case:

> Source (4) Reasons for predominantly white senates
>
> *Blacks lacked education, organisation and experience.*
>
> ■ *Blacks were accustomed to white leadership and domination.*
>
> ■ *The black community was divided. Ex-slaves resented free-born blacks who saw themselves as superior.*
>
> ■ *Blacks were a minority in most states.*
>
> ■ *Sure of the black vote, the Republican Party usually put forward white candidates in the hope of attracting more white votes.*
>
> ■ *White Republicans usually considered blacks to be less able to govern than whites.*
>
> ■ *Southern black leaders were usually moderates who had no desire to exclude ex-Confederates from office.*
>
> From V. Saunders, *Race Relations in the USA 1863–1980*, published in 2006.

EXAM TIP

Comparing two sources.

In the exam you will be required to compare and contrast sources. Sometimes the similarities are very obvious. What obvious similarities can you detect in both the content and provenance of Sources 1 and 2? Sometimes the similarities are less obvious. What are the similarities between clause 1 of Amendment 14 (Source 2) and clause 1 of Amendment 13 (Source 1)? If this is your own book use a highlighter pen to identify key phrases.

Disenfranchised

To be deprived of the right to vote.

THINK LIKE AN HISTORIAN

Comparing three sources.

What are the main similarities and differences between Sources 1, 2 and 3?

In a final gesture of 'Reconstruction', the Republican-dominated Congress passed a second Civil Rights Act in 1875 to end segregation. It declared that:

ACTIVITY

How might the conservative white owner of a private inn or theatre have felt that the 1875 Act contravened his own civil rights?

> **Source 5** The 1875 Civil Rights Act
>
> *... all persons within the jurisdiction of the United States shall be entitled to the full and equal enjoyment of the accommodations, advantages, facilities, and privileges of inns, public conveyances on land or water, theaters, and other places of public amusement; subject only to the conditions and limitations established by law, and applicable alike to citizens of every race and color, regardless of any previous condition of servitude*
>
> The Civil Rights Act, 1875.

Confederate

The Confederate states were those that broke away from the United States and fought against the North in the Civil War.

From 1877, when federal troops were withdrawn from the former '**Confederate**' states, the South was given more autonomy by the federal government based in Washington in the North. This included control over such matters as voting procedures and education.

The Supreme Court and segregation

In the 1880s the Supreme Court proved to be far less progressive than the Republican Congress of the 1870s. The Civil Rights Act of 1875 was found to be unlawful by the Supreme Court in 1883 on the grounds that it undermined the sovereignty of the state legislatures and denied individuals their rights. Justice Joseph P. Bradley argued that the 14th Amendment guaranteed equal protection before the law for American citizens but it did not outlaw the principle of segregation. He argued that:

ACTIVITY

To what extent, if at all, did the 13th and 14th Amendments support legislation for desegregation? Explain your answer with reference to these Amendments.

> **Source 6** A judge's views on segregation
>
> *On the whole, we are of opinion that no countenance of authority for the passage of the law in question can be found in either the thirteenth or fourteenth amendment of the constitution; and no other ground of authority for its passage being suggested, it must necessarily be declared void, at least so far as its operation in the several states is concerned.*
>
> US Supreme Court cases, 109 US 3 (1883).

Also in 1883 the Supreme Court found the Ku Klux Klan Act of 1871, designed to deal with Klan offences in the federal courts when state courts would not hear them, to be unlawful.

From the start, the campaign for advancing the civil rights of African Americans was associated with the Republican party which had dominated in the Reconstruction period between 1863 and 1877. In the later 1870s, in the South particularly, the Democrats were in the ascendant. Here new Black Codes disenfranchised ex-slaves by declaring in the 'Grandfather' clauses that only Americans whose families had been enfranchised for two generations were entitled to vote. In Mississippi in 1890, and subsequently in other southern states, literacy tests and income thresholds were introduced to determine who could vote. By 1900 a mere 3 per cent of southern Blacks were permitted to vote.

EXAM TIP

Testing a hypothesis.

In the exam you will be required to evaluate interpretations on the basis of the available evidence. How far do Sources 1, 2 and 3 substantiate the claim of Source 6? Use key phrases from these sources to explain your opinion. How does the need for a Civil Rights Act in 1875 (Source 5) further substantiate this claim?

Even before the end of the Reconstruction and the findings of the Supreme Court regarding the 1875 Civil Rights Act, laws were being passed in the South at state level that enforced segregation. These were the notorious 'Jim Crow' laws that remained the target of civil rights campaigners up until 1965. These laws forbade such things as inter-racial marriages ('miscegenation'), mixed schools, mixed residential areas, mixed libraries, and mixed toilet and washing facilities.

As such legislation increased in conservative Democrat-dominated states, a group of liberals in Los Angeles in 1892 set about challenging segregation in the courts. They called themselves the Citizens' Committee to Test the Constitutionality of the Separate Car Law. In 1890 a law was passed in Louisiana that prohibited the sharing of railroad carriages by people of different races. In 1892 one of their members, Homer Plessy, who was one-eighth African American and fair-skinned, bought a ticket and found a seat in a whites-only carriage. He was soon arrested for refusing to move to another part of the train. Subsequently the critical *Plessy v. Ferguson* test case was heard by the Supreme Court in 1896. The defence argued that Plessy's arrest denied his rights to equal protection under the terms of the 14th Amendment and that such treatment amounted to the condition of slavery vilified in the 13th Amendment. However, the majority of the Court supported the counter-argument that:

> Source (7) A court's view on equality
>
> *Legislation is powerless to eradicate racial instincts or to abolish distinctions based on physical differences, and the attempt to do so can only result in accentuating the differences of the present situation. If the civil and political rights of both races be equal, one cannot be inferior to the other civilly or politically. If one race be inferior to the other socially, the Constitution of the United States cannot put them on the same plane.*
>
> Plessy v. Ferguson, US Supreme Court cases, 163 US 537 (1896).

ACTIVITY

1   To what extent do you think the 14th Amendment was a purely 'political' statement? Explain your answer with reference to the Amendment.

2   What distinction does Source 7 seem to make between 'civil' rights and 'social' rights?

They argued that such laws separated people equally in as much as whites were prohibited from using 'coloreds-only' carriages. This 'equal but separate' doctrine became the central plank of justifications for segregation from this point on until the argument was overturned by the *Brown v. Board of Education* case of 1954 (see Chapter 5).

The US Army, Native Americans, treaties and reservations

In a series of treaties between 1851 and 1861, the federal government deprived Native Americans of tens of millions of acres of their tribal territories. By confining them to smaller reservations, these treaties shattered their hunter-gatherer economy, a situation worsened by the destruction of the great herds of buffalo upon which certain tribes traditionally depended.

Native American retaliation led to the '**Plains Wars**' of the 1860s. In 1876, following a revival of the conflict and the Battle of Little Big Horn in which General Custer and a third of his Ninth Cavalry regiment were killed, the federal government handed over the 'Indian Problem' to the army to sort out. The brutality with which the reservations were managed was epitomised by the 1890 'Massacre at Wounded Knee' when 200 unarmed men, women and children were killed.

The extermination of Native Americans, advocated by extremists, was rejected by Congress in favour of a policy of 'civilising' them. This led to the Dawes Act of 1887, section 6 of which granted them the status of American citizens:

THINK LIKE AN HISTORIAN

Reading beyond the face value of sources.

It would be easy to infer from a piece of legislation that it had some effect in preventing that which it legislated against. Use Source 7 to explain why this might not have been the case with the 1875 Civil Rights Act (Source 5). What additional evidence would you need to find out about the full effect of this law?

the Plains Wars

Series of conflicts between the US Army and Native Americans in the 1860s.

45

Source ⑧ The Dawes Act

… every Indian born within the territorial limits of the United States to whom allotments [i.e. farm land on the reservations] shall have been made under the provisions of this act, or under any law or treaty, and every Indian born within the territorial limits of the United States who has voluntarily taken up, within said limits, his residence separate and apart from any tribe of Indians therein, and has adopted the habits of civilized life, is hereby declared to be a citizen of the United States, and is entitled to all the rights, privileges, and immunities of such citizens…

The Dawes Act, 1887.

The object of the Act was to break up the communal tribes and to re-establish them along western capitalist lines in which land on the reservations, the allotments referred to in the source, would be owned as property by independent farmers. The civilising mission also led to the establishment of white-run boarding schools for Native-American children.

Source ⑨

■ Two photographs showing the same person, Tom Torlino of the Navajo, on his arrival at the Carlisle Indian Industrial School in 1882 (left) and three years later.

THINK LIKE AN HISTORIAN

Looking for ambiguities.

The analysis of sources involves being attentive to both what is clearly stated and that which invites interpretation. What ambiguous statement concerning definitions appears in Source 8? How might this loophole have been exploited by racists? With reference to both Sources 8 and 9 explain why the Dawes Act (Source 8) itself can be described as racist despite its association with promoting civil rights.

ACTIVITY

'A respectable desire to 'civilise' explains white attitudes towards Native Americans in the last quarter of the 19th century.' How far do you think Sources 8 and 9 support this interpretation? If, on the evidence of these sources, you disagree with the statement, suggest an alternative interpretation.

ACTIVITY

For discussion

1   In what ways was the treatment of Native Americans in the later 19th century both segregationist and integrationist?

2   Why was this likely to cause future problems?

EXAM TIP

Although the history of race and American society in modern times has been dominated by the struggle of African Americans for racial equality, don't forget that you need to know about the experience of other minority racial groups. You are likely to be presented with a source that focuses on one of these or an organisation that represented the interests of all racial minorities.

President Theodore Roosevelt (1901–09) and lynch law

The Republican President Theodore Roosevelt's position on racial issues is hard to determine. According to the following source he had his doubts regarding the extent to which legislation could resolve the race issue:

> Source **10**   Race legislation
>
> *The difference between what can and what cannot be done by law is well exemplified by our experience with the negro problem... The negroes were formerly held in slavery. This was a wrong which legislation could remedy, and which could not be remedied except by legislation. Accordingly they were set free by law. This having been done, many of their friends believed that in some way, by additional legislation, we could at once put them on an intellectual, social, and business equality with the whites. The effort has failed completely. In large sections of the country the negroes are not treated as they should be treated, and politically in particular the frauds upon them have been so gross and shameful as to awaken not merely indignation but bitter wrath; yet the best friends of the negro admit that his hope lies, not in legislation, but in the constant working of those often unseen forces of the national life which are greater than all legislation.*
>
> From How Not To Help Our Poorer Brother, an article in the *Review of Reviews*, January, 1897.

THINK LIKE AN HISTORIAN

Considering tone.

In the exam you may be presented with sources that draw similar conclusions despite being written from very different perspectives. What broad conclusions regarding legislation, race and American society are shared by the authors of Sources 10 and 7? Using extracts from both sources explain how the tone of each reveals how they approach the subject from a different perspective.

THINK LIKE AN HISTORIAN

Why should an historian treat evidence like Source 10 with caution when evaluating the views of Roosevelt *as President*?

More controversial was his State of the Union Address of 1906 concerning the problem of lynching.

Source (11) Race and lynching

In connection with the delays of the law, I call your attention and the attention of the Nation to the prevalence of crime among us, and above all to the epidemic of lynching and mob violence that springs up, now in one part of our country, now in another… A great many white men are lynched, but the crime is peculiarly frequent in respect to black men. The greatest existing cause of lynching is the perpetration, especially by black men, of the hideous crime of rape - the most abominable in all the category of crimes, even worse than murder. Mobs frequently avenge the commission of this crime by themselves torturing to death the man committing it; thus avenging in bestial fashion a bestial deed, and reducing themselves to a level with the criminal.

Lawlessness grows by what it feeds upon; and when mobs begin to lynch for rape they speedily extend the sphere of their operations and lynch for many other kinds of crimes, so that two-thirds of the lynchings are not for rape at all; while a considerable proportion of the individuals lynched are innocent of all crime…

The white people of the South indict the whole colored race on the ground that even the better elements lend no

assistance whatever in ferreting out criminals of their own color. The respectable colored people must learn not to harbor their criminals, but to assist the officers in bringing them to justice. This is the larger crime, and it provokes such atrocious offenses as the one at Atlanta. The two races can never get on until there is an understanding on the part of both to make common cause with the law-abiding against criminals of any color.

… Every colored man should realize that the worst enemy of his race is the negro criminal, and above all the negro criminal who commits the dreadful crime of rape; and it should be felt as in the highest degree an offense against the whole country, and against the colored race in particular, for a colored man to fail to help the officers of the law in hunting down with all possible earnestness and zeal every such infamous offender. Moreover, in my judgment, the crime of rape should always be punished with death, as is the case with murder… Let justice be both sure and swift; but let it be justice under the law, and not the wild and crooked savagery of a mob.

From Theodore Roosevelt's State of the Union Address, 1906.

EXAM TIP

The provenance of sources.

In part **b** of the exam you will be asked to consider the limitations of sources. This involves asking questions. You need to consider who produced the source and for what reasons. Taking this into consideration why should an historian be cautious in taking Source 11 at face value?

ACTIVITY

'The worst enemy of his race is the negro criminal.' How far do you think Sources 6, 7, 10, 11 and 12 support President Roosevelt's claim? If, on the evidence of these sources, you disagree with the statement, suggest an alternative interpretation.

In his address Roosevelt concluded that education offered the solution to racial problems.

Source (12) Race and education

…The white man, if he is wise, will decline to allow the Negroes in a mass to grow to manhood and womanhood without education. Unquestionably education such as is obtained in our public schools does not do everything towards making a man a good citizen; but it does much. The

lowest and most brutal criminals, those for instance who commit the crime of rape, are in the great majority men who have had either no education or very little; just as they are almost invariably men who own no property; for the man who puts money by out of his earnings, like the man who

acquires education, is usually lifted above mere brutal criminality. Of course the best type of education for the colored man, taken as a whole, is such education as is conferred in schools like Hampton and Tuskegee; where the boys and girls, the young men and young women, are trained industrially as well as in the ordinary public school branches. The graduates of these schools turn out well in the great majority of cases, and hardly any of them become criminals, while what little criminality there is never takes the form of that brutal violence which invites lynch law. Every graduate of these schools - and for the matter of that every other colored man or woman - who leads a life so useful and honorable as to win the good will and respect of those whites whose neighbor he or she is, thereby helps the whole colored race as it can be helped in no other way; for next to the negro himself, the man who can do most to help the negro is his white neighbor who lives near him; and our steady effort should be to better the relations between the two. Great tho the benefit of these schools has been to their colored pupils and to the colored people, it may well be questioned whether the benefit, has not been at least as great to the white people among whom these colored pupils live after they graduate.

From Theodore Roosevelt's State of the Union Address, 1906.

ACTIVITY

1   In what ways might civil rights campaigners have considered that Roosevelt's views on education in Source 12 were inherently racist?

2   To what extent, according to Source 12, does Roosevelt appear to support the principle of segregation?

President Woodrow Wilson (1913–21) and segregation

Woodrow Wilson was a deeply conservative Democrat and the first Southerner to be elected President after the Civil War. He was far less ambivalent regarding race issues than Theodore Roosevelt and brought to the White House the values of the South's 'Jim Crow' laws. He openly admired the historic role of the KKK in undermining Reconstruction in the South and he considered slavery an institution that had advanced the condition of Africans. His views on the KKK were celebrated in D. Griffith's influential and racist *The Birth of a Nation* silent movie in a slide quoting from Wilson's book *History of the American People* (1902).

Source (13)

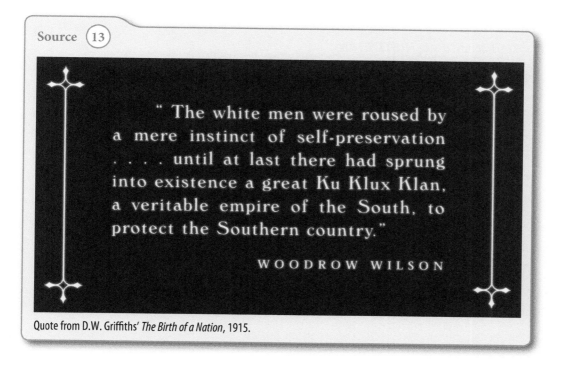

" The white men were roused by a mere instinct of self-preservation . . . . until at last there had sprung into existence a great Ku Klux Klan, a veritable empire of the South, to protect the Southern country."

WOODROW WILSON

Quote from D.W. Griffiths' *The Birth of a Nation*, 1915.

Disliking the idea of shared toilet facilities or black men having any contact with white women, Wilson did his bit in promoting segregation in his own workplace: federal government offices. Although when the KKK was revived after the First World War he was deeply critical of its excesses, there is no doubt that he contributed in no small way to continuing racial discrimination.

However, Wilson's racism is not found in his most famous speeches such as his address at the Gettysburg battlefield in 1913:

Source 14   Woodrow Wilson's Gettysburg Speech, 1913

I have been chosen the leader of the Nation. I cannot justify the choice by any qualities of my own, but so it has come about, and here I stand. Whom do I command? The ghostly hosts who fought upon these battlefields long ago and are gone? These gallant gentlemen stricken in years whose fighting days, are over, their glory won? What are the orders for them, and who rallies them? I have in my mind another host, whom these set free of civil strife in order that they might work out in days of peace and settled order the life of a great Nation. That host is the people themselves, the great and the small, without class or difference of kind or race or origin; and undivided in interest, if we have but the vision to guide and direct them and order their lives aright in what we do. Our constitutions are their articles of enlistment. The orders of the day are the laws upon our statute books. What we strive for is their freedom, their right to lift themselves from day to day and behold the things they have hoped for, and so make way for still better days for those whom they love who are to come after them. The recruits are the little children crowding in. The quartermaster's stores are in the mines and forests and fields, in the shops and factories. Every day something must be done to push the campaign forward; and it must be done by plan and with an eye to some great destiny.

From Woodrow Wilson's Gettysburg Speech, 1913.

President Franklin D. Roosevelt (1933–45) and the New Deal

The economic crisis ushered in by the Wall Street Crash of 1929 had a greater impact in advancing African-American economic interests than the work of the various civil rights organisations established since the start of the century. The Democrat President Roosevelt came to office in 1933 with a promise to address the depression in a much more interventionist and forthright way than his Republican predecessor, Herbert Hoover. His ensuing '**New Deal**' provided homes, jobs and training for tens of thousands of people, regardless of their colour.

> **Source 15 On discrimination in the defence industries**
>
> *By the virtue of the authority vested in me by the Constitution, and as a prerequisite to the successful conduct of our national defence production effort, I do hereby reaffirm the policy of the United States that there shall be no discrimination in the employment of workers in defence industries or government because of race, creed, color, or national origin, and I do hereby declare that it is the duty of employers and of labor organizations to provide for the equitable participation of workers in defence industries.*
>
> From President Roosevelt's Executive Order 8802, 25 June, 1941 (quoted in J.R. Franklin and I. Starr, *The Negro in Twentieth Century America*, published in 1967).

The effectiveness of the federal aid New Deal programme, despite some discrimination in its application in parts of the South, inspired many black voters, especially in the North, to switch from the Republican Party to the Democrats. Although Roosevelt did not legislate against segregation, his New Deal obliged Democrats to consider the promotion of civil rights as a path to securing the black Democrat vote. Roosevelt's wife, Eleanor, was particularly active in cultivating African-American support for the party and her husband's presidency, and she encouraged Roosevelt to appoint capable black men to senior positions in his administration.

One piece of legislation from the Roosevelt era did directly address the civil rights of one ethnic group: the Native Americans. This was the Indian Reorganisation Act of 1934, otherwise known as the 'Indian New Deal'. It countered the allotment principle of the earlier Dawes Act, that had encouraged the breaking up of the reservations, by making it harder to buy or sell reservation land. It also strengthened the control of tribal councils over their homelands and helped restore, over the next twenty years, more than two million acres to the reservations through federal proclamation or purchase.

New Deal

Series of economic initiatives to combat America's economic depression taken by the administration of President Roosevelt from 1933.

ACTIVITY

What links are suggested by Source 15 between the war effort in America during the Second World War and presidential support for racial equality?

Source 16

PERSONAL AND CONFIDENTIAL.

THE WHITE HOUSE
WASHINGTON

March 19, 1936

Ack'd W+W. 3-21-36

My dear Mr. White:

        Before I received your letter today I
had been in to the President, talking to him about
your letter enclosing that of the Attorney General.
I told him that it seemed rather terrible that one
could get nothing done and that I did not blame you
in the least for feeling there was no interest in
this very serious question. I asked him if there
were any possibility of getting even one step taken,
and he said the difficulty is that it is unconsti-
tutional apparently for the Federal Government to
step in in the lynching situation. The Government
has only been allowed to do anything about kidnapping because of its interstate aspect, and even that
has not as yet been appealed so they are not sure
that it will be declared constitutional.

        The President feels that lynching is
a question of education in the states, rallying
good citizens, and creating public opinion so that
the localities themselves will wipe it out. However, if it were done by a Northerner, it will
have an antagonistic effect. I will talk to him
again about the Van Nuys resolution and will try
to talk also to Senator Byrnes and get his point
of view. I am deeply troubled about the whole
situation as it seems to be a terrible thing to
stand by and let it continue and feel that one cannot speak out as to his feeling. I think your next
step would be to talk to the more prominent members
of the Senate.

        Very sincerely yours,

        Eleanor Roosevelt

Letter, Eleanor Roosevelt to Walter White, secretary of the NAACP, detailing her lobbying efforts for federal action against lynchings, 19 March 1936.

ACTIVITY

'The views on racial issues of powerful individuals helped change the views of American society as a whole.' How far do you think Sources 10–16 support this claim? You may, if you wish, amend the interpretation or suggest a different interpretation. If you do this, you must use the sources to support the changes you make.

EXAM TIP

In part **a** questions you are invited to suggest a different interpretation and you should do so. Although you will need some of your own knowledge and understanding to make full sense of the sources provided you must resist the temptation to use this as the basis for forming your new interpretation. The examiner is looking for evidence that you appreciate how historical interpretations rely on the available evidence which, in this case, means the six or seven sources provided. Your new interpretation therefore must be fully justified by the evidence of the exam paper in front of you.

President Harry S. Truman (1945–53) and the Committee on Civil Rights

Harry Truman, a white Southerner with typically racist southern views, was serving as Roosevelt's vice-president when the President died in 1945. Truman replaced him and served as President from 1945 to 1953. Unlike Roosevelt, despite his background, Truman was much more pro-active in addressing the issue of racial inequality. Most importantly he established, in 1946, the President's Committee on Civil Rights. However, his attempts to pass civil rights legislation were thwarted by Congress and the 'Jim Crow' laws remained intact in the South. His main achievement in this area came in 1948 when, as Commander-in-Chief, he ordered an end to discriminatory practices in the Armed Forces. His position on civil rights won him black votes but lost him those of southern supremacist whites. His enthusiasm for advancing civil rights seems to have been genuine and, as the leader of the 'free world' in the struggle against Communist dictatorships in the Cold War, any other position would have exposed him to charges of hypocrisy.

The following sources help explain President Truman's conviction that he needed to take the lead in promoting racial equality.

Source (17) President Truman's comments on racist violence against black soldiers in the Southern states in 1946

[My stomach] turned over when I learned that Negro soldiers, just back from overseas, were being dumped out of army trucks in Missouri and beaten. Whatever my inclinations as a native of Missouri might have been, as President I know this is bad. I shall fight to end evils like this... I am not asking for social equality, because no such things exist, but I am asking for equality of opportunity for all human beings... When a mayor and a City Marshal can take a Negro Sergeant off a bus in South Carolina, beat him up and put out one of his eyes, and nothing is done about it by the State Authorities, something is radically wrong with the system.

From V. Saunders, *Race Relations in the USA 1863–1980*, published in 2006.

Source (18) President Truman's State of the Union Address, 1947

We have recently witnessed in this country numerous attacks upon the constitutional rights of individual citizens as a result of racial and religious bigotry. Substantial segments of our people have been prevented from exercising fully their right to participate in the election of public officials, both locally and nationally. Freedom to engage in lawful callings has been denied.

The will to fight these crimes should be in the hearts of every one of us.

For the Federal Government that fight is now being carried on by the Department of Justice to the full extent of the powers that have been conferred upon it. While the Constitution withholds from the Federal Government the major task of preserving peace in the several States, I am not convinced that the present legislation reached the limit of federal power to protect the civil rights of its citizens.

I have, therefore, by Executive Order, established the President's Committee on Civil Rights to study and report on the whole problem of federally-secured civil rights, with a view to making recommendations to the Congress.

From President Truman's State of the Union Address, 1947.

Source (19) Private comments made by President Truman to his sister in June 1947

I have got to make a speech to the Society for the Advancement of Colored People tomorrow, and I wish I didn't have to make it. Mrs Roosevelt [who was also speaking] has spent her public life stirring up trouble between white and black – and I am in the middle. Mamma won't like what I say because I wind up by quoting old Abe [Abraham Lincoln]. But I believe what I say and I am hopeful we may implement it.

From V. Saunders, *Race Relations in the USA 1863–1980*, published in 2006.

THINK LIKE AN HISTORIAN

The provenance of sources.

In the exam you will be given a range of sources of different types and from different times. In the case of Sources 17 to 19 you can read three sources that have much in common but fundamental differences in terms of their target audience. How does this affect your reading of Sources 18 and 19? In what ways is the information regarding its provenance inadequate for the historian handling Source 17?

ACTIVITY

1   What do Sources 17–19 reveal regarding the reasons why President Truman, whose racist views as a younger man are well-attested, developed a more liberal approach to the race issue?

2   What might a white supremacist Southern Democrat conclude was the main reason for Truman's commitment to improving the lives of African Americans?

3   To what extent, if at all, do these three sources address the issue of segregation? Explain your answer with reference to the sources.

President Dwight D. Eisenhower (1953–61) and the Civil Rights Acts

Although in his inaugural addresses the Republican President Eisenhower paid lip service to Truman's call for racial equality, in practice he was rather more conservative, less prepared to push for anti-discriminatory legislation, and he was firmly opposed to desegregation. However, his presidency coincided with the take-off of the post Second World War civil rights movement and events of monumental importance such as the outcome of the *Brown v. Board of Education* case (1954), the Montgomery Bus Boycott (1955–56), the Little Rock crisis (1957), student sit-ins, and the arrival on the scene of dynamic civil rights leaders such as Martin Luther King and Malcolm X (see Chapter 6). With the race issue having such a high profile as Eisenhower's first term of office reached its end, the Republican Party pursued the black vote to get him re-elected. This led to a civil rights bill that led to the Civil Rights Act of 1957. It included the setting up of a Commission to investigate certain practices that, allegedly, disenfranchised black voters.

Source (20) The 1957 Civil Rights Act

The Commission shall… investigate allegations in writing under oath or affirmation that certain citizens of the United States are being deprived of their right to vote and have that vote counted by reason of their color, race, religion, or national origin; which writing, under oath or affirmation, shall set forth the facts upon which such belief or beliefs are based;

… No person, whether acting under color of law or otherwise, shall intimidate, threaten, coerce, or attempt to intimidate, threaten or coerce any other person for the purpose of interfering with the right of such other person to vote or to vote as he may choose, or of causing such other person to vote for, or not to vote for, any candidate for the office of President, Vice President, presidential elector, Member of the Senate, or Member of the house of Representatives, Delegates or Commissioners from the Territories or possessions, at any general special, or primary election held solely or in part for the purpose of selecting or electing any such candidate.

From the Civil Rights Act, 1957.

ACTIVITY

How far does Source 20 support the hypothesis that politics, as opposed to ethics, led to the Civil Rights Act of 1957? Explain your answer.

A second civil rights bill was presented in 1958 in the context of escalating KKK violence that included the bombing of black churches and other atrocities. It led to the Civil Rights Act of 1960.

> **Source** **The 1960 Civil Rights Act**
>
> *Whoever transports or aids and helps another in transporting in interstate or foreign commerce any explosive, with the knowledge or intent that it will be used to damage or destroy any building or other real or personal property for the purpose of interfering with its use for educational, religious, charitable, residential, business, or civic objectives or of intimidating any person pursuing such objectives, shall be subject to imprisonment for not more than one year, or a fine of not more than $1,000, or both; and if personal injury results shall be subject to imprisonment for not more than ten years or a fine of not more than $10,000, or both; and if death results shall be subject to imprisonment for any term of years or for life, but the court may impose the death penalty if the jury so recommends.*
>
> From the Civil Rights Act, 1960.

ACTIVITY

Why, on the evidence of Source 21, can the reasons for the Civil Rights Act of 1960 be considered 'open to interpretation'?

EXAM TIP

Change over time.

A key concept in this unit, and the main theme of Chapter 1, is change and continuity over time. In the exam you will need to find opportunities to comment on how the sources reveal this. You will find that the sources selected span most of the period from 1865 to the 1970s. Try comparing and contrasting the Civil Rights Acts from which Sources 5, 20 and 21 are extracts. In what ways do these three sources reveal both change and continuity in the historical record?

These acts seem to have had little immediate effect but they did give hope to civil rights activists that legislation was the way forward and they set a precedent for the much more effective Civil Rights Act of 1964.

President John F. Kennedy (1961–63) and the Civil Rights Act of 1964

Despite having shown no previous interest in promoting civil rights as a young senator in the 1950s, the Democrat contender, John F. Kennedy, played the 'race card' in the elections that made him President in 1961. Once in office he stayed true to his electoral promises to promote, albeit slowly, racial equality. Thus he appointed far more African Americans to posts in the federal administration than his predecessors, and a good number of prosecutions in the South were made for violation of school desegregation and voting obstruction rules.

However his civil rights legislation, like that of Eisenhower, was a reaction to new circumstances and not the outcome of some long-term plan. In Kennedy's case the pressure on him for change, in the certain knowledge that this would lead to the loss of many white votes, came in the form of the violent response to the Freedom Rides (1961), and the massive March on Washington demonstration (1963) (see Chapter 6). Many historians are of the opinion that without these dramatic occurrences, Kennedy would have prevaricated over the need to introduce more comprehensive civil rights legislation.

Source **22 On segregation**

We are confronted primarily with a moral issue. It is as old as the Scriptures and is as clear as the American Constitution. The heart of the question is whether all Americans are to be afforded equal rights and equal opportunities; whether we are going to treat our fellow Americans as we want to be treated.

If an American, because his skin is dark, cannot eat lunch in a restaurant open to the public; if he cannot send his children to the best public schools available; if he cannot vote for the public officials who represent him; if, in short, he cannot enjoy the full and free life which all of us want, then who among us would be content to have the color of his skin changed and stand in his place?

… The fires of frustration and discord are burning in every city, North and South. Where legal remedies are not at hand, redress is sought in the streets in demonstrations, parades and protests, which create tensions and threaten violence – and threaten lives…

I am, therefore, asking the Congress to enact legislation giving all Americans the right to be served in facilities which are open to the public – hotels, restaurants and theatres, retail stores and similar establishments. This seems to me to be an elementary right…

J. F. Kennedy's radio and television report to the American people on civil rights, 11 June 1963 (from B.J. Dierenfield, *The Civil Rights Movement*, published in 2004).

ACTIVITY

1 What two explanations for Kennedy's advocacy of civil rights are revealed in Source 22?

2 Why should historians be wary of taking a source such as this at face value?

Kennedy did not live to see his civil rights bill of 1963 become law; he was killed by an assassin's bullet on 22 November 1963.

ACTIVITY

Hypothesis 1: President Kennedy played the leading role in bringing about the 1964 Civil Rights Act.

Hypothesis 2: Civil Rights activists played the leading role in bringing about the 1964 Civil Rights Act.

Based on what you have read, which hypothesis do you find more convincing? Make a list of evidence for and against each one to justify your choice.

Source (23) The 1964 Civil Rights Act

All persons shall be entitled to the full and equal enjoyment of the goods, services, facilities, and privileges, advantages, and accommodations of any place of public accommodation, as defined in this section, without discrimination or segregation on the ground of race, color, religion, or national origin.

Each of the following establishments which serves the public is a place of public accommodation within the meaning of this title if its operations affect commerce, or if discrimination or segregation by it is supported by State action:

(1) any inn, hotel, motel, or other establishment which provides lodging to transient guests, other than an establishment located within a building which contains not more than five rooms for rent or hire and which is actually occupied by the proprietor of such establishment as his residence;

(2) any restaurant, cafeteria, lunchroom, lunch counter, soda fountain, or other facility principally engaged in selling food for consumption on the premises, including, but not limited to, any such facility located on the premises of any retail establishment; or any gasoline station;

(3) any motion picture house, theater, concert hall, sports arena, stadium or other place of exhibition or entertainment…

… The provisions of this title shall not apply to a private club or other establishment not in fact open to the public.

From the Civil Rights Act, 1964.

ACTIVITY

'American presidents in the middle years of the 20th century failed to make significant advances in civil rights.' Explain how far Sources 17–23 support this interpretation. You may, if you wish, amend the interpretation or suggest a different interpretation. If you do this, you must use the sources to support the changes you make.

EXAM TIP

When evaluating sources always be careful to distinguish *intent* from what actually happened. For example, you may be presented with sources that provide evidence of presidential proposals as well as laws, such as civil rights acts, that were actually passed.

President Lyndon B. Johnson (1963–69) and the 'Great Society'

When Vice-President Johnson took over the presidency on Kennedy's death, he brought to the White House a seemingly genuine commitment to promoting the interests of the more deprived American citizens, including the poor and black people. His critics accused him of posing as a defender of civil rights for purely political reasons while others praised him for risking his political career by bravely challenging social inequality. In anticipation of the 1964 presidential elections, he announced his dream of a 'Great Society', a dream that he was warned by some doubters would lose him the election.

Source (24) The Great Society

The purpose of protecting the life of our Nation and preserving the liberty of our citizens is to pursue the happiness of our people. Our success in that pursuit is the test of our success as a Nation.

For a century we labored to settle and to subdue a continent. For half a century we called upon unbounded invention and untiring industry to create an order of plenty for all of our people.

The challenge of the next half century is whether we have the wisdom to use that wealth to enrich and elevate our national life, and to advance the quality of our American civilization.

Your imagination, your initiative, and your indignation will determine whether we build a society where progress is the servant of our needs, or a society where old values and new visions are buried under unbridled growth. For in your time we have the opportunity to move not only toward the rich society and the powerful society, but upward to the Great Society.

The Great Society rests on abundance and liberty for all. It demands an end to poverty and racial injustice, to which we are totally committed in our time. But that is just the beginning.

From Johnson's 'Great Society' speech at the University of Michigan, 1964.

ACTIVITY

1   What was the purpose of this speech (Source 24)?

2   How might the purpose of this speech have affected its content?

3   Does this affect its value as historical evidence? Explain your answer.

4   What similarities and differences were there between Roosevelt's 'New Deal' and Johnson's vision of a 'Great Society'?

In addition to pushing through the 1964 Civil Rights Act, Johnson, in 1965, produced Education Acts and the Social Security Act, all of which advanced opportunities for black Americans. Most significantly, in the same year, the violent response to Martin Luther King's march from Selma to challenge discriminatory voting practices (see Chapter 6) persuaded Johnson to risk the hostility of southern Congressmen by calling for a new Voting Rights Act.

Source (25) We shall overcome

I speak tonight for the dignity of man and the destiny of Democracy. I urge every member of both parties, Americans of all religions and of all colors, from every section of this country, to join me in that cause.

… There is no cause for pride in what has happened in Selma. There is no cause for self-satisfaction in the long denial of equal rights of millions of Americans. But there is cause for hope and for faith in our Democracy in what is happening here tonight.

… There is no Negro problem. There is no Southern problem. There is no Northern problem. There is only an American problem.

… To apply any other test, to deny a man his hopes because of his color or race or his religion or the place of his birth is not only to do injustice, it is to deny Americans and to dishonor the dead who gave their lives for American freedom.

… Many of the issues of civil rights are very complex and most difficult. But about this there can and should be no argument: every American citizen must have an equal right to vote. There is no reason which can excuse the denial of that right. There is no duty which weighs more heavily on us than the duty we have to insure that right. Yet the harsh fact is that in many places in this country men and women are kept from voting simply because they are Negroes.

Every device of which human ingenuity is capable, has been used to deny this right. The Negro citizen may go to register only to be told that the day is wrong, or the hour is late, or the official in charge is absent. And if he persists and, if he manages to present himself to the registrar, he may be disqualified because he did not spell out his middle name, or because he abbreviated a word on the application. And if he manages to fill out an application, he is given a test. The registrar is the sole judge of whether he passes this test. He may be asked to recite the entire Constitution, or explain the most complex provisions of state law.

And even a college degree cannot be used to prove that he can read and write. For the fact is that the only way to pass these barriers is to show a white skin. Experience has clearly shown that the existing process of law cannot overcome systematic and ingenious discrimination. No law that we now have on the books, and I have helped to put three of them there, can insure the right to vote when local officials are determined to deny it. In such a case, our duty must be clear to all of us. The Constitution says that no person shall be kept from voting because of his race or his color.

… What happened in Selma is part of a far larger movement which reaches into every section and state of America. It is the effort of American Negroes to secure for themselves the full blessings of American life. Their cause must be our cause too. Because it's not just Negroes, but really it's all of us, who must overcome the crippling legacy of bigotry and injustice.

And we shall overcome.

From President Johnson's Address to a Joint Session of Congress on Voting Legislation, 15 March 1965.

EXAM TIP

Supporting an interpretation.

In part **a** of the exam you will be asked to use a range of sources to test a hypothesis. In part **b** you will need to consider the limitations of the selection. Although you need to look for evidence that challenges the given interpretation you will also need to find evidence to support it in order to arrive at a balanced conclusion. Try looking for evidence in Sources 12, 22, 24 and 25 that supports the hypothesis that presidents had more confidence in education than legislation as a means of resolving America's racial problems. Which of these sources, in this context, is the odd one out? Explain your answer. Now use this source to try amending the interpretation. How complete is this selection of sources for this purpose? What are the limitations of this selection?

ACTIVITY

1   Why did Johnson on two occasions in this speech (Source 25) use the phrase 'we shall overcome' – the title of the civil rights 'anthem' of this period?

2   Why is this speech considered a masterpiece of political rhetoric? Explain your answer with reference to the source.

The Voting Rights Act was passed in the August of 1965; it had a massive impact in extending the franchise in the Southern states, and upon the election of African-American representatives to public office. However, the riots of 1965, 1966 and 1968 (see Chapter 7) revealed, despite the substantial legislation of 1964 and 1965, how far America was from fulfilling Johnson's dream of a 'Great Society'. Ironically, at the end of the presidency that had produced the most far-reaching civil rights legislation, and, conceivably, because of it, racial relations seemed to be at their lowest ebb since the end of the Reconstruction era. The Kerner Report, commissioned by Johnson in 1967 to investigate the troubles, clarified how legal desegregation had failed to eliminate the actual segregation in cities between relatively affluent white communities and the black ghettos and slums that were most afflicted by riots.

Source (26) Two societies

This is our basic conclusion: Our nation is moving toward two societies, one black, one white - separate and unequal.

Reaction to last summer's disorders has quickened the movement and deepened the division. Discrimination and segregation have long permeated much of American life; they now threaten the future of every American.

From the National Advisory Commission on Civil Disorders (The Kerner Report), 1967.

ACTIVITY

What does Source 26 reveal of the condition of the civil rights movement in the later 1960s?

Exam practice

Interpretation: 'The real hero of this struggle is the American Negro.' (President Johnson, quoted in Sanders, V. (2006) *Race Relations in the USA 1863–1980*)

a   Explain how far the sources in this chapter support this interpretation. You may, if you wish, amend the interpretation or suggest a different interpretation. If you do this you must use the sources to support the changes you make.

   Remember not to simply take the sources at face value. Use your knowledge of the period to interpret and evaluate them.

b   Explain how these sources are both useful and raise problems and issues for a historian using them.

Summary – what you have learned in Chapter 3

This chapter has introduced you to the role of state and federal authorities in the history of America's civil rights movement. You have been introduced to the systems of state and federal authority and the role of Congress and the Supreme Court in the legislative process.

This chapter has also introduced you to some key pieces of federal legislation and important racist state legislation, especially in the South. You have encountered two political parties, the Democrats and the Republicans, and explored their influence through Congress and the Presidency upon the course of the history of race and society in America between 1863 and the 1970s. You have studied in particular the contribution of seven presidents.

By working through the various *Activity* and *Think like an historian* tasks you have practised and developed important skills for the examination:

- understanding concepts and key issues including the nature of government in the USA
- understanding how and why race legislation changed over time
- analysing sources to develop an understanding of the attitudes and motives of those in authority
- comparing and contrasting different presidential initiatives
- considering how different people would have felt about different presidential initiatives
- comparing two or more sources
- using a group of sources to test a hypothesis
- reading beyond the face value of sources
- looking for ambiguities
- considering tone
- considering the provenance of sources
- using a group of sources to support an interpretation.

Now take a look at the Exam Café at the back of the book for more advice and practice.

Resistance from below: evidence concerning the role of groups and organisations

4

Overview

By the start of the 20th century, campaigners for racial equality had recognised the importance of national organisations in promoting their work. This chapter explores, through the evidence of primary sources, how such organisations emerged and developed in the first half of the 20th century. It also considers the role of groups opposed to racial equality and their contribution to hindering or, perhaps, inadvertently assisting, progress towards equality.

> **Key Questions:**
>
> 1   What were the aims of these groups and organisations?
>
> 2   What were their methods?
>
> 3   How effective were they in achieving their objectives?
>
> 4   What part did the trade unions and the labour movement play in the struggle for equality in the inter-war period?

The National Association of Colored Women (NACW)

NACW

The National Association of Colored Women formed in 1896.

The **NACW** was formed in Washington in 1896 from the merger of two earlier groups: the National Federation of African-American Women and the National League of Colored Women. Apart from the Church, this organisation, still running, has the longest history of all African-American organisations. Furthermore, as its website (www.nacwc. org) proudly proclaims, it is 'America's Oldest Women's Organization'. Its original constitution opened with the following declaration:

> **Source** **The Constitution of the NACW**
>
> *"We, the Colored Women of the United States of America, feeling the need of united and sympathetic effort, and hoping to furnish evidence of the moral, mental and material progress made by our people, do hereby unite in a National Association."*
>
> Preamble to the Constitution of the National Association of Colored Women, 1897.

> ### EXAM TIP
>
> **Identifying change and continuity.**
>
> Recognising change and continuity over time is a key skill tested in the exam. As you work through this chapter consider how far the guiding principles of the NACW underpinned other organisations as they emerged in the 20th century. How inclusive/exclusive were they? What were their objectives? Were they all 'national' organisations?'

Organised around clubs, the NACW had around 200,000 individual members by 1920. In the following passage one of the movement's founders and first President, Mary Church Terrell, explained the need for the NACW in her first Presidential address.

Source 2 Genteel militancy

We call ourselves an Association to signify that we have joined hands one with the other to work together in a common cause: to proclaim to the world that women of our race have become partners in the great firm of progress and reform. We denominate ourselves colored, not because we are narrow, and wish to lay emphasis on the color of our skin... But we refer to the fact that this is an association of colored women, because our peculiar status in this country at the present time seems to demand that we stand by ourselves in the special work for which we have been organised.

... Listen to the cry of the children, my sisters. Upon you they depend for the light of knowledge, and the blessing of a good example.

From, Sharon Harley 'Mary Church Terrell: Genteel Militant', in *Black Leaders of the Nineteenth Century*, Ed. Leon F. Litwack, published in 1991.

ACTIVITY

1   There were other women's organisations in America at the end of the 19th century. What do you think Terrell meant when she said 'our peculiar status in this country at the present time seems to demand that we stand by ourselves' (Source 2)?

2   How did her rhetoric aim to appeal to a female audience?

3   What does the closing sentence of this source reveal regarding the objectives of the NACW?

Although it started out as an organisation 'to furnish evidence of the moral, mental and material progress made by people of color through the efforts of our women', the NACW soon became involved in campaigning against the 'Jim Crow' laws, the anti-lynching movement, temperance campaigns, and from 1912, the call for women's suffrage.

In the following source, a modern historian explains the importance of the organisation's principle publication, *The National Notes*.

Source 3 The National Notes

The National Notes served as a unifying force in the expansion of the NACW, by keeping black women informed about what other individuals and groups were doing to advance the race, but, more importantly, giving black women a sense of belonging and pride in their accomplishments. The newsletter served as the primary vehicle to advance the issues agenda of the organization. By doing so, it increased the ties among black women from across the country who learned that women in Kansas were concerned about the same kinds of issues as women in South Carolina, or women in Maryland. The publication also gave hope to the idea that, with effort and by working together, racial prejudice could be reduced. The major themes present in the publication over the years reflect to a great degree both the organization's goals and the concerns and issues of the day. For example, while unity within the organization was an important theme in early issues of the publication—and a necessity in order for the organization to grow and prosper—the unity theme grew less important as other issues arose and as the organization was able to achieve agreement among members about its role as both an activist organization and a social organization.

From Dulcie Straughan, "Lifting as We Climb": The Role of The National Association Notes in Furthering the Issues Agenda of the National Association of Colored Women, 1897–1920, in *Media History Monographs*, published in 2006.

ACTIVITY

1 Why were rising levels of literacy among African Americans so important in the history of the campaign for racial equality?

2 On the basis of the evidence of Sources 1–3, how representative of African-American women was the NACW? Explain your answer.

3 What further information would an historian find helpful in answering question 2?

Despite its longevity, some historians, as in the following source, have stressed the limited success and appeal of the NACW.

> Source A modern historian's verdict on the NACW
>
> *The black clubwomen's movement was very much a middle class movement. Members looked down on the common law marriages and emotional worship habits of lower class blacks. The lack of broad-based support, internal squabbling and snobbery, and the power of white supremacists meant that the NACW declined by the second quarter of the twentieth century, but they had raised awareness of social issues and established schools, orphanages, clinics, hospitals and homes for the elderly.*
>
> From V. Saunders, *Race Relations in the USA 1863–1980*, published in 2006.

ACTIVITY

1 Source 4 is from a modern historian. What kinds of primary evidence might have been used to construct this account?

2 What does Source 4 reveal regarding the limitations of national organisations as vehicles for promoting reform?

3 What sort of evidence would lead an historian to these conclusions? Make a list.

EXAM TIP

Using own knowledge in the analysis of sources.

In part **a** of the exam you will need to use your own knowledge and understanding of changes and developments across the period to make inferences from the sources. Use the information in Sources 3 and 4 to consider how far the NACW seems to have stuck to the original aims and objectives stated in Sources 1 and 2.

The Niagara Movement

A movement founded by a group of 32 African-American intellectuals in 1905 at a location near Niagara Falls.

The Niagara Movement

The **Niagara Movement** was founded by a group of 32 African-American intellectuals in 1905 at a location near Niagara Falls. The most important outcome of this inaugural meeting was a manifesto: 'Niagara's Declaration of Principles'.

Source ⑤ The Niagara Movement

▌ The Niagara Movement 1905 (W.E.B. Du Bois, middle row, second from right).

ACTIVITY

1   For what reason, other than the geographical location of its first meeting, do you think this organisation chose to name itself after the Niagara Falls?

2   On the evidence of this photograph (Source 5), what sort of people set up the Niagara Movement? What additional evidence would you need to support/prove your hypothesis?

EXAM TIP

Analysing photographs.

There is a good chance that one of the seven sources provided in the exam will be a photograph. When you are asked to consider usefulness of sources and the problems they present, be sure to link your commentary to the specific topic. For example, with this photograph the fact that the men in the picture are wearing hats is not of particular significance but their generally 'respectable' appearance is. When you consider the problems presented by the source you need to consider the questions a historian of race and American society is likely to ask. Generic comments on the limitations of photographs, such as 'photos can be edited', are not useful unless they are linked directly to the photo in question and the associated historical theme.

The movement's principle member, W.E.B. Du Bois, summarised its objectives in a speech the following year at the organisation's second meeting:

Source 6   **Aims of the Niagara Movement**

In detail our demands are clear and unequivocal. First, we would vote; with the right to vote goes everything: Freedom, manhood, the honor of your wives, the chastity of your daughters, the right to work, and the chance to rise, and let no man listen to those who deny this.

We want full manhood suffrage, and we want it now, henceforth and forever.

Second. We want discrimination in public accommodation to cease. Separation in railway and street cars, based simply on race and color, is un-American, un-democratic, and silly. We protest against all such discrimination.

Third. We claim the right of freemen to walk, talk, and be with them that wish to be with us. No man has a right to choose another man's friends, and to attempt to do so is an impudent interference with the most fundamental human privilege.

Fourth. We want the laws enforced against rich as well as poor; against Capitalist as well as Laborer; against white as well as black. We are not more lawless than the white race, we are more often arrested, convicted, and mobbed. We want justice even for criminals and outlaws. We want the Constitution of the country enforced. We want Congress to take charge of Congressional elections. We want the Fourteenth amendment carried out to the letter and every State disfranchised in Congress which attempts to disfranchise its rightful voters. We want the Fifteenth

amendment enforced and No State allowed to base its franchise simply on color.

The failure of the Republican Party in Congress at the session just closed to redeem its pledge of 1904 with reference to suffrage conditions at the South seems a plain, deliberate, and premeditated breach of promise, and stamps that party as guilty of obtaining votes under false pretense.

Fifth, We want our children educated. The school system in the country districts of the South is a disgrace and in few towns and cities are Negro schools what they ought to be. We want the national government to step in and wipe out illiteracy in the South. Either the United States will destroy ignorance or ignorance will destroy the United States.

And when we call for education we mean real education. We believe in work. We ourselves are workers, but work is not necessarily education. Education is the development of power and ideal. We want our children trained as intelligent human beings should be, and we will fight for all time against any proposal to educate black boys and girls simply as servants and underlings, or simply for the use of other people. They have a right to know, to think, to aspire.

These are some of the chief things which we want. How shall we get them? By voting where we may vote, by persistent, unceasing agitation; by hammering at the truth, by sacrifice and work.

W.E.B. Du Bois, extract from the 'Harpers Ferry' speech, 1906.

EXAM TIP

Considering the completeness of sources.

The sources you are presented with in the exam will be a lot shorter than Source 6. Furthermore they will probably be incomplete. Sometimes they might be missing important details and this will affect the way in which they are interpreted. Imagine if point 4 was missing from this list of aims. How would this affect your reading of the source? What important views of the Niagara Movement are expressed here but not elsewhere in the document? It is important, especially in your answer to part **b** of the exam, to ask yourself 'What might be missing from this source?'.

ACTIVITY

1   In what ways does this evidence (Source 6) reveal that the Niagara Movement's approach to resolving the race issue was based upon full integration? Make a list.

2   How does this source reveal that race was a *political* as well as a *social* issue?

3   Historians need to find the authentic voices of the period they are studying. How far does Du Bois's 1906 speech (Source 6) provide us with an 'authentic voice' of the civil rights movement of this period?

Stretch and challenge

The movement's second meeting was held at a place called Harpers Ferry, in West Virginia. Use the internet to find out why this was such an appropriate location for an organisation promoting racial equality.

The movement's first white member, Mary White Ovington, joined in 1908. Troubled by funding and leadership issues, most members, including Du Bois, had joined the National Association for the Advancement of Colored People (NAACP) by 1911. Compared to the NAACP, the Niagara Movement was minuscule, a mere 19 members were recorded as attending at their 1908 convention held in Oberlin, Ohio.

The reasons for the emergence of organisations like the Niagara Movement, and the NACW and NAACP before and after it, at the turn of the century, are complex. The following source however provides the historian with some useful clues. It is an extract from the report of the committee of the Niagara Movement delivered at their 1908 Annual Convention.

Source 7   The revolt against discrimination

The Niagara movement at its fourth annual meeting congratulates ten million Negro Americans on their unparalleled opportunity to lead the greatest moral battle of modern times - the fight for the abolition of the color line. In Europe, Asia, and Africa the revolt against mere denomination of color and race has begun. The triumph of the highest civilization is the hope of all races, and that civilization is not and never was the property of any one race or color.

The modern attempt to make it so is the last grasp of barbarism, and has caused a moral deterioration which today threatens the peace and progress of the world. Nowhere has the fearful cost of using crime and lies as a weapon to force races into subjection been so apparent as right here in the United States. This nation has stolen the black man's labor, and has so learned theft; it has lied away the liberties of black litigants, and so learned lawlessness; it has prostituted the ballot and so shaken the foundation of Democracy. Fellow Americans, does it pay? Is the superiority of the white race demonstrated by burning human beings, lynching innocent workingmen, stealing black men's votes and insulting black women?

The program laid down by the Negro haters of America is the most tremendous mistake this nation ever made. It is uncivilized, illogical, and wrong; it cannot triumph unless the Christian religion is a lie. Yet the converts to race segregation and subjection are growing alarmingly. We are today fighting for free common schools in Pennsylvania, for free ballots in Maryland, and for freedom of travel in the nation. The cause of human freedom shrieks aloud in our every step. It is not because of our poverty, it is not because of ignorance, it is not because of crime, it is not even because of race antipathy; it is simply the crude and brutal desire to oppress and abuse and murder wherever and

whenever there is no fear of public opinion or courts of law or just retaliation. Once we were told: Be worthy and fit and the ways are open. Today the avenues of advancement in the army, navy, and civil service, and even in business and professional life, are continually closed to black

applicants of proven fitness, simply on the bald excuse of race and color.

This is the spirit and practice which the Niagara Movement is fighting, and will never cease to fight.

From the *Oberlin Tribune*, published on September 4, 1908.

ACTIVITY

With reference to Source 7 and your own knowledge explain what factors, in America and abroad, help explain the emergence of civil rights organisations around the start of the 20th century.

In the second part of this report, the committee outlined strategies that should be adopted to promote equal rights:

THINK LIKE AN HISTORIAN

To what extent were the approaches of the Niagara Movement the same as those of the NACW?

EXAM TIP

Cross-referencing sources.

Cross-referencing is a key skill for success in the exam. Have a look at Sources 6, 7 and 8 and write down ways in which the message of each source reinforces that of the others. Incidentally, all three sources can be considered as examples of propaganda. Does this make them any less reliable as historical evidence? Explain your answer.

Source (8) Legal and political strategies

First: We say to our own: Obey the law, defend no crime, conceal no criminal, seek no quarrel; but arm yourselves, and when the mob invades your home, shoot, and shoot to kill.

Secondly: We say to voters: Register and vote whenever and wherever you have a right. Vote not in the past, but in the present. Remember that the conduct of the Republican party toward Negroes has been a disgraceful failure to keep just promises. The dominant Roosevelt faction has sinned in this respect beyond forgiveness. We therefore trust that every black voter will uphold men like Joseph Benson Foraker, and will leave no stone unturned to defeat William H. Taft. Remember Brownsville, and establish next November the principle of Negro independence in voting, not only for punishing enemies, but for rebuking false friends.

Let no bribe of money, office nor influence seduce the Negro American to betray the great principles of liberty, equality and opportunity… And the men today who think they can club ten million Negro Americans into inferiority and submission forget that God reigns and the Government at Washington still lives.

From the *Oberlin Tribune*, published on September 4, 1908.

The National Association for the Advancement of Colored People (NAACP)

The NAACP's centenary was celebrated on 12 February 2009, just weeks after America's first African-American president took office. Still a vibrant organisation with around 400,000 members, the NAACP was founded in the wake of the 1908 race riot in Springfield, Illinois. The Niagara Movement's W.E.B. Du Bois once again played a central role from the organisation's inception taking on the role of Director of Publicity and Research and editor of the organisation's journal, *The Crisis*. Although the Niagara Movement had a few white members, the NAACP had a much greater ethnic diversity. Indeed, Du Bois was its only African-American director at the outset, the board being dominated by white Jewish Americans. From the outset, the NAACP championed the civil rights of all groups, including Native Americans and recent immigrants.

The NAACP started life as the National Negro Committee in 1909. This subscription form contains its mission statement ('platform').

Source ⑨ NAACP subscription form

Platform Adopted by the National Negro Committee, 1909

We denounce the ever-growing oppression of our 10,000,000 colored fellow citizens as the greatest menace that threatens the country. Often plundered of their just share of the public funds, robbed of nearly all part in the government, segregated by common carriers, some murdered with impunity, and all treated with open contempt by officials, they are held in some States in practical slavery to the white community. The systematic persecution of law-abiding citizens and their disfranchisement on account of their race alone is a crime that will ultimately drag down to an infamous end any nation that allows it to be practiced, and it bears most heavily on those poor white farmers and laborers whose economic position is most similar to that of the persecuted race.

The nearest hope lies in the immediate and patiently continued enlightenment of the people who have been inveigled into a campaign of oppression. The spoils of persecution should not go to enrich any class or classes of the population. Indeed persecution of organized workers, peonage, enslavement of prisoners, and even disfranchisement already threaten large bodies of whites in many Southern States.

We agree fully with the prevailing opinion that the transformation of the unskilled colored laborers in industry and agriculture into skilled workers is of vital importance to that race and to the nation, but we demand for the Negroes, as for all others, a free and complete education, whether by city, State or nation, a grammar school and industrial training for all and technical, professional, and academic education for the most gifted.

But the public schools assigned to the Negro of whatever kind or grade will never receive a fair and equal treatment until he is given equal treatment in the Legislature and before the law. Nor will the practically educated Negro, no matter how valuable to the community he may prove, be given a fair return for his labor or encouraged to put forth his best efforts or given the chance to develop that efficiency that comes only outside the school until he is respected in his legal rights as a man and a citizen.

We regard with grave concern the attempt manifest South and North to deny black men the right to work and to enforce this demand by violence and bloodshed. Such a question is too fundamental and clear even to be submitted to arbitration. The late strike in Georgia is not simply a demand that Negroes be displaced, but that proven and efficient men be made to surrender their long-followed means of livelihood to white competitors.

As first and immediate steps toward remedying these national wrongs, so full of peril for the whites as well as the blacks of all sections, we demand of Congress and the Executive:

(1). That the Constitution be strictly enforced and the civil rights guaranteed under the Fourteenth Amendment be secured impartially to all.

(2). That there be equal educational opportunities for all and in all the States, and that public school expenditure be the same for the Negro and white child;

(3). That in accordance with the Fifteenth Amendment the right of the Negro to the ballot on the same terms as other citizens be recognized in every part of the country.

I herewith subscribe $_____ to the National Negro Committee, and desire to become a member of the permanent organization growing out of the present Conference.

_____

(Make checks payable to Oswald G. Villard, Treasurer).

Platform adopted by the National Negro Committee, 1909. Courtesy of the NAACP.

ACTIVITY

1   Compare Sources 6 and 9. What points of similarity and difference are there between the mission of the National Negro Committee and the objectives of the NACW and the Niagara Movement?

2   What emotive words and phrases appear in this text (Source 9)? Make a list. What is their purpose?

In the following source, Mary White Ovington, the first white person to join the NAACP, explains its origins.

Source (10) **An early account of the origins of the NAACP**

The National Association for the Advancement of Colored People is five years old, old enough, it is believed, to have a history; and I, who am perhaps, its first member, have been chosen as the person to recite it... In the summer of 1908, the country was shocked by the account of the race riots at Springfield, Illinois. Here, in the home of Abraham Lincoln, a mob containing many of the town's "best citizens," raged for two days, killed and wounded scores of Negroes, and drove thousands from the city. Articles on the subject appeared in newspapers and magazines. Among them was one in the Independent of September 3rd, by William English Walling, entitled "Race War in the North." After describing the atrocities committed against the colored people, Mr. Walling declared:

"Either the spirit of the abolitionists, of Lincoln and of Love-joy must be revived and we must come to treat the Negro on a plane of absolute political and social equality, or Vardaman and Tillman will soon have transferred the race war to the North." And he ended with these words, "Yet who realizes the seriousness of the situation, and what large and powerful body of citizens is ready to come to their aid?"

It so happened that one of Mr. Walling's readers accepted his question and answered it. For four years I had been studying the status of the Negro in New York. I had investigated his housing conditions, his health, his opportunities for work. I had spent many months in the South, and at the time of Mr. Walling's article, I was living in a New York Negro tenement on a Negro Street. And my investigations and my surroundings led me to believe with the writer of the article that "the spirit of the abolitionists must be revived."

So I wrote to Mr. Walling, and after some time, for he was in the West, we met in New York in the first week of the year of 1909. With us was Dr. Henry Moskowitz, now prominent in the administration of John Purroy Mitchell, Mayor of New York. It was then that the National Association for the Advancement of Colored People was born. It was born in a little room of a New York apartment. It is to be regretted that there are no minutes of the first meeting, for they would make interesting if unparliamentary reading.

From Mary White Ovington, *How NAACP Began*, published in 1914.

ACTIVITY

1   How reliable do you find the account in Source 10?

2   To what extent is the establishment of organisations entirely reliant upon the inspiration of individuals? Explain your answer with reference to this and other organisations you have read about in this chapter.

How does Mary White Ovington's account of the origins of the NAACP compare to the following?

> **Source 11 A modern account of the origins of the NAACP**
>
> *Visiting Springfield to witness the effects [of the 1908 race riot] was an inspiration for the labor leader and settlement house activist William English Walling. He wrote an article for The Independent magazine called "The Race War in the North," published September 3, 1908. Walling called for an integrated movement of all Americans to end the violence and oppression that he compared to the treatment of Jews he had just seen on a visit to Russia. Marie White Ovington, a leader of the settlement house movement researching the conditions for African Americans, had already seen the potential of connecting the ideas of Booker T. Washington and W.E.B. Du Bois's Niagara Movement with progressive social reform. Under the inspiration of Walling's article, she began to gather intellectual reformers in meetings first called the National Negro Committee and then the National Association for the Advancement of Colored People. The NAACP, then, would bring together several communities into one larger and thus more effective community.*
>
> *From its origins, therefore, the NAACP had both a chronological history and a rhetorical history. After Walling's inspiration, Oswald Garrison Villard, president of the New York Evening Post, drafted "The Call," a manifesto, signed by many prominent American progressives, urging "all the believers in democracy to join in a national conference for the discussion of present evils, the voicing of protests, and the renewal of the struggle for civil and political liberty." The first meetings included representatives from, among others, the progressive movement, the settlement house movement... the Niagara Movement, the African-American churches, the abolitionist movement's descendents and the anti-lynching crusade personified in Ida B. Wells-Barnett. The organization brought W. E. B. Du Bois into its research and publicity management and, within a year, he began editing the NAACP's official magazine, The Crisis: A Record of the Darker Races.*
>
> From Collins, S., Sturdevant, K.S., 'The history and rhetoric of the NAACP: the origins', in *Black History Bulletin* published in 2008.

ACTIVITY

1 In what ways did the NAACP have both a 'chronological' and a 'rhetorical' history?

2 How would black **separatists** or white supremacists have been likely to respond to Villard's manifesto?

3 What points of difference and similarity can you identify in Sources 10 and 11? How can the differences be explained?

Despite the breadth of its programme the NAACP, with around 90,000 members by the early 1920s, did not recruit the vast membership its founders must have hoped for. Like the NACW, it seemed to appeal more to the middle-class, particularly in the North, than the working-class. Nor, despite fighting some successful court cases on behalf of its members, did it make much headway in achieving its objectives: segregation and the 'Jim Crow' laws remained intact well into the 1930s.

The Universal Negro Improvement Association (UNIA)

The **UNIA**, established by a West Indian activist, Marcus Garvey, in Jamaica in 1914, was a very different organisation to the NAACP: launched by Garvey in America in 1917, it became numerically much stronger, with a membership of over a million in the USA by 1925. It appealed particularly to northern urban working-class blacks and migrants from

Separatists

Term used to describe any white and non-white Americans who believed that the integration of the races was either wrong or impractical.

UNIA

Universal Negro Improvement Association formed in 1914 by Marcus Garvey.

THINK LIKE AN HISTORIAN

Use all of the sources in this section to summarise the role of events, ideas and actions in the founding of the NAACP.

the South, and it adopted a radically different approach to the equality issue. Garvey competed with Du Bois' NAACP *The Crisis* for readers by launching his own weekly, *The Negro World*, in 1918.

Garvey's position and that of the UNIA, by the 1920s, was far removed from that of earlier organisations and race leaders like Booker T. Washington and W.E.B. Du Bois:

Source 12 'What we believe'

The Universal Negro Improvement Association advocates the uniting and blending of all Negroes into one strong, healthy race. It is against miscegenation and race suicide.

It believes that the Negro race is as good as any other, and therefore should be as proud of itself as others are.

It believes in the purity of the Negro race and the purity of the white race.

It is against rich blacks marrying poor whites.

It is against rich or poor whites taking advantage of Negro women.

It believes in the spiritual Fatherhood of God and the Brotherhood of Man.

It believes in the social and political physical separation of all peoples to the extent that they promote their own ideals and civilization, with the privilege of trading and doing business with each other.

It believes in the promotion of a strong and powerful Negro nation in Africa.

It believes in the rights of all men.

Marcus Garvey, January 1, 1924.

ACTIVITY

1   In what ways, on the basis of the evidence of Source 12 did the objectives of the UNIA differ to those of the NACW (Sources 1 and 2), the Niagara Movement (Source 6), and the NAACP (Source 9)? Make a list.

2   What do the views expressed in Source 12 have in common with those of white supremacists?

By the year in which this statement was published, however, Garvey's popularity and that of his movement was in decline; largely as a result of failed UNIA commercial enterprises and the corruption charges that would lead to a spell of imprisonment in 1925 and deportation in 1927 for its president.

In the following source, a modern historian highlights some of the problems inherent in Garvey's programme for the UNIA which some felt may have hindered more than helped promote the campaign for racial equality.

Source 13 Garvey's views on those of mixed-race ancestry

In New York, the effective headquarters of the Garvey movement, the UNIA benefited from the presence of a sizable West Indian community… Generally better educated and more assertive of their civil rights than native black Americans, West Indian immigrants were an important potential source of grassroots leadership. Moreover, West Indians had a particular reputation for success in business, and for this reason were nicknamed the 'Jews of their race'.

... *[W.E.B. Du Bois] believed that Garvey was seeking to instil inappropriate West Indian values and attitudes in black American society. In Jamaica racial divisions took different forms from in the United States. Whites comprised only about 2 per cent of the inhabitants of the island. A black labouring class made up 80 per cent of the population. In between these two groups was a mixed-race caste, accounting for some 18 per cent of the island's residents. This middle group aspired to acceptance and inclusion within the white community, and tended to look down on the majority black population as social inferiors. Coming from this background Garvey displayed a consistent distrust of blacks of mixed-race ancestry within the United States. He suspected light-skinned African Americans, like Du Bois, of lacking racial loyalty and being motivated primarily by a desire for social recognition from whites.*

From K. Verney, *Black Civil Rights in America*, published in 2000.

ACTIVITY

1   How does Source 13 reveal the complexities of the politics of race?

2   How might Garvey's background have prompted him into developing an alternative to the 'accommodationist'/'**integrationist**' approaches of his contemporaries?

The UNIA may not have achieved reforms before its demise in the later 1920s, but it did succeed in becoming America's first black/civil rights mass movement, and its figurehead became an inspiration for generations of future activists.

THINK LIKE AN HISTORIAN

1   For what reasons do you think the UNIA was more successful than other organisations in attracting working class members?

2   You have now read a series of pro-civil rights campaigning programmes. What do you think might be the main benefits and drawbacks of using such documents to understand the struggle for and against civil rights in the USA?

The Ku Klux Klan (KKK)

The Ku Klux Klan was formed in Tennessee in 1865 by white 'supremacist' demobbed Confederate soldiers who were determined to prevent black people from exercising their new found civil rights, such as the right to vote, at the end of the American Civil War. They soon adopted a costume – the infamous white robes and conical hats – and engaged in acts of intimidation, sometimes violent, including attacks on property, and murder. In addition to blacks they targeted known liberal-minded Republicans. Membership of the KKK in this first phase is estimated at around 550,000. After 1870 the movement was crushed by the Force Act that banned their activities and resulted in thousands of arrests and hundreds of trials.

The movement was revived in 1915 in Atlanta, Georgia, and membership soared after the end of the First World War to 4 million in 1924. Where the original Klan had been a southern phenomenon, this was truly national, with plenty of support in the North, particularly the state of Michigan. This, in part, can be explained by the 'Great Migration', starting around 1910, of poor blacks from the South to the industrial cities of the North. In addition to the black population, immigrants, Catholics, communists, trade unionists, and Jews were now potential KKK victims. The KKK advocated the

EXAM TIP

Using own knowledge in the analysis of sources.

Although in the exam it is vital to avoid writing long descriptive passages based on your own knowledge, you do need to find opportunities to show that you understand the context in which the sources are set and how this affects their content and the way in which historians interpret them. What information contained in Source 13 is helpful in interpreting Source 12? What likely misconceptions does this contextual knowledge correct?

Integrationist

The concept of people of different racial origins mixing in the workplace and in public spaces.

WASPs

White Anglo-Saxon
Protestants

supremacy of white people with an Anglo-Saxon Protestant heritage ('**WASPs**'); these, in the jargon of the day, were the 'Native Americans', not the indigenous 'Indians'. President Woodrow Wilson (1913–21), America's first southern president, was sympathetic to the cause and the Klan was glorified in the very popular 1915 movie, *The Birth of a Nation*. Membership rapidly declined in the later 1920s amid charges of corruption within the organisation.

Source (14) The Imperial Wizard's address to the Imperial Klonvokation, 1924

I greet you, the Imperial Klonvokation, representing the millions of native-born, white, Gentile, Protestant citizens who have united under the banner of the Knights of the Ku Klux Klan for the protection of our nation and race. You have assembled here at a time of great crisis. Events of overwhelming importance are waiting in the womb of history. The future of America, and the white race, hangs in the balance.

… We are laying the foundations of the greatest structure in the history of human progress [i.e. modern America]. Therefore, we cannot afford to make gigantic blunders. The Klan leadership must insure to this country conditions which will make it possible for our descendants through succeeding centuries to adequately perform the high duties of citizenship, and the still higher duties of leadership – not only of America, but of civilisation itself. If representative government is to endure and possess the earth (and it must), there must be not only a high level in average intelligence (a level which history proves, and current events are proving, has never been reached except by Nordic and Anglo-Saxon peoples), but every generation must produce enough men and women of unusual attainment to lead their fellow citizens in every sphere of national life – men and women who are 'the salt of the earth', who ever lead the way to higher things.

The blood which produces human leadership must be protected from inferior blood, and from the competition which saps the vitality of leadership because it makes the struggle for existence such a burden that people stagger under it. You are of this superior blood. You are more – you are leaders in the only movement in the world, at present, which exists solely to establish a civilisation that will insure these things. Klansmen and Klanswomen are verily 'the salt of the earth' upon whom depends the future of civilisation.

… White Protestant Americans everywhere are turning to the Klan for guidance in the present world-shaking crisis. And they will turn to it in ever increasing numbers as the crisis becomes more acute, and as the Klan leadership becomes stronger and more effective in the cause of righteousness.

… We will make America a perfect nation, thus fulfilling the ideals of the great Statesman and Father who laid the foundation upon which to build a civilisation better than the world has ever known, wherein free men may live and rear their children in liberty, security and justice – untainted by the blood of alien races and unhampered by mental and spritual tyranny.

From 'The Klan of Yesterday and of Today', an address by The Imperial Wizard in Knights of the Ku Klux Klan Incorporated, *Proceedings of the Second Imperial Klonvocation*, published in 1924.

EXAM TIP   **Considering the range of sources.**

This chapter is rich in the mission statements of various organisations. Why are these so valuable to historians? In part **b** of the exam you will probably be presented with two or more sources of a similar kind. As well as considering their particular value, and remember that all historical sources have value, you should also consider the problems they present. What problems are presented by mission statements as historical evidence? In the exam consider what useful source types are missing or are under-represented from the selection. What sources should the historian of race organisations consider in addition to their own mission statements?

ACTIVITY

Use Source 14 to help you answer the following questions:

1   Identify a short passage that reveals the *racist* views of the speaker.

2   Identify a short passage that reveals the *nationalist* views of the speaker.

3   On the evidence of this source, what strategies did the KKK employ to attract support?

4   Historical sources sometimes reveal more than their authors intended. What does this account reveal about the confidence of the KKK in its own strength?

5   For what reasons might people living in America in 1924 have cause to think they were living 'at a time of great crisis'?

6   What aspects of the Klan's activities are missing from this account? Why?

7   The author may not have provided a balanced view of US society, but in what ways is this source still useful to historians?

One supposed victim of the Ku Klux Klan was the father of the race leader Malcolm X. The following source is his own account of what happened to his father.

Source 15   The death of Malcolm X's father

I remember waking up to the sound of my mother's screaming again. When I scrambled out, I saw the police in the living-room; they were trying to calm her down. She had snatched on her clothes to go with them. And all of us children who were staring knew without anyone having to say it that something terrible had happened to our father.

My mother was taken by the police to the hospital, and to a room where a sheet was over my father in a bed, and she wouldn't look, she was afraid to look. Probably it was wise that she didn't. My father's skull, on one side, was crushed in, I was told later. Negroes in Lansing have always whispered that he was attacked, and then laid across some tracks for a streetcar to run over him. His body was cut almost in half.

He lived two and a half hours in that condition… It was morning when we children at home got the word that he was dead. I was six. I can remember a vague commotion, the house filled up with people crying, saying bitterly that the white Black Legion [a branch of the KKK] had finally gotten him.

From Malcom X and Alex Haley, *The Autobiography of Malcolm X*, first published in 1965.

THINK LIKE AN HISTORIAN

'The UNIA and the Klan shared common beliefs in racial pride and racial separatism.' (K. Verney, *Black Civil Rights in America* (2000))

How acceptable is this hypothesis? Use the evidence in this section and in the section on the UNIA to make a list of the evidence for and against it. If the list against contains significant points, try to modify and rewrite the hypothesis so that it takes into account this additional evidence.

You may conclude that the interpretation is entirely wrong and that 'The UNIA and the Klan shared no common beliefs' or that it is partially correct but needs amending to 'The UNIA and the Klan shared a common belief, racial separatism, but their differences greatly outweighed their similarities.'

ACTIVITY

1   It is commonly believed that Malcolm X's father was murdered. To what extent does the account in Source 15 support that hypothesis? Explain your answer.

2   'The death of his father at the hands of the Black Legion was a turning point in the life of Malcolm X.' What evidence would you need to support this hypothesis?

3   What is the value and what are the limitations of autobiographies, like this one, as historical evidence?

It is reasonable to conclude that the atrocities of the KKK were self-defeating by highlighting the race issue and they obliged administrations to address it and, ultimately, to legislate against inequality.

ACTIVITY

Test your understanding by using the sources in this chapter and your own knowledge to answer each of the following questions regarding the race issue in the period 1865–1935:

1   How did the approaches of groups and organisations change during the period?

2   How did the aims of groups and organisations change during the period?

3   To what extent did the objectives and methods of these groups and organisations remain constant during the period?

4   To what extent did groups and organisations succeed in developing or restricting racial equality?

What part did the trade unions and the labour movement play in the struggle for equality in the inter-war period?

The watchwords of the American Left in the 1930s were 'organise' and 'unionise'. Trade unions exist, primarily, to secure, usually through the threat of strike action, decent wages and working conditions for their members; by organising themselves into unions workers hope to have the power to take on oppressive employers. Consequently if workers in inter-war America had chosen not to co-operate with one another on the grounds of colour or creed they would have weakened themselves in their economic struggles with the bosses. Thus the Committee of Industrial Organization (CIO) was formed by trade unionists to establish a federation of American and Canadian unions, and to promote the non-discriminatory unionisation of all industrial workers. Being unionised did not end discrimination in the workplace, however, and the average earnings of African-American workers were lower, perhaps half as much, as those of their white counterparts. Furthermore, as the following source, a report from 1929, reveals, they were sometimes more likely to be assigned to dirty and dangerous jobs.

Source (16) The employment of African-Americans in the automobile industry

"As one Ford employment official has stated, 'Many of the Negroes are employed in the foundry and do work that nobody else would do.' The writer noticed in one Chevrolet plant that Negroes were engaged on the dirtiest, roughest and most disagreeable work, for example, in the painting of axles. At the Chrysler plant they are used exclusively on paint jobs, and at the Chandler-Cleveland plant certain dangerous emery wheel grinding jobs were given only to Negroes."

From Robert W. Dunn, *Labor and Automobiles*, published in 1929.

ACTIVITY

1   To what extent can Source 16 be used as evidence for racial discrimination? Explain your answer.

2   What are the limitations of this source as historical evidence?

The demands of American socialists for economic equality were attractive to both trade unionists and to those seeking racial equality. Asa Philip Randolph, who like so many other blacks had migrated from the South to the North shortly before the First World War, was one such socialist who saw unionisation as a path towards racial equality. In common with other race leaders he disseminated his views through his own journal called the *Messenger*, and established a trade union for black railway workers in 1925 named the Brotherhood of Sleeping Car Porters (**BSCP**). As the membership of the union rose (7000 by 1934) the railway bosses were obliged to recognise its existence and, eventually, in 1937, to agree to a contract that resulted in higher wages and shorter hours for their black employees. Its New York Office has been described as 'the political headquarters of black America' by one historian (J. Anderson, quoted in Saunders V. *Race Relations in the USA 1863–1980* (2006)), a meeting place for leading activists including, later on, Martin Luther King. In 1935 A. Philp Randolph was a founder member of the National Negro Congress (NNC) that was set up to try to help black people during the Depression. One of its campaigns, using the slogan 'Don't Buy Where You Can't Work', was to persuade black shoppers to boycott stores that did not employ black workers.

Although A. Philip Randolph refused to align himself with the Communist Party of the United States of America (**CPUSA**) and the Soviet inspired politic of the Communist International that it subscribed to, the CPUSA was also committed to the principle of racial equality and became the dominant force in the NNC. Its activities included the promotion of unions and the provision of legal assistance, most notably in a high profile trial of nine young black men on rape charges in Alabama; the Scottsboro case of 1931. Not surprisingly many blacks and others disadvantaged because of their ethnicity joined the CPUSA and the more extreme left wing trade unions. The Food, Tobacco, Agricultural and Allied Workers Union (FTA), for example, was predominantly both black and communist.

EXAM TIP

The analysis of historical sources involves the ability to be able to recognise what is inferred by the source in addition to what is explicitly stated. It is always important to be wary of taking a source at face value.

BSCP

The Brotherhood of Sleeping Car Porters, a trade union for black railway workers formed in 1925.

CPUSA

The Communist Party of the United States of America.

ACTIVITY

Exam practice

'Divisions within the movement for racial equality in America explain its failure to achieve its objectives between 1865 and 1935.'

a   Explain how far the sources in this chapter support this interpretation. You may, if you wish, amend the interpretation or suggest a different interpretation. If you do this you must use the sources to support the changes you make

Remember not to simply take the sources at face value. Use your knowledge of the period to interpret and evaluate them.

b   Explain how these sources are both useful and raise problems and issues for a historian using them.

Summary – what you have learned in Chapter 4

This chapter has introduced you to five of the earliest and most significant organisations in the history of race and American society.

You have also read about developments in the history of trade unions and the labour movement that had a bearing on the struggle for equality in the inter-war period.

You have learned that different groups and organisations had different aims and used different strategies, even if they claimed to be united in reaching the same goals.

You have also learned, through such evidence as the manifestos of the different organisations and other statements of intent, that different organisations had different aims. The most fundamental difference between them is that some were integrationist and some were separatist in their approach.

By working through the various *Activity* and *Think like an historian* tasks you have practised and developed important skills for the examination:

- the comparison and contrast of sources
- the consideration of what is missing from sources as well as what they contain
- the ability to infer meaning from sources
- using groups of sources to test hypotheses
- using groups of sources to form interpretations
- identifying change and continuity
- using own knowledge in the analysis of sources
- analysing photographs
- cross-referencing sources.

Now take a look at the Exam Café at the back of the book for more practice and advice.

ACTIVITY

Construct a table in three columns headed 'Type of sources', 'Usefulness', 'Things to watch out for'. In the left column, list each type of source used in this chapter and then against it fill in what you think should be noted for the middle and right-hand columns. The information set out in the table will help you to evaluate the sources you are given in the classroom and in the exam. If you apply these specific ideas when discussing particular sources, you will gain much higher marks than if you write a very general answer.

5 Ideas and actions: evidence concerning the role of individuals

Overview

Some of the most accessible evidence for students of Race and American Society can be found in the various biographies and autobiographies of that history's leading figures. Individuals often take centre stage in history: sometimes because they genuinely played a very central role in historical developments; sometimes because they are colourful, though possibly ineffectual, characters; and sometimes because historians are convinced by their propaganda or the extravagant claims of their supporters. Furthermore, building historical accounts around individuals can make it easier for us to navigate our way through the complex landscapes of the past and the millions of lives it represents.

In this chapter you will encounter four eminent activists, their beliefs and their actions. As you work through the evidence you should be prepared to interrogate it by asking fundamental questions such as:

> **THINK LIKE AN HISTORIAN**
>
> Read an autobiography of one of the leaders mentioned in this chapter. A good place to start is Booker T. Washington's *Up from Slavery* (1901) which you can find online in its entirety.

Key Questions:

1 What motivated these individuals?

2 What impact did these individuals have upon other people?

3 Would the history of race relations have been significantly different without these individuals' involvement?

Accomodationism, confrontation and separatism: the contributions of Booker T. Washington, W.E.B. Du Bois and Marcus Garvey

Booker T. Washington (1856–1915)

An educationalist and founder and first principal of the Tuskegee Negro National Institute, Alabama, Booker T. Washington was the son of an African slave. His father, who he never met, was white. Freed from slavery when a child, his formative years were recorded in his autobiography *Up from Slavery*, which reveals his conviction that education and self-help were the key to future racial equality. His was essentially an optimistic vision based upon the assumption that whites and blacks could live in harmony.

Source ① The memories of a former slave

I had no schooling whatever while I was a slave, though I remember on several occasions I went as far as the schoolhouse door with one of my young mistresses to carry her books. The picture of several dozen boys and girls in a schoolroom engaged in study made a deep impression upon me, and I had the feeling that to get into a schoolhouse and study in this way would be about the same as getting into paradise.

… As a rule, not only did the members of my race entertain no feelings of bitterness against the whites before and during the war, but there are many instances of Negroes tenderly caring for their former masters and mistresses who for some reason have become poor and dependent since the war. I know of instances where the former masters of slaves have for years been supplied with money by their former slaves to keep them from suffering. I have known of still other cases in which the former slaves have assisted in the education of the descendants of their former owners.

From Booker T. Washington, *Up from Slavery* published in 1901.

ACTIVITY

In small groups consider the following questions:

1   How far should Source 1 be taken at face value?

2   What purpose(s) might it have served Washington and the movement for racial equality when he penned it before his death in 1915?

3   What particular problems do reminiscences present as evidence for historians?

EXAM TIP

When considering the problems presented by sources, take care not to be too negative in your comments. After all, each source is a unique piece of historical evidence and it has been selected for the examination, primarily, because it has significant historical value.

Washington eventually received an education at the Hampton Institute in his home-state of Virginia, set up in 1868 by whites to teach vocational skills to recently-freed black slaves. From here he progressed to a career as a teacher, first of Native Americans and then blacks. At Tuskegee he promoted the teaching of agricultural, industrial and housekeeping skills to enhance the chances of black boys and girls finding paid work.

Invited to speak about his role as a black educationalist at the opening of the Atlanta World Fair (the Atlanta Cotton States and International Exposition) in 1895, Washington delivered a controversial speech, subsequently known as his 'Alabama Compromise'.

Source ② The 'Alabama Compromise'

Mr. President and Gentlemen of the Board of Directors and Citizens:

One-third of the population of the South is of the Negro race. No enterprise seeking the material, civil, or moral welfare of this section can disregard this element of our population and reach the highest success. I but convey to you, Mr. President and Directors, the sentiment of the masses of my race when I say that in no way have the value and manhood of the American Negro been more fittingly and generously recognized than by the managers of this magnificent Exposition at every stage of its progress. It is a recognition that will do more to cement the friendship of the two races than any occurrence since the dawn of our freedom.

... A ship lost at sea for many days suddenly sighted a friendly vessel. From the mast of the unfortunate vessel was seen a signal, "Water, water; we die of thirst!" The answer from the friendly vessel at once came back, "Cast down your bucket where you are." A second time the signal, "Water, water; send us water!" ran up from the distressed vessel, and was answered, "Cast down your bucket where you are." And a third and fourth signal for water was answered, "Cast down your bucket where you are." The captain of the distressed vessel, at last heeding the injunction, cast down his bucket, and it came up full of fresh, sparkling water from the mouth of the Amazon River. To those of my race who depend on bettering their condition in a foreign land or who underestimate the importance of cultivating friendly relations with the Southern white man, who is their next-door neighbor, I would say: "Cast down your bucket where you are"— cast it down in making friends in every manly way of the people of all races by whom we are surrounded.

... Our greatest danger is that in the great leap from slavery to freedom we may overlook the fact that the masses of us are to live by the productions of our hands, and fail to keep in mind that we shall prosper in proportion as we learn to dignify and glorify common labour, and put brains and skill into the common occupations of life... No race can prosper till it learns that there is as much dignity in tilling a field as in writing a poem. It is at the bottom of life we must begin, and not at the top. Nor should we permit our grievances to overshadow our opportunities.

To those of the white race who look to the incoming of those of foreign birth and strange tongue and habits for the prosperity of the South, were I permitted I would repeat what I say to my own race, "Cast down your bucket where you are." Cast it down among the eight millions of Negroes whose habits you know, whose fidelity and love you have tested in days when to have proved treacherous meant the ruin of your firesides. Cast down your bucket among these people who have, without strikes and labour wars, tilled your fields, cleared your forests, builded your railroads and cities, and brought forth treasures from the bowels of the earth, and helped make possible this magnificent representation of the progress of the South. Casting down your bucket among my people, helping and encouraging them as you are doing on these grounds, and to education of head, hand, and heart, you will find that they will buy your surplus land, make blossom the waste places in your fields, and run your factories. While doing this, you can be sure in the future, as in the past, that you and your families will be surrounded by the most patient, faithful, law-abiding, and unresentful people that the world has seen. As we have proved our loyalty to you in the past, in nursing your children, watching by the sick-bed of your mothers and fathers, and often following them with tear-dimmed eyes to their graves, so in the future, in our humble way, we shall stand by you with a devotion that no foreigner can approach, ready to lay down our lives, if need be, in defense of yours, interlacing our industrial, commercial, civil, and religious life with yours in a way that shall make the interests of both races one. In all things that are purely social we can be as separate as the fingers, yet one as the hand in all things essential to mutual progress.

... Nearly sixteen millions of hands will aid you in pulling the load upward, or they will pull against you the load downward. We shall constitute one-third and more of the ignorance and crime of the South, or one-third [of] its intelligence and progress; we shall contribute one-third to the business and industrial prosperity of the South, or we shall prove a veritable body of death, stagnating, depressing, retarding every effort to advance the body politic.

... The wisest among my race understand that the agitation of questions of social equality is the extremest folly, and that progress in the enjoyment of all the privileges that will come to us must be the result of severe and constant struggle rather than of artificial forcing. No race that has anything to contribute to the markets of the world is long in any degree ostracized. It is important and right that all privileges of the law be ours, but it is vastly more important that we be prepared for the exercise of these privileges. The opportunity to earn a dollar in a factory just now is worth infinitely more than the opportunity to spend a dollar in an opera-house.

Extract from the 'Alabama Compromise' speech, Booker T. Washington, 1895.

EXAM TIP

Interrogating the evidence.

Historians ask questions. They use historical evidence to find the answers. Evaluating sources in relation to the questions historians ask is a key skill in answering part **b** questions. What questions does this source help answer? Make a list.

ACTIVITY

Consider the following questions:

1 Why did this speech come to be known as a 'compromise'?

2 How would these views be likely to be regarded by the following groups:
   a black militants seeking racial equality
   b segregationists
   c white supremacists?

Explain your answer to each with specific references to the text (Source 2).

Washington's autobiography, *Up from Slavery*, promoting self-help and racial harmony, was an inspiration for many, including Marcus Garvey. Washington was committed to education and self-help, rather than force, as the route to gaining racial equality. Such was his reputation by the closing years of the 19th century that he became a presidential advisor on racial affairs. This was a role he retained through several presidencies until the election of the southern-born and overtly segregationist President Woodrow Wilson in 1912.

W.E.B. Du Bois (1868–1963)

W.E.B. Du Bois was a leading light in the early history of the NAACP for whom he edited the magazine *Crisis*. His family were landowning free African Americans from Massachusetts. Compared to Washington he was uncompromising and, ultimately, became a fierce critic of Washington's position regarding the race issue. As a freeman born in the North, Du Bois was less exposed to prejudice than Washington. An academic, he became a professor of sociology at Atlanta University in 1897. Unlike Washington, initially he argued that equality could not be separated from full integration and that, ultimately, it relied upon recognition in law. His was a more assertive, even confrontational, stance than Washington's and it became the dominant principle in the struggle for equality in place of Washington's '**accommodationism**'. When Du Bois formed the Niagara Movement for racial equality in 1905 Washington was not invited to join; nor did he join the NAACP into which it evolved in 1909.

The following source is an extract from Du Bois' 'Harpers Ferry' speech of 1906 in which he outlined the objectives of his Niagara Movement, formed two years earlier.

Accommodationism

A word, often used derisively, to describe a willingness to compromise the struggle for political and legal racial equality in order to achieve economic advances for minority races.

Source 3 The 'Harpers Ferry' speech

The men of the Niagara Movement coming from the toil of the year's hard work and pausing a moment from the earning of their daily bread turn toward the nation and again ask in the name of ten million the privilege of a hearing. In the past year the work of the Negro hater has flourished in the land. Step by step the defenders of the rights of American citizens have retreated. The work of stealing the black man's ballot has progressed and the fifty and more representatives of stolen votes still sit in the nation's capital. Discrimination in travel and public accommodation has so spread that some of our weaker brethren are actually afraid to thunder against color discrimination as such and are simply whispering for ordinary decencies.

Against this the Niagara Movement eternally protests. We will not be satisfied to take one jot or little less than our full manhood rights. We claim for ourselves every single right that belongs to a freeborn American, political, civil and social; and until we get these rights we will never cease to protest and assail the ears of America. The battle we wage is not for ourselves alone but for all true Americans. It is a fight for ideals, lest this, our common fatherland, false to its founding, become in truth the land of the thief and the home of the Slave…

Never before in the modern age has a great and civilized folk threatened to adopt so cowardly a creed in the treatment of its fellow-citizens born and bred on its soil. Stripped of verbiage and subterfuge and in its naked nastiness the new American creed says: Fear to let black men even try to rise lest they become the equals of the white. And this is the land that professes to follow Jesus Christ. The blasphemy of such a course is only matched by its cowardice.

… We do not believe in violence, neither in the despised violence of the raid nor the lauded violence of the soldier, nor the barbarous violence of the mob, but we do believe in John Brown, in that incarnate spirit of justice, that hatred of a lie, that willingness to sacrifice money, reputation, and life itself on the altar of right. And here on the scene of John Brown's martyrdom we reconsecrate ourselves, our honor, our property to the final emancipation of the race which John Brown died to make free.

Our enemies, triumphant for the present, are fighting the stars in their courses. Justice and humanity must prevail. We live to tell these dark brothers of ours - scattered in counsel, wavering and weak - that no bribe of money or notoriety, no promise of wealth or fame, is worth the surrender of a people's manhood or the loss of a man's self-respect. We refuse to surrender the leadership of this race to cowards and trucklers. We are men; we will be treated as men. On this rock we have planted our banners.

We will never give up, though the trump of doom finds us still fighting.

And we shall win. The past promised it, the present foretells it.

… We appeal to the young men and women of this nation, to those whose nostrils are not yet befouled by greed and snobbery and racial narrowness: stand up for the right, prove yourselves worthy of your heritage and whether born north or south dare to treat men as men. Cannot the nation that has absorbed ten million foreigners into its political life without catastrophe absorb ten million Negro Americans into that same political life at less cost than their unjust and illegal exclusion will involve?

Courage brothers! The battle for humanity is not lost or losing. All across the skies sit signs of promise. The Slav is raising in his might, the yellow millions are tasting liberty, the black Africans are writhing toward the light, and everywhere the laborer, with ballot in his hand, is voting open the gates of Opportunity and Peace. The morning breaks over blood-stained hills. We must not falter, we may not shrink. Above are the everlasting stars.

Extract from the 'Harpers Ferry' speech, W.E.B. Du Bois, 1906.

ACTIVITY

Try writing short answers to the following questions:

1   What is the tone of Du Bois' speech (Source 3)? Cite examples to justify your view.

2   Explain how it compares to the tone of Washington's 'Alabama Compromise' speech (Source 2).

3   In what ways does the content of Du Bois' speech differ from that of Washington's? Show this by specific references from each text.

4   How might these differences have impacted upon the progress of the movement for racial equality at the start of the 20th century?

5   Why should historians be cautious of taking political speeches at face value?

Garveyist

Attitudes in line with the views of Marcus Garvey.

BSL

The Black Star Line steamship company set up by Marcus Garvey in 1919 to promote international commerce and unity among black people.

Marcus Garvey (1887–1940)

Jamaica-born Marcus Garvey was the flamboyant and charismatic founder of the UNIA. In his promotion of black pride, he called for the separation of whites and blacks; declared that both God and Christ were black; and styled himself as the 'President of Africa' in his 'Back to Africa' campaign. Such views came to be known as **Garveyist**. The organisation he set up in 1920 to promote his ideas, and, some suspected, himself, was the UNIA. In 1919 he established a short-lived steamship company, the Black Star Line (**BSL**) to promote black commercial interests and international black unity. Just as his influence can be detected in the work of later activists such as Malcolm X, he was inspired by others, notably by Booker T. Washington through his autobiography *Up* from *Slavery* (1901) and his advocacy of self-improvement. His ideas were disseminated through his books, such as *The Negro Race and its Problems* (1914) and *School of African Philosophy* (1937), and his weekly newspaper, *Negro World*.

Just as Du Bois had clashed with Booker T. Washington, Garvey was highly critical of the arguments and methods advocated by Du Bois. This is very evident in the following extracts from a speech he gave in New York in 1923.

> **THINK LIKE AN HISTORIAN**
>
> In what way did Garvey differ from Washington regarding the issue of integration?

Source ④ Marcus Garvey and the UNIA

Let me tell you: Some fellows like Randolph and Owen and that Du Bois bunch think that my greatest ambition is to be where I am. They mistake the man. I wish you had not kept me here so long. They by their jealousy and maliciousness seem to think that Marcus Garvey feels that he has reached the height of his ambition. I knew when I started, I knew when I came here and I know now that the Negro cannot accomplish anything in a white man's civilization, surrounded by the white man's environment, and it is a waste of time for Marcus Garvey to live within the British Empire or the French Empire or within the American commonwealth. So the height of Marcus Garvey's ambition is not to be a successful Britisher or a successful Frenchman or a successful American. The height of Marcus Garvey's ambition is to settle down in Africa, among millions of other Negroes (applause) and in conjunction with them build up a civilization as our contribution to the world, as our contribution to the human race. Marcus Garvey feels that two years hence the Universal Negro Improvement Association's program will be so developed that we won't have to be wasting time around here with such insignificant Negroes as Du Bois and that bunch. The white folks will take care of them. Marcus Garvey knows that neither the Universal Negro Improvement Association nor any other Negro association can get anywhere in the white man's civilization. So long as the white man sits there as President, so long as he sits there as Governor, so long as he sits there as Mayor, so long as he sits there as Police Commissioner, so long as he sits there as Judge of the Municipal Court and the Supreme Court, so long will Negroes never accomplish anything in a white people's country. Therefore, Marcus Garvey realizes for the Negro to accomplish anything he must have a government of his own, that he must have his own President, his own Governor, his own Mayor, his own

Police Commissioner, his own Municipal and Supreme Court Judges, and even his own jail to put unruly Negroes in. (laughter) So long as you build up a white man's country so long will he, directly or indirectly, destroy your progress. So long as he is to correct the evils within your race for the possibility of your success so long will they remain uncorrected. If you are waiting on the white man to give you protection for the possibility of your development, you and I will wait until eternity.

Therefore, the Universal Negro Improvement Association and Marcus Garvey and those of us who lead feel that the only solution of the Negro problem is to create a government of our own, where Negroes will rule Negroes; where Negroes will be compelled to be honest and true to Negroes because of the correction that will be enforced upon them by the laws made by Negroes for their own racial development. (applause) When you can make laws to punish unruly and treacherous Negroes as the Russians did when they were making the Russian Empire and as the British did when they were making the British Empire and as the fathers of this country did when they were making the American nation, then and only then will this race of ours go forward and enjoy the things that we have mapped out for the program of the Universal Negro Improvement Association. Fooling around with Negroes under white people's civilization will never get you or anybody anywhere. But the time is coming when through the efforts of the Universal Negro Improvement Association we will establish a system of government by which we will be able to correct our own evils and give an inspiration to those who desire to follow in the right way for the development of this race of ours.

From Marcus Garvey, 'The Handwriting On The Wall', published in *Negro World*, 1923.

EXAM TIP

Amending an interpretation.

In part **a** of the exam you are required to evaluate the accuracy of an interpretation using the evidence of the seven sources provided. This involves finding ways in which the sources support the interpretation and looking for ways in which they suggest an alternative or amended interpretation. Use Sources 2, 3 and 4 to test this interpretation: 'African-American leaders in the early 20th century were united by their common demand for racial equality.' Try to write an amended or alternative interpretation on the basis of this evidence.

ACTIVITY

Test your understanding of Source 4 by considering the following questions:

1   Explain how Garvey's claims differ from those of both Washington and Du Bois.

2   Use the source to explain why some observers and subsequent historians suggested Garvey had the makings of a military dictator along the lines of his contemporary Benito Mussolini (Italy's Prime Minister from 1922).

3   Why did Du Bois consider Garvey 'the most dangerous enemy of the Negro race'?

4   Suggest and justify, using the evidence in this section, an alternative interpretation of his contribution to the lives of African-American people.

In the following passage, Kevern Verney has explained some of the reasons why Garvey is a controversial figure in America's civil rights history.

Source 5   A summary of the achievements of Marcus Garvey

The contribution and achievements of Garvey as a race leader have been the subject of much controversy. By 1922 the Black Star Line was in a state of economic ruin… following a series of poor investments and disastrous commercial undertakings. In 1925 Garvey himself was convicted of fraud for continuing to advertise shares in the line. Jailed for two years, he was released in 1927 and deported… he died in London in 1940, a largely forgotten figure.

Between 1920 and 1924 W.E.B. Du Bois wrote a series of articles in Crisis that were highly critical of Garvey. These accused him of promoting fanciful and grandiose schemes to attract investments from poor blacks who could ill afford to engage in such speculation… Like Garvey, Du Bois supported the goal of decolonization and believed that black Americans should strongly identify with their ancestral heritage in Africa. However, this should take the form of a spiritual rediscovery of African culture and values rather than simplistic notions of physical migration back to the Dark Continent.

From K. Verney, *Black Civil Rights in America*, published in 2000.

ACTIVITY

1   On the evidence of Source 5, consider the interpretation that Marcus Garvey caused more harm than good in the struggle for civil rights.

2   What additional information would an historian need to test this hypothesis?

3   Do you agree with this interpretation? If not provide an alternative interpretation on the basis of your understanding of the evidence in this section.

4   How might Du Bois' mixed race ancestry have influenced his assessment of Garvey, for whom the 'blackest' black people were the 'best'?

As a West Indian, some influential black Americans were suspicious of the colonial influence upon Garvey's views. They thought his vision of a new black elite he called the 'Knights of the Nile', and the founding of a militaristic black state replete with an 'African Legion' and a 'Garvey Militia' were all highly suspect. His separatist views in America caused scandal when, in 1922, he met with leaders of the KKK to discuss their common beliefs on this matter.

The impact of Garvey's message upon the young Malcolm X is clear in this extract from his autobiography, first published in 1965:

Source (6) Malcolm X's memories of Marcus Garvey

I knew that the collections my father got for his preaching were mainly what fed and clothed us, and he also did other odd jobs, but still the image of him that made me proudest was his crusading and militantly campaigning with the words of Marcus Garvey. As young as I was then, I knew from what I overheard that my father was saying something that made him a 'tough' man. I remember an old lady, grinning and saying to my father, 'You're scaring these white folks to death!'

… I remember seeing the big, shiny photographs of Marcus Garvey that were passed from hand to hand. My father had a big envelope of them that he always took to these [UNIA] meetings. The pictures showed what seemed to me millions of Negroes thronged in parade behind Garvey riding in a fine car, a big black man dressed in a dazzling uniform with gold braid on it, and he was wearing a thrilling hat with tall plumes. I remember hearing that he had black followers not only in the United States but all around the world, and I remember how the meetings always closed with my father saying, several times, and the people chanting after him, 'Up, you mighty race, you can accomplish what you will!'

From Malcom X and Alex Haley, *The Autobiography of Malcolm X*, first published in 1965.

ACTIVITY

In pairs, discuss the following questions:

1   Is Source 6 a primary or secondary source? Explain your answer.

2   In what ways does the evidence of Source 6 reveal that Marcus Garvey was a 'charismatic' leader?

3   To what extent, and why, does Source 6 draw different conclusions to Source 5 regarding the role of Marcus Garvey in the history of the struggle for civil rights in America?

EXAM TIP

Recognising continuity in history.

In part **a** of the exam you should look out for opportunities to comment on how the sources provide evidence of both change and continuity in the historical record. Garvey and Du Bois are recognised as two of the most important early advocates of the two main approaches associated with the civil rights movement: integration (Du Bois) and separation (Garvey). When you get to Chapters 6 and 7 look for links between the views of Du Bois in the work of Martin Luther King, and between those of Garvey and Malcolm X.

Source 7

Marcus Garvey dressed in the ceremonial costume of the commander-in-chief of the Universal African Legion.

ACTIVITY

Have another look at Source 7.

1   To what extent does the evidence of this source confirm that of Source 6?

2   Why did Garvey's dressing in colonial-style military uniform provoke controversy among those campaigning for racial equality in 20th-century America? Refer to Sources 2, 3, 4 and 8 in your answer.

The Princess of the Press: Ida B. Wells (1862–1931)

Like Booker T. Washington, Ida Wells was the child of a slave. She also became a teacher. However she was far less 'accommodating' than Washington: expelled from school as a pupil for aggressive behaviour, she would be expelled from the teaching profession for her open criticism of existing teaching practices regarding racial segregation. Once when an attempt was made to remove her from a first-class train carriage, she bit the conductor and sued the railway company! She found her true vocation in journalism, earning herself the nickname 'Princess of the Press' for her contributions to the *Memphis Free Speech* weekly newspaper. In this capacity she became particularly associated with her vigorous campaign against lynching. In the 1890s she spoke on the subject in a number of American cities and also in Britain.

In an article in 1900, Wells provided four arguments for why the white majority should no longer tolerate the savagery of the lynch mobs:

> Source 8 The unacceptability of lynching

… this question affects the entire American nation, and from several points of view:

First, on the ground of consistency. Our watchword has been "the land of the free and the home of the brave." Brave men do not gather by thousands to torture and murder a single individual, so gagged and bound he cannot make even feeble resistance or defense. Neither do brave men or women stand by and see such things done without compunction of conscience, nor read of them without protest. Our nation has been active and outspoken in its endeavors to right the wrongs of the Armenian Christian, the Russian Jew, the Irish Home Ruler, the native women of India, the Siberian exile, and the Cuban patriot. Surely it should be the nation's duty to correct its own evils!

Second, on the ground of economy. To those who fail to be convinced from any other point of view touching this momentous question, a consideration of the economic phase might not be amiss. It is generally known that mobs in Louisiana, Colorado, Wyoming, and other States have lynched subjects of other countries. When their different governments demanded satisfaction, our country was forced to confess her inability to protect said subjects in the several States because of our State-rights doctrines, or in turn demand punishment of the lynchers. This confession, while humiliating in the extreme, was not satisfactory; and, while the United States cannot protect, she can pay. This she has

done, and it is certain will have to do again in the case of the recent lynching of Italians in Louisiana. The United States already has paid in indemnities for lynching nearly a half million dollars, as follows:

Paid China for Rock Springs (Wyo.) massacre $147,748.74

Paid China for outrages on Pacific Coast $276,619.75

Paid Italy for massacre of Italian prisoners at New Orleans $24,330.90

Paid Italy for lynchings at Walsenburg, Col $10,000.00

Paid Great Britain for outrages on James Bain and Frederick Dawson $2,800.00

GRAND TOTAL $461,499.99

Third, for the honor of Anglo-Saxon civilization. No scoffer at our boasted American civilization could say anything more harsh of it than does the American white man himself who says he is unable to protect the honor of his women without resort to such brutal, inhuman, and degrading exhibitions as characterize "lynching bees." The cannibals of the South Sea Islands roast human beings alive to satisfy hunger. The red Indian of the Western plains tied his prisoner to the stake, tortured him, and danced in fiendish glee while his victim writhed in the flames. His savage, untutored mind suggested no better way than that of

wreaking vengeance upon those who had wronged him. These people knew nothing about Christianity and did not profess to follow its teachings; but such primary laws as they had they lived up to. No nation, savage or civilized, save only the United States of America, has confessed its inability to protect its women save by hanging, shooting, and burning alleged offenders.

Finally, for love of country. No American travels abroad without blushing for shame for his country on this subject. And whatever the excuse that passes current in the United States, it avails nothing abroad. With all the powers of government in control; with all laws made by white men, administered by white judges, jurors, prosecuting attorneys, and sheriffs; with every office of the executive department filled by white men – no excuse can be offered for exchanging

the orderly administration of justice for barbarous lynchings and "unwritten laws." Our country should be placed speedily above the plane of confessing herself a failure at self-government. This cannot be until Americans of every section, of broadest patriotism and best and wisest citizenship, not only see the defect in our country's armor but take the necessary steps to remedy it. Although lynchings have steadily increased in number and barbarity during the last twenty years, there has been no single effort put forth by the many moral and philanthropic forces of the country to put a stop to this wholesale slaughter. Indeed, the silence and seeming condonation grow more marked as the years go by.

From Ida B. Wells-Barnett, 'Lynch Law in America', *The Arena*, published in 1900.

ACTIVITY

Discuss the following questions with your neighbour:

1   How, on the basis of the evidence of Source 8, would you categorise the strategy of Ida Wells as a campaigner for race equality?

2   In her approach do you consider Wells closest to Washington, Du Bois, or Garvey? Justify your selection.

Wells relied not just on the 'common sense' approach revealed above, but also the shock value of harrowing descriptions of lynchings:

Source ⑨ Lynching and public participation

Not only are two hundred men and women put to death annually, on the average, in this country by mobs, but these lives are taken with the greatest publicity. In many instances the leading citizens aid and abet by their presence when they do not participate, and the leading journals inflame the public mind to the lynching point with scare-head articles and offers of rewards.

Whenever a burning is advertised to take place, the railroads run excursions, photographs are taken, and the same jubilee is indulged in that characterized the public hangings of one hundred years ago. There is, however, this difference: in those old days the multitude that stood by was permitted only to guy or jeer. The nineteenth century lynching mob cuts off ears, toes, and fingers, strips off flesh, and distributes portions of the body as souvenirs among the crowd. If the leaders of the mob are so minded, coal-oil is poured over the

body and the victim is then roasted to death. This has been done in Texarkana and Paris, Tex., in Bardswell, Ky., and in Newman, Ga. In Paris the officers of the law delivered the prisoner to the mob. The mayor gave the school children a holiday and the railroads ran excursion trains so that the people might see a human being burned to death. In Texarkana, the year before, men and boys amused themselves by cutting off strips of flesh and thrusting knives into their helpless victim. At Newman, Ga., of the present year, the mob tried every conceivable torture to compel the victim to cry out and confess, before they set fire to the faggots that burned him. But their trouble was all in vain – he never uttered a cry, and they could not make him confess.

From Ida B. Wells-Barnett, 'Lynch Law in America', *The Arena*, published in 1900.

ACTIVITY

Try answering the following questions to test your understanding of the content of Source 9 and its value as historical evidence:

1   What evidence could an historian use to substantiate the claims in this source?

2   For what reasons might the fact that Wells was female have helped or hindered the campaign for racial equality? Explain your answer.

3   Is this source propagandist? If so, does that make it unreliable? Explain your answer.

4   Consider why this source would be useful to historians.

EXAM TIP

When considering the reliability of sources you must remember that this is determined by the use to which the source is being put by the historian. For example, even the most untruthful propaganda is excellent evidence for the views and methods of the propagandist, despite the fact that it might be utterly unreliable as evidence for the alleged 'facts' it contains.

Convinced that organisation was essential for success, Wells was active in the NACW, a founder member of the NAACP and later joined Garvey's UNIA. In the opinion of Du Bois her greatest contribution was to the 'wakening of the conscience of the nation'.

The views of historians regarding the places of Washington, Du Bois, Garvey and Wells in the history of race and American society

The four people profiled in this chapter are some of the most controversial figures in the history of race relations in the USA. Sources 10–13 provide overviews of their roles and of some of the debates that surround them.

> **Source** (10) **Different assessments by historians of Booker T. Washington**
>
> *Booker T. Washington has always provoked very different assessments. W.E.B. Du Bois claimed that Washington's conciliatory approach made Southern whites even worse to blacks.*
>
> *In the 1960s, historians found evidence of Washington's 'secret life', which demonstrated greater militancy but also greater vanity than had been thought. Donald J. Calista (1964) pointed out that 'beneath his ingratiating manner', Washington 'boiled with contempt for injustices done to his race' but knew that the open protest strategy of Wells and Du Bois would only alienate whites further.*
>
> *Robert Sherer (1977) pointed out the fate of 'uppity' black college principals in 1887: one was forced to resign for suing against railroad segregation; another had his school closed.*
>
> *Adam Fairclough (2001) gives an excellent, balanced account of Washington, 'a product of black powerlessness' whose accommodationism psychologically damaged blacks. Fairclough criticized Washington's inability to accept black critics' ideas, insisting that they were motivated by jealousy and political ambition. Washington was loath, says Fairclough, to concede any of his own power.*
>
> *Washington's most thorough biographer, Louis Harlan (1983), portrayed Washington as a devious, manipulative, power-hungry tyrant and a failure. However, Virginia Denton (1992), using Washington's papers (edited by Harlan!) concluded that he was an unselfish servant and great leader of his race, 'dominated by purpose, not power'.*
>
> From V. Saunders, *Race Relations in the USA 1863–1980*, published in 2006.

ACTIVITY

In a small group discuss the following questions:

1   Why do famous men and women of history find admirers and detractors both in their lifetimes and in the writings of historians?

2   To what extent is this controversy a matter of historical evidence? Explain your thoughts on this with reference to Source 10.

3   Why should historians be aware of historical context in explaining the actions of people in the past? Explain with reference to Source 10.

4   On the evidence of this passage and your own knowledge, consider the hypothesis that Washington did more harm than good to the civil rights campaign in early 20th century America.

Source (11) The rivalry between Du Bois and Washington

Du Bois was born a free man in the North. He experienced very little racial prejudice until he attended Fisk, a Southern black university... Du Bois typified the elitist Northern black intellectuals, Washington the more pragmatic and lower class Southerners who had to co-exist with whites... Washington favoured 'separate but equal' while Du Bois sought rapid integration. Washington, frightened by the increasing number of lynchings, felt that Du Bois' more aggressive approach would serve only to alienate whites.

... The rivalry between [Du Bois and Washington] became increasingly bitter... Some blacks thought that these divisions damaged the black cause, but Washington stressed that Northern and Southern states required very different handling. His sharp distinction between racial problems in the North and the South made it extremely difficult to sustain his position as a black national leader.

From V. Saunders, *Race Relations in the USA 1863–1980*, published in 2006.

ACTIVITY

Test your understanding of Source 11 by considering the following questions:

1   How might Du Bois' background account for his different approach to Washington regarding the race issue? Explain your answer.

2   In what ways does this source reveal the danger of presuming that a leader's views reflect those of the people he claims to represent?

3   In what ways does this source support the hypothesis that black race leaders in the early 20th century did more harm than good to the cause of racial equality?

> **Source 12** Historians' views on the achievements of Marcus Garvey
>
> The contribution and achievements of Garvey as a race leader have been the subject of much controversy. By 1922 the Black Star Line was in a state of economic ruin… In 1925 Garvey himself was convicted of fraud for continuing to advertise shares in the line… Garvey never succeeded in fulfilling his vision of an independent black African republic. He died in London in 1940, a largely forgotten figure.
>
> … historians have been divided in their views on Garvey. Some… have seen him as a dangerous extremist… [others] have been more positive. They perceive Garvey as ahead of his time: a visionary who inspired future independence movements in Africa and later black nationalist leaders in the United States, like Malcolm X.
>
> … Garvey was the first black nationalist leader to build up a mass organisation and following in the United States. This achievement was a testimony to his unique abilities as a race leader. It was equally a measure of despair of many black Americans over the state of US race relations.
>
> From K. Verney, *Black Civil Rights in America*, published in 2000.

ACTIVITY

1 Try writing one paragraph on the extent to which Source 12 provides evidence in support of the hypothesis that history is essentially the story of 'great men'. Remember to consider its limitations in this context.

2 If you disagree with this hypothesis, provide an alternative and explain why it is a better fit for the historical evidence.

> **Source 13** The rediscovery of Ida Wells
>
> Wells believed that one motive of lynching was to 'get rid of Negroes who were acquiring wealth and property and thus keep the race terrorised.' She wrote anti-lynching articles for many newspapers… One Memphis minister accused her of 'stirring up', while a black Kansas newspaper called her that 'crazy… animal from Memphis'. Before her marriage, her sexuality and morality were frequently called into question.
>
> … By the end of her life, Ida B. Wells was an increasingly isolated crusader. However, W.E.B. Du Bois credited her with beginning 'the awakening of the conscience of the nation', saying her 'work has easily been forgotten because it was taken up on a much larger scale by the NAACP and carried to greater success.' Although Wells failed to get the federal government to legislate against lynching, she put the issue in the public eye. Other factors (such as Southern white fear of the loss of black labour when blacks migrated North) contributed to the post-1892 decrease in lynching, but Wells also deserves credit. She was an activist role model for all blacks, but particularly for women. Her strategies were adapted by subsequent activists.
>
> For many years after her death, Wells was virtually forgotten outside Chicago, where she lived from 1895 to 1931. Her daughter struggled for 40 years to get her mother's autobiography published, finally succeeding in 1970. By that date, greater black militancy and feminism led to greater interest in and sympathy with Ida B. Wells. Much has been written about her since.
>
> From V. Saunders, *Race Relations in the USA 1863–1980*, published in 2006.

ACTIVITY

Discuss the following questions with your neighbour:

1 What evidence would help historians to evaluate Wells' claim (Source 13) regarding the motives behind lynchings?

2 What might have motivated southern blacks in their vociferous criticism of Wells' activities?

3 Source 13 was written by a woman and published in 2006. To what extent, if at all, is it appropriate to consider the sex of the author and the date of first publication when evaluating an historian's interpretations?

Stretch and challenge

Investigate the role of other individuals who played a role in the struggle for racial equality in the late 19th century and early 20th century, such as:

- Frederick Douglass
- Walter White
- Eleanor Roosevelt
- A. Philip Randolph.

ACTIVITY

Exam practice

Interpretation: Leading civil rights activists in early 20th century America had little in common except a dream of racial equality.

a Explain how far the sources in this chapter support this interpretation. You may, if you wish, amend the interpretation or suggest a different interpretation. If you do this you must use the sources to support the changes you make.

Remember not to simply take the sources at face value. Use your knowledge of the period to interpret and evaluate them.

b Explain how these sources are both useful and raise problems and issues for a historian using them.

Summary – what you have learned in Chapter 5

This chapter has introduced you to four of the most influential figures in the earlier history of America's civil rights movement.

You have been encouraged to consider their importance in the history of the struggle for civil rights and you have also learned about their association with several organisations.

You have also been introduced to a range of approaches of leading activists in the early years of the American civil rights movement.

By working through the various *Activity* and *Think like an historian* tasks you have practised and developed important skills for the examination:

- understanding the role of important individuals
- understanding their different strategies in their common struggle for greater racial equality
- understanding why historians have arrived at different interpretations regarding their contributions
- the analysis and evaluation of political speeches and other polemical literature
- interrogating the evidence
- amending an interpretation
- recognising continuity in history.

Now take a look at the Exam Café at the back of the book for more practice and advice.

The civil rights movement: integrationists and non-violent protest

Overview

This chapter explores the non-violent aims and methods of the civil rights movement and focuses on the key campaigns of the 1950s and 1960s. Its leading proponents were either directly or indirectly influenced by the example of the Indian national and spiritual leader Mahatma Gandhi (1869–1948). A protestor against racial discrimination in South Africa and colonialism in India he advocated the strategies of non-violent civil disobedience, hunger strikes and boycotts. He became an inspiration for freedom fighters the world over and for individual activists such as Martin Luther King. The non-violent methods of King and others in the American civil rights movement were wide-ranging and effective. The primary sources in this chapter have been selected to reveal what they were, how they worked, and with what success. Information on the key figures, their particular strategies, and the organisations and events with which they are associated, provides the context in which the sources are set.

Key Questions:

1   What was the role of individuals in the post-war civil rights movement?

2   How did the aims of civil rights' movements develop in the middle years of the 20th century?

3   How effective were the methods of non-violent civil rights activists in the 1950s and 1960s?

Oliver Brown, Kenneth B. Clark, the NAACP and school segregation

Oliver Brown was a preacher and welder in Topeka in the northern state of Kansas who, in 1954, challenged the segregation principle by demanding the right to send his daughter, Linda, to a whites-only school two blocks away from their home instead of the school for African-American children more than a mile away. His cause was taken up by the NAACP before the Supreme Court in the celebrated case *Brown v. The Board of Education, Topeka, Kansas* (1954). Brown was represented by the NAACP lawyer, Thurgood Marshall, who argued for Brown on the grounds that school segregation contravened the terms of the 14th Amendment and that segregation was psychologically damaging for young African Americans. In his argument he referred to the findings of psychologists Kenneth B. Clark and his wife Mamie who, in 1940, had carried out a series of interviews with black children and published their findings in the *Journal of Experimental Education*. Although some other NAACP lawyers questioned the relevance of Clark's report, it proved to be the most important factor in influencing the decision of the white Chief Justice Earl Warren's finding in favour of Brown.

Source (1) 'How children learn about race'

Are children born with racial feelings? Or do they have to learn, first, what color they are and, second, what color is 'best'?

Less than fifty years ago, some social theorists maintained that racial and religious prejudices are inborn – that they are inherent and instinctive. These theorists believed that children do not have to learn to dislike people who differ from them in physical characteristics; it was considered natural to dislike those different from oneself and to like those similar to oneself.

However, research over the past thirty years has refuted these earlier theories... there is now no doubt that children learn the prevailing social ideas about racial differences early in their lives.

... To determine the extent of consciousness of skin color in these children between three and seven years old, we showed the children four dolls all of the same mold and dressed alike; the only difference in the dolls was that two were brown and two were white... In an effort to determine their racial preferences, we asked the children the following questions:

1 'Give me the doll that you like to play with' or 'the doll you like best.'

2 'Give me the doll that is the nice doll.'

3 'Give me the doll that looks bad.'

4 'Give me the doll that is a nice color.'

The majority of these negro children at each age indicated an unmistakable preference for the white doll and a rejection of the brown doll... The fact that young Negro children would prefer to be white reflects their knowledge that society prefers white people.

... Some children as young as three years of age begin to express racial and religious attitudes similar to those held by adults in their society... although children tend to become more tolerant in their general social attitudes as they grow older, they become less tolerant in their attitudes toward the Negro. This may reflect the fact that the things children are taught about the Negro and the experiences they are permitted to have usually result in the development of racial intolerance.

Kenneth B. Clark, *Prejudice and your child*, published by Beacon Press, 1955.

ACTIVITY

1   What does Source 1 reveal about changing approaches to resolving the race issue in American society?

2   Why, do you think, did such evidence have a greater impact upon the judge's verdict than the more traditional reliance upon the Constitution of the USA (the 14th Amendment)?

3   On the basis of the evidence of the final paragraph, what might a judge conclude regarding the implications of the segregation of children and the maintenance of law and order? Explain your answer.

EXAM TIP

Recognising the uniqueness of sources.

In the part **b** question in the exam you are asked to consider how the sources provided are both useful and raise problems for historians. Sometimes you may be presented with a source that has an unusual and unique perspective on the subject. Why is Source 1 so 'special'? What are its limitations as historical evidence?

The following source contains extracts from Judge Earl Warren's summing up in this case:

THINK LIKE AN HISTORIAN

Recognising continuity in history.

In what ways does the position taken in Source 2 show continuity in the thinking of civil rights activists? Refer to chapters four and five.

> **Source** **Brown v. Board of Education**
>
> *In approaching this problem, we cannot turn the clock back to 1868 when the [14th] Amendment was adopted... We must consider public education in the light of its full development and its present place in American life throughout the Nation. Only in this way can it be determined if segregation in public schools deprives these plaintiffs of the equal protection of the laws...*
>
> *... To separate [black children] from others of similar age and qualifications solely because of their race generates a feeling of inferiority as to their status in the community that may affect their hearts and minds in a way unlikely ever to be undone...*
>
> *We conclude that in the field of public education the doctrine of 'separate but equal' has no place. Separate educational facilities are inherently unequal. Therefore, we hold that the plaintiffs and others similarly situated for whom the actions have been brought are, by reason of the segregation complained of, deprived of the equal protection of the laws guaranteed by the Fourteenth Amendment...*
>
> From *Brown v. Board of Education of Topeka, Kansas* 347 US 483 (1954).

ACTIVITY

1   On the basis of the evidence of Source 2, what appears to have been the most important factor in this landmark case: the findings of Kenneth B. Clark or the terms of the 14th Amendment? Explain your answer.

2   Use your response to question 1 to formulate a one sentence hypothesis that best explains the outcome of this court case.

By finding in favour of Brown, segregation in state-owned schools was effectively outlawed. However it took a long time, as much as 15 years in some places, to be brought to an end. Most of the representatives of the Southern states in the US Congress (101 of 128) signed the Southern Manifesto in which they committed themselves to resistance to integration by legal means.

> **Source** **The Southern Manifesto**
>
> *This unwarranted exercise of power by the Court, contrary to the Constitution, is creating chaos and confusion in the States principally affected. It is destroying the amicable relations between the white and Negro races that have been created through 90 years of patient effort by the good people of both races. It has planted hatred and suspicion where there has been heretofore friendship and understanding.*
>
> *Without regard to the consent of the governed, outside agitators are threatening immediate and revolutionary changes in our public-school systems. If done, this is certain to destroy the system of public education in some of the States.*
>
> *With the gravest concern for the explosive and dangerous condition created by this decision and inflamed by outside meddlers... We decry the Supreme Court's encroachments on rights reserved to the States and to the people, contrary to established law, and to the Constitution.*
>
> From the Southern Manifesto, 1956.

ACTIVITY

1   What does the evidence of Sources 2 and 3 reveal about the problems inherent in the American Constitution?

2   On what grounds could those subscribing to the Southern Manifesto (Source 3) claim that relations between white Americans and African Americans had gradually improved since the end of the Civil War?

3   On what grounds might this claim have been rejected?

4   What 'hidden agenda' is revealed in the second and third paragraphs regarding the main purpose of the Southern Manifesto?

5   Are you surprised by (a) the language and tone, and (b) the content of the Manifesto?

6   What evidence might you use to see how closely these Southern senators reflected the views of their voters?

7   How does this evidence help to explain the rise in Southern racial violence in the aftermath of the *Brown* verdict?

EXAM TIP

When examining sources like this in the exam, remember to think carefully about the PROVENANCE of each; this is of great importance in the evaluation process. Remember to ask the key questions:

Who produced it?

When?

Why?

Much of this information will be revealed in the headings for each source but sometimes it will rely upon a certain amount of your own contextual knowledge so make sure you know all the key facts before sitting the exam.

Six Southern states, Alabama, Georgia, Louisiana, Mississippi, South Carolina, and Virginia, rejected the verdict out of hand and withheld funding from schools that proposed implementing integration. Meanwhile, membership of the KKK soared. Further court cases reinforced the *Brown* ruling but resistance at a local level continued. Members of the NAACP in the South were harassed by officialdom; the KKK intimidated black families and carried out lynchings and other atrocities; mobs, sometimes with the active support of the authorities, barred entry by African Americans to 'white' schools; and, most spectacularly of all, state schools in Prince Edward County, Virginia, were closed between 1959 and 1964, depriving black children of an education while white children attended whites-only private schools. Just 6.4 per cent of black schoolchildren in the South attended integrated schools as late as 1960. Nevertheless, the *Brown* ruling was a landmark, groundbreaking event in the disintegration of the 'Jim Crow' laws.

THINK LIKE AN HISTORIAN

The *Brown v. Board of Education* case involved several key figures including:

- Oliver and Linda Brown
- Kenneth and Mamie Clark
- Thurgood Marshall
- Earl Warren

1 Who in this list do you think played the most important part in promoting racial equality in America? Explain your answer.

2 Why could historians use the same evidence to make a case for any one of these individuals as the key player in this drama? What does that tell you about the nature of historical evidence?

3 To what extent do you think the evidence of this section supports the interpretation that individuals played the key role in the American civil rights movement? Explain your answer.

4 If you disagree with the interpretation in question 3, work out an alternative interpretation of your own and explain why it is a better fit for the historical evidence.

EXAM TIP

Amending an interpretation.

Although in the part **a** question in the exam you are not obliged to amend or change the interpretation provided, it is usually good practice to do so; the chances are the sources will contain information that challenges the premise of the interpretation.

Remember though that your amended or alternative interpretation must be based upon the evidence provided in the exam. If it is based mainly on your broad general knowledge of the subject you will be throwing away marks. The exam, after all, is to do with the principle that historians' interpretations are formed from the *available* evidence which, in this case, is the six or seven sources you will find in the exam paper.

The Little Rock Nine

One of the most significant events leading on directly from the *Brown* case occurred at Little Rock, Arkansas in 1957. On the eve of Little Rock's Central High School admitting its first nine black children, Arkansas governor, Orval Faubus, declared in a news conference broadcast on television that it would 'not be possible to restore or maintain order… if forcible integration is carried out tomorrow' and that 'blood will run in the streets if Negro pupils should attempt to enter Central High School' (quoted in P. Engelbert (1999) *American Civil Rights*).

THINK LIKE AN HISTORIAN

1 To what extent was Governor Faubus likely to reveal his real reasons for preventing school integration in Little Rock in a televised conference? Explain your answer.

2 Why do historians need to take into account the purpose and intended audience of a source?

The following day, September 3, on Faubus' orders the school was surrounded by 250 National Guards, barring entry to the 'Arkansas Nine'. They didn't attempt to get in on that occasion but two days later, plans were put in place, by the president of the Arkansas NAACP, Daisy Bates, who had obtained a federal court order guaranteeing their right to admission, to have them taken into school in two police cars. One student, 15-year-old Elizabeth Eckford, did not receive the details of where they were to meet and ended up walking to the school alone. Her encounter with the waiting mob, as recalled by an eyewitness, Benjamin Fine, a Jewish journalist, is described here in the memoirs of Daisy Bates.

Source 4 | Benjamin Fine, eyewitness

I was standing in front of the school that day. Suddenly there was a shout – 'They're here! The niggers are coming!' I saw a sweet little girl who looked about fifteen, walking alone. She tried several times to pass through the guards. The last time she tried, they put their bayonets in front of her. When they did this, she became panicky. For a moment she just stood there trembling. Then she seemed to calm down and started walking towards the bus stop with the mob baying at her heels like a pack of hounds. The women were shouting, 'Get her! Lynch her!' The men were yelling, 'Go home, you bastard of a black bitch!' She finally made it to the bus stop and sat down on the bench. I sat down beside her and said 'I'm a reporter from the New York Times, may I have your name?' She just sat there, her head down. Tears were streaming down her cheeks from under her sunglasses. Daisy, I don't know what made me put my arm around her, lifting her chin, saying, 'Don't let them see you cry.' Maybe she reminded me of my fifteen-year-old daughter, Jill.

There must have been five hundred around us by this time. I vaguely remember someone hollering, 'get a rope and drag her over to this tree.' Suddenly I saw a white-haired, kind-faced woman fighting her way through the mob, 'Leave this child alone! Why are you tormenting her? Six months from now you will hang your heads in shame.' The mob shouted, 'Another nigger-lover. Get out of here!' The woman, who I later found out was Mrs. Grace Lorch, wife of Dr. Lee Lorch, professor at Philander Smith College, turned to me and said, 'We have to do something. Let's try to get a cab.'

... [when] the bus came... Mrs. Lorch and Elizabeth got on... the mob closed in around me. 'We saw you put your arm around that little bitch. Now it's your turn.' A drab, middle-aged woman said viciously, 'Grab him and kick him in the balls!' A girl I had seen hustling in one of the local bars screamed, 'A dirty New York Jew! Get him!' A man asked me, 'Are you a Jew?' I said, 'Yes.' He then said to the mob, 'Let him be! We'll take care of him later.'

The irony of it all, Daisy, is that during all this time the national guardsmen made no effort to protect Elizabeth or to help me. Instead they threatened to have me arrested – for inciting to riot.

From Daisy Bates, *The Long Shadow of Little Rock: a Memoir*, published in 1962.

ACTIVITY

1   On the basis of the evidence of Source 4, for what reasons were Elizabeth Eckford and Benjamin Fine attacked by the mob at Arkansas?

2   On the basis of this evidence, what motivated the national guardsmen: racism or the duty to maintain law and order? Explain your answer.

3   For what reasons should an historian be careful of taking the validity of this source at face value?

Daisy Bates also recorded in her autobiography Elizabeth's recollections of the same events shortly afterwards. As with Fine's account, it is unclear as to whether or not Bates wrote down their exact words.

Source 5 Daisy Bates, eyewitness

When I got right in front of the school, I went up to a guard again. But this time he just looked straight ahead and didn't move to let me pass. I didn't know what to do… When I tried to squeeze past him, he raised his bayonet and then the other guards closed in and raised their bayonets.

They glared at me with a mean look and I was very frightened and didn't know what to do. I turned around and the crowd came toward me.

They moved closer and closer. Somebody started yelling, 'Lynch her! Lynch her!'

… They came closer, shouting, 'No nigger bitch is going to get in our school. Get out of here!'

I turned back to the guards but their faces told me I wouldn't get help from them. Then I looked down the block and saw a bench at the bus stop. I thought, 'If I can only get there I will be safe.'

… When I finally got there, I don't think I could have gone another step. I sat down and the mob crowded up and began shouting all over again. Someone hollered, 'Drag her over to this tree! Let's take care of the nigger.' Just then a white man sat down beside me, put his arm around me and patted my shoulder. He raised my chin and said, 'Don't let them see you cry.'

Then a white lady – she was very nice – she came over to me on the bench. She spoke to me but I don't remember now what she said. She put me on the bus and sat next to me. She asked me my name and tried to talk to me but I don't think I answered.

From Daisy Bates, *The Long Shadow of Little Rock: a Memoir,* published in 1962.

ACTIVITY

1. To what extent does Source 5 corroborate the evidence of the previous source? Give examples.

2. How useful are memoirs as historical evidence? Explain your answer.

EXAM TIP

Cross-referencing sources.

Always look for opportunities to cross-reference sources, especially in answer to the part **a** question. Examiners do not look favourably on 'shopping list' approaches (i.e. answers that consider sources one by one).

In a 2004 interview, another of the Little Rock Nine, Melba Pattillo, recalled her memories of the same incident.

Source 6 Melba Pattillo, eyewitness

Arrangements, prior arrangements had been made that each of the children would come to Central High School as individuals, with their families or whatever. Some carpooled. We were to meet at a specific point. No one anticipated, although there had been radio announcements of mobs gathering, sporadic fighting, or what-not, no one anticipated that there would be a mob in front of the school. Uh, the school, you must picture, is this castle so therefore the front of it is a block long and within that block perimeter, it was filled with layers and layers of red-faced angry people. And I came up behind this group of people on the opposite, you know, just across the street from Central High School to see Elizabeth Eckford walking across the street with the mob jeering at her. And at first, you know, I was standing on tippy-toes, trying to see what everybody in front of me was looking at. You know, what was going on, had there been some [gap] of accident, why were all these people there? Why, you know. All those questions in my mind. Angry, angry people, it was like, you know when you go to a football game or rodeo, just angry, angry crowds of people. And we walked up behind these people, my mother and I. My mother was behind me, and uh, they were jeering at Elizabeth who was across the street and, so one of them turns and says, "Now we got us a nigger." And it was at that point that my mother said, "Get to the car, don't wait for me, don't stop, Melba, just go for it." And I couldn't drive. She said, "Get to the car," and so we were driving this Chevrolet and um, the guys had their t-shirts off and they had ropes, and they, they were sweating and, I saw all these faces looking at me and I remember thinking, 'cause at first you know, when these people turn around, you want to say, "Hi, how are you?" you know. You don't understand that what they're turning around for is to kill you. And so, I uh, I back up in astonishment, you know, like with both my hands up and my mother just screamed at me, she said, "I tell you, get to the car now! Listen to me, leave me if you have to, get to the car!" She was just screaming at me to get in this car, we both got in the car, she jammed the car to reverse and we backed down this mob. And this was my first day at Central High School.

From an interview with Melba Pattillo, Washington University Libraries, 2004.

ACTIVITY

1 In what ways does Source 6 corroborate the accounts of Benjamin Fine and Elizabeth Eckford (Sources 4 and 5)?

2 What additional information does it provide?

3 What potential problems face the historian working with older people's recollections as historical evidence?

4 Is the scene in the film *Forrest Gump* (1994) depicting forcible integration in Alabama of any value to historians?

Eventually, all nine students began to attend classes at Little Rock Central High. However their troubles were not over: on the first day in school they were nearly lynched and they were subjected to violent race-hate from within the school after things quietened down outside. In the following source, Melba Pattillo describes that terrifying first day.

Source (7) Melba Pattillo's first day at Little Rock Central High School

Um, I'd only been in the school a couple of hours and by this time it was apparent that the mob was just uh, over running the school. Policemen were throwing down their uh, their badges and uh, the mob was getting past the wooden sawhorses because the police would no longer fight their own in order to keep, to protect us. And so we were all called into the principal's office and there was great fear that we would not get out of this building. Uh, we were trapped. And I thought, "O.K., so I'm going to die here, school." And I remember you know, thinking back to what I'd been told that uh, understand the realities of where you are and pray. And uh, at one point, someone in this crowd, this crowd of adults were panicked. This is the other thing that I could see is that even the adults, the school officials were panicked like no protection. And somebody made a suggestion, a couple of the kids, the black kids that were with me were crying and uh, someone made a suggestion that if they allowed the mob to hang one kid, while they were hanging the one kid, um, they could then get the rest out. And a gentleman, who I believed to be the Police Chief said, "Huh uh, which one? How are you going to choose, you're going to let them draw straws?" He said, "I'll get them out." And we were taken to the basement of this place, and we were put into two cars, grayish-blue colored Fords. And the uh, man instructed them, he said, "Once you start driving, do not stop." And he told us to put our heads down. So um, the guy revved up the engine there was a whole, you know, there was a [gap] that elapsed, they got the gas together and got these cars. This guy revved up his engine and he came up out of the bowels of this building and as he came up, I could just see hands reaching across this car, I could hear the yelling, I could see guns, uh, and he was told not to stop. If you hit somebody you keep rolling, 'cause the kids are dead. And he did just that, and he didn't hit anybody, but he certainly was forceful and aggressive in the way he exited this driveway because people tried to stop him and uh, he dropped me off at home. And I remember saying, "Thank you for the ride," and I should've said, "Thank you for my life."

From an interview with Melba Pattillo, Washington University Libraries, 2004.

The arrival of soldiers from the 101 Airborne Division sent in by President Eisenhower to protect the children and enforce desegregation, made life a little safer for Melba but, nevertheless, she was subjected to all manner of cruelties that included having her eyesight damaged when acid was sprayed in her face.

EXAM TIP

The comparison of sources is a fundamental activity of historians. As you read through the sources on the exam paper, try to identify points of similarity and difference between them. Make sure that you endeavour to cross-reference these sources throughout your answer; try to avoid discussing sources in isolation from each other.

ACTIVITY

What does this evidence reveal about the degree of white hostility to African Americans in Little Rock in 1957?

THINK LIKE AN HISTORIAN

Assessing the value of oral history.

Source 7 is an example of oral history: an exact transcription of someone's recorded memories. What do you think are the reasons historians regard oral history as both useful and problematic? Have a look at the Oral History Society's website for more information on this fascinating approach to the past.

Daisy Bates concluded, 'Events in history occur when the time has ripened for them, but they need a spark. Little Rock was the spark at that stage of the struggle of the American Negro for justice.' (quoted in P. Engelbert (1999) *American Civil Rights*).

Rosa Parks, the NAACP and the Montgomery bus boycott

Although the African-American campaign for racial equality was well over half a century old by 1956, the Montgomery Bus Boycott of that year is often regarded as the beginning of America's civil rights movement. This claim to fame is based upon two factors:

- The boycott was sustained for 13 months and revealed the power of African Americans when they were united in a common cause.
- It produced a new figurehead for the movement: Dr Martin Luther King.

The Montgomery Bus Boycott was launched in December 1955 when Rosa Parks refused to give up her place on a crowded bus to enable a white man to sit down. As a consequence she was arrested. What could be thought of as the entirely spontaneous action of a tired woman at the end of a busy day, that had such unexpected repercussions when Parks' case was taken up by the NAACP, proves to be rather more 'contrived' when the historian delves further into the available evidence. The following source demonstrates how important it is for historians to consider the context in which historical events such as this are set.

> ### Source (8) The Montgomery Bus Boycott
>
> *Parks, a trim, soft-spoken, bespectacled 42-year-old seamstress at the Montgomery Fair department store, prepared for that decisive day all her life. She married a civil rights activist and… joined the NAACP… When James Blake forced her off his Cleveland Avenue bus in 1943, Parks vowed never to ride with him again, and she kept that vow for twelve years… In the summer of 1955, Virginia Dunn [Alabama civil rights activist] arranged for Parks to attend a desegregation workshop…*
>
> *… On Thursday, 1 December, a weary Rosa Parks absentmindedly entered Blake's bus once more. Holding her purse and a grocery bag on her lap, she sat right behind the white section. As the bus filled, a white man was left standing. An indignant Blake yelled at Parks and three other blacks in her row to step to the rear: 'Move y'all, I want those two seats.' When no one budged, Blake spluttered, 'Y'all better make it light on yourselves and let me have those seats.' The three blacks sitting next to Parks moved immediately. Parks stayed put because she was 'tired of giving in' to racism… When Parks refused to move, a flustered Blake found two policemen who quizzed her motives. Parks held her ground: 'Why do you all push us around?' The policeman shrugged, replying, 'I don't know, but the law is the law, and you're under arrest.'*
>
> From B.J. Dierenfield, *The Civil Rights Movement*, published in 2004.

ACTIVITY

1   What evidence in Source 8 suggests that Parks' action on December 1, 1955, was spontaneous?

2   What evidence in this source suggests Parks had been planning to make some kind of anti-segregation gesture before she got on Blake's bus on December 1, 1955?

A similar event had occurred in Montgomery just a few weeks earlier when a bus driver, slamming his foot on the accelerator, had intentionally jolted a black woman's two small children off the whites-only seats she had placed them on while she looked for money to pay her fare. Back in March 1955, a 15-year-old black girl, Claudette Colvin, had also refused to give up her seat to allow a white person to sit down and she ended up being kicked and dragged off the bus by a policeman. The NAACP had considered challenging Colvin's treatment in court but feared that her 'moral' character (Colvin was pregnant at the time) might undermine their case. The impeccably respectable Rosa Parks was a more viable proposition.

Inspired by the example of the Baton Rouge bus boycott two years earlier, Rosa Parks, secretary of the Alabama NAACP branch and its president, E.D. Nixon, launched a leafleting campaign, urging people to stay off the buses. By choosing to get to work on foot, bicycle, or in shared cars and taxis, the black community threatened the ruin of the bus company, and by not going into town to shop they damaged the prospects of numerous businesses. The Montgomery Improvement Association (**MIA**) was established to co-ordinate the campaign, and the man chosen to lead it was a promising 26-year-old pastor named Martin Luther King.

> ### THINK LIKE AN HISTORIAN
>
> 1 What does the evidence tell you about how the authorities aimed to defeat the civil rights protestors in the 1950s?
> 2 'The Montgomery Bus Boycott was more the work of organizations than individuals.' How far does the evidence support this interpretation? Explain your answer.

As the boycott escalated, the white response hardened. Rosa Parks lost her job; black pedestrians were abused by white passers-by, hurling rotten eggs and spraying urine over them; black drivers were harassed by police and charged with all manner of petty offences; and black churches, cars purchased for the MIA's car-sharing scheme and King's home were all bombed.

Finally the boycott was triumphant when the Supreme Court ruled that Montgomery's segregation laws contravened the 14th Amendment. Boycotts followed in other places and southern cities rapidly abandoned bus segregation. Further white supremacist violence continued, however, including the bombing of more churches and the homes of black ministers, including King's, assaults on individuals, and the killing by the KKK of a black lorry driver. However, there would be no turning back now that the 'MIA's interlocking strategy of local boycott, nonviolent protest, and federal lawsuit' (B.J. Dierenfield, (2004) *The Civil Rights Movement*) had proved so successful.

Martin Luther King, the SCLC and civil rights marches

Following his triumph in Montgomery, Martin Luther King helped establish with other black preachers the Southern Christian Leadership Conference (**SCLC**), dedicated to non-violent direct-action approaches to attaining full racial equality. This offered an alternative approach to that of the NAACP which relied heavily upon the litigation approach. From its headquarters in Atlanta, Georgia, Martin Luther King, the president of the SCLC until his death in 1968, campaigned for something much bigger than desegregated buses: the elimination of all obstacles that stood in the way of black peoples' right to vote. In 1957 King organised the first of his marches in Washington in which 20,000 people assembled to hear him speak out at the Lincoln Memorial for the right of African Americans to vote. Despite its general disorganisation, pressure from

MIA

The Montgomery Improvement Association, led by Martin Luther King, was established in 1956 to co-ordinate the Montgomery bus boycott campaign.

SCLC

Southern Christian Leadership Conference formed in 1957 by Martin Luther King.

the SCLC and the desirability of winning black voters in the next presidential election helped bring about the Civil Rights Act of 1960 which criminalised any actions, such as interference with the voter registration process, designed to prevent individuals from voting.

Although his critics accused him of indecisiveness and some historians regard him as more of a follower than initiator of direct action in the period before 1963, in that year he staged the events that raised his profile as the most dynamic of all the American civil rights leaders and helped shape the King legend. The first of these was his SCLC co-ordinated march in Birmingham, Alabama. Knowing that this was a city where the white community was split on the race issue between white supremacists and business leaders who, for economic reasons, advocated integration, he knew it provided the volatile conditions in which a desegregation march was bound to receive more than just local attention. As he had anticipated, the march in April 1963 was broken up with shows of violence by the police and he ended up in prison for having ignored a court order not to march. From here, on toilet paper and the margins of newspapers, he wrote his famous *Letter from Birmingham City Jail* which addressed a series of objections made by the 'Fellow Clergymen' to which it was addressed.

Source ⑨ **King's letter from Birmingham Jail**

I think I should give the reason for being in Birmingham... I am here... because we were invited here. I am here because I have organizational ties here.

Beyond this, I am in Birmingham because injustice is here... I cannot sit idly by in Atlanta and not be concerned with what happens in Birmingham. Injustice anywhere is a threat to justice everywhere. We are caught in an inescapable network of mutuality, tied in a single garment of destiny... Whatever affects one directly affects all indirectly. Never again can we afford to live with the narrow, provincial 'outside agitator' idea. Anyone who lives in the United States can never be considered an outsider anywhere in this country.

You deplore the demonstrations that are currently taking place in Birmingham... I would not hesitate to say that it is unfortunate that so-called demonstrations are taking place in Birmingham at this time, but I would say in more emphatic terms that it is even more unfortunate that the white power structure of this city left the Negro with no other alternative.

From Martin Luther King, *Letter from Birmingham City Jail*, 1963.

ACTIVITY

What does the evidence of Source 9 reveal about divisions within the civil rights movement in the early 1960s?

THINK LIKE AN HISTORIAN

Forming an interpretation.

In the exam you will need to consider, and probably amend, an interpretation. Use Source 9 and your knowledge of the civil rights movement in earlier times to form an interpretation regarding the degree of unity between those involved in the struggle.

The Birmingham Letter outlined the campaign strategy King had developed and would rely upon for the rest of his life.

Source 10 Non-violent protest

In any nonviolent campaign there are four basic steps: collection of the facts to determine whether injustices exist; negotiation; self-purification; and direct action. We have gone through all these steps in Birmingham. There can be no gainsaying the fact that racial injustice engulfs this community. Birmingham is probably the most thoroughly segregated city in the United States. Its ugly record of brutality is widely known. Negroes have experienced grossly unjust treatment in the courts. There have been more unsolved bombings of Negro homes and churches in Birmingham than in any other city in the nation. These are the hard, brutal facts of the case. On the basis of these conditions, Negro leaders sought to negotiate with the city fathers. But the latter consistently refused to engage in good-faith negotiation.

Then, last September, came the opportunity to talk with leaders of Birmingham's economic community. In the course of the negotiations, certain promises were made by the merchants --- for example, to remove the stores' humiliating racial signs... As the weeks and months went by, we realized that we were the victims of a broken promise. A few signs, briefly removed, returned; the others remained.

... We had no alternative except to prepare for direct action... Mindful of the difficulties involved, we decided to undertake a process of self-purification. We began a series of workshops on nonviolence, and we repeatedly asked ourselves: "Are you able to accept blows without retaliating?" "Are you able to endure the ordeal of jail?" We decided to schedule our direct-action program for the Easter season, realizing that, except for Christmas, this is the main shopping period of the year. Knowing that a strong economic withdrawal program would be the by-product of direct action, we felt that this would be the best time to bring pressure to bear on the merchants for the needed change.

From Martin Luther King, *Letter from Birmingham City Jail*, 1963.

ACTIVITY

1   What was King's reason for explaining his strategy in such detail in 1963 (in Source 10)?

2   How might NAACP leaders have responded to King's argument that 'We had no alternative except to prepare for direct action'?

Source 11 'when the cup of endurance flows over'

... We have waited for more than 340 years for our constitutional and God-given rights. The nations of Asia and Africa are moving with jet-like speed toward gaining political independence, but we still creep at horse-and-buggy pace toward gaining a cup of coffee at a lunch counter. Perhaps it is easy for those who have never felt the stinging dart of segregation to say, "Wait." But when you have seen vicious mobs lynch your mothers and fathers at will and drown your sisters and brothers at whim; when you have seen hate-filled policemen curse, kick and even kill your black brothers and sisters; when you see the vast majority of your twenty million Negro brothers smothering in an airtight cage of poverty in the midst of an affluent society; when you suddenly find your tongue twisted and your speech stammering as you seek to explain to your six-year-old daughter why she can't go to the public amusement park that has just been advertised on television, and see tears welling up in her eyes when she is told that Funtown is closed to colored children, and see ominous clouds of inferiority beginning to form in her little mental sky, and see her beginning to distort her personality by developing an unconscious bitterness toward white people; when you have to concoct an answer for a five-year-old son who is asking: "Daddy, why do white people treat colored people so mean?"; when you take a cross-county drive and find it necessary to sleep night after night in the uncomfortable corners of your automobile because no motel will accept you; when you are humiliated day in and day out by nagging signs reading "white" and "colored"; when your first name becomes "nigger," your middle name becomes "boy" (however old you are) and your last name becomes "John," and your wife and mother are never given the respected title "Mrs."; when you are harried by day and haunted by night by the fact that you are a Negro, living constantly at tiptoe stance, never quite knowing what to expect next, and are plagued with inner fears and outer resentments; when you are forever fighting a degenerating sense of "nobodiness" then you will understand why we find it difficult to wait. There comes a time when the cup of endurance runs over, and men are no longer willing to be plunged into the abyss of despair. I hope, sirs, you can understand our legitimate and unavoidable impatience.

From Martin Luther King, *Letter from Birmingham City Jail*, 1963.

King's letter from Birmingham reads like a speech. The earlier logically-argued text of the speech leads into highly emotive, impassioned and powerful **rhetoric**:

rhetoric

Language, such as that of presidential election campaign speeches, that is designed to persuade and impress.

ACTIVITY

1   What techniques did King employ in this passage (Source 11) to put across his message?

2   What does the *Letter from Birmingham City Jail* tell us about how King saw himself?

3   How does it help explain King's central place in the history of the civil rights movement?

4   Explain why historians need to be cautious when reading what protestors claim about their motives?

Although his critics in 1963 accused him of provoking violence by marching in the first place, King's advocacy of non-violent direct action gave the movement the moral high ground. By exposing themselves as targets for white hostility the marchers made more public the brutality of white supremacists. Furthermore, by condemning in this letter and elsewhere the white 'moderates' who turned a blind eye to the race issue he encouraged whites, particularly those of the middle-classes, to take a position.

Source 12 'white moderates'

… I must make two honest confessions to you, my Christian and Jewish brothers. First, I must confess that over the past few years I have been gravely disappointed with the white moderate. I have almost reached the regrettable conclusion that the Negro's great stumbling block in his stride toward freedom is not the White Citizens' 'Counciler' or the Ku Klux Klanner, but the white moderate, who is more devoted to 'order' than to justice; who prefers a negative peace which is the absence of tension to a positive peace which is the presence of justice; who constantly says: "I agree with you in the goal you seek, but I cannot agree with your methods of direct action"; who paternalistically believes he can set the timetable for another man's freedom; who lives by a mythical concept of time and who constantly advises the Negro to wait for a 'more convenient season.' Shallow understanding from people of good will is more frustrating than absolute misunderstanding from people of ill will. Lukewarm acceptance is much more bewildering than outright rejection.

From Martin Luther King, *Letter from Birmingham City Jail*, 1963.

ACTIVITY

1   What do you think King meant by 'direct action' (Source 12)? Give some examples.

2   What was the propaganda value of this paragraph in the Birmingham Letter (Source 13), soon to be published and circulated by the American Friends Service Committee?

THINK LIKE AN HISTORIAN

Considering an interpretation.

Use Sources 9–12 and your own knowledge to test the interpretation that 'the civil rights movement had more to do with individuals than organisations'. If you disagree with this interpretation try writing a more accurate one.

The Birmingham campaign, which escalated into considerable violence, perpetrated by both whites and African Americans, certainly generated the media attention King was looking for even though he was accused of having provoked the violence he claimed to abhor. The events in Birmingham in the spring of 1963 paved the way for further protests throughout the South in the summer. On 1 June King confidently declared, 'We are on the threshold of a significant breakthrough and the greatest weapon is the mass demonstration' (quoted in V. Saunders, (2006) *Race Relations in the USA 1863–1980*).

In August 1963 King led the March on Washington for civil rights and black employment opportunities. To 250,000 people, at the Lincoln Memorial, he delivered his 'I have a dream' speech, one of the most famous speeches made in the 20th century.

Source **13 The March on Washington**

I am happy to join with you today in what will go down in history as the greatest demonstration for freedom in the history of our nation.

… the Negro…finds himself an exile in his own land. And so we've come here today to dramatize a shameful condition.

… This is no time to engage in the luxury of cooling off or to take the tranquilizing drug of gradualism. Now is the time to make real the promises of democracy. Now is the time to rise from the dark and desolate valley of segregation to the sunlit path of racial justice. Now is the time to lift our nation from the quicksands of racial injustice to the solid rock of brotherhood. Now is the time to make justice a reality for all of God's children.

It would be fatal for the nation to overlook the urgency of the moment. This sweltering summer of the Negro's legitimate discontent will not pass until there is an invigorating autumn of freedom and equality. 1963 is not an end, but a beginning. And those who hope that the Negro needed to blow off steam and will now be content will have a rude awakening if the nation returns to business as usual. And there will be neither rest nor tranquility in America until the Negro is granted his citizenship rights. The whirlwinds of revolt will continue to shake the foundations of our nation until the bright day of justice emerges.

… The marvelous new militancy which has engulfed the Negro community must not lead us to a distrust of all white people, for many of our white brothers, as evidenced by their presence here today, have come to realize that their destiny is tied up with our destiny. And they have come to realize that their freedom is inextricably bound to our freedom.

We cannot walk alone.

And as we walk, we must make the pledge that we shall always march ahead.

We cannot turn back.

From Martin Luther King's March on Washington speech, 1963.

ACTIVITY

1 Why might those in authority have been alarmed by the rhetoric of King's March on Washington speech? Use extracts from Source 13 to explain your answer.

2 What phrases in Source 13 support the interpretation that King was a social revolutionary?

3 How, on the basis of this evidence, had the civil rights movement progressed in the 1960s?

4 Why should historians be cautious in taking speeches like this at face value?

The impact of the March on Washington has been disputed by historians ever since. However it seems certain that it contributed to the passing of the Civil Rights bill in 1964. In December of that year King was awarded the Nobel Peace Prize.

In 1965 King replicated his 1963 Birmingham strategy by targeting the town of Selma, Alabama, with a public protest to help invigorate the SCLC. In this segregated community, with an even numerical split of African Americans and whites but where only three per cent of blacks were registered to vote, King and the SCLC joined forces

with the disenfranchised attempting to register at the Selma County Court. His initial protest march from Selma to Montgomery, the state capital, was broken up by state troopers with such violence that the day became known as 'Bloody Sunday'. The violence of the white community, such as the throwing of poisonous snakes into the crowd, in preventing the march and King's subsequent arrest, provided the media attention and propaganda opportunities King was looking for. A second attempted march proved equally unsuccessful. Ten days after 'Bloody Sunday' a federal judge declared the protest legitimate and, consequently, the final, triumphant march received the protection of the state troopers. The Selma victory prompted similar marches in several northern cities and played a big part in pushing through the Voting Rights Act in August 1965. In the opinion of some historians this was the highpoint of King's career. His campaigning would continue as he took on new causes including the anti-Vietnam War campaign and became an advocate of socialist principles and economic equality. In 1968 he was killed by an assassin's bullet in Memphis where he was supporting a sanitation workers' strike.

THINK LIKE AN HISTORIAN

1   On the basis of this evidence, to what extent and why had King moved beyond the race issue by the end of his life?

2   How might this have been perceived by other 'race leaders'?

Historians have debated the significance of Martin Luther King's role in the civil rights movement. While none doubt his importance, many modern historians believe this one individual has been given too much of the credit owed to others and that his failings have tended to be overlooked. A summary of such views can be found in Kevern Verney's book *Black Civil Rights in America* (2000):

THINK LIKE AN HISTORIAN

Why might an historian be prone to exaggerating the influence of individuals in the history of the civil rights movement?

Source (14) **A modern historian's view of the part played by Martin Luther King in the civil rights movement**

It is now recognized that civil rights campaigns were more than just an extension of the personality of Dr King. The Montgomery bus boycott would have taken place without him, for it was not he who initiated it. The major civil rights campaigns in the 1950s and 1960s were not the by-products of his messianic persona, but rather the culmination of growing black consciousness and protest at grassroots level that dated back to the 1930s and 1940s. Similarly, the break-up of the civil rights coalition was already underway before King's death and a result of complex political, social and economic factors. During his lifetime Martin Luther King's leadership was a subject of criticism even within the civil rights movement. His successful campaigns were offset by, at times, bitter disappointments, failure and self-doubt.

From Kevern Verney, *Black Civil Rights in America*, published in 2000.

Some sources reveal that he was not always revered quite as highly as he has been since his death. Indeed, some of his fellow activists, including Malcolm X, despised his methods. On the evidence of the following sources it could be suggested that his role in the civil rights movement at the start of the 1960s was relatively minor but that by the time of his death in 1968 his legendary status had been established.

Source **15 A student activist's view of Martin Luther King**

The individual who had probably the most influence on us was Gandhi, more than any single individual. During the time that the Montgomery Bus Boycott was in effect, we were tots for the most part and barely heard of Martin Luther King. Yes, Martin Luther King's name was well-known when the sit-in movement was in effect, but to pick Martin Luther King as a hero... I don't want you to misunderstand what I'm about to say: Yes, Martin Luther King was a hero... No, he was not the individual that we had upmost in mind when we started the sit-in movement.

From an interview with Franklin McCain, a black student who staged, with three others, a lunch-counter sit-in in the Woolworth's department store in Greensboro, North Carolina, on February 1, 1960, in Carson C. et al, *The Eyes on the Prize Civil Rights Reader*, published in 1991.

Source 16 Introductory speech for Martin Luther King at the Jewish Rabbinical Assembly annual convention

Where in America today do we hear a voice like the voice of the prophets of Israel? Martin Luther King is a sign that God has not forsaken the United States of America. God has sent him to us. His presence is the hope of America. His mission is sacred, his leadership is of supreme importance to every one of us.

[...] Martin Luther King is a voice, a vision, and a way. I call upon every Jew to harken to his voice, to share his vision, to follow in his way. The whole future of America will depend upon the impact and influence of Dr King.

May everyone present give his strength to this great spiritual leader, Martin Luther King.

From Professor Abraham Joshua Heschel's introductory speech welcoming Martin Luther King to the 68th annual convention of the Jewish Rabbinical Assembly as a visiting speaker, March 25, 1968 in Carson C. et al, *The Eyes on the Prize Civil Rights Reader*, published in 1991.

ACTIVITY

Use Sources 15 and 16 to form your own interpretation of the role of Martin Luther King in the civil rights movement.

THINK LIKE AN HISTORIAN

Reconciling conflicting sources of evidence.

In the exam you are likely to be presented with sources that seem to conflict with each other. Sometimes, as in the apparent differences of opinion between Sources 15 and 16 these differences can be reconciled. Use your understanding of provenance and the questions historians ask to explain these differences.

Ella Baker, the SNCC and sit-ins

Ella Baker, convinced that co-ordinated involvement of ministers would boost popular interest in the civil rights movement, was the person who persuaded Martin Luther King to set up the SCLC in 1957. She was an experienced former NAACP organiser and she also became the key figure in the establishment of the young people's branch of the SCLC, the Student Non-violent Coordinating Committee (**SNCC**).

SNCC

Student Non-violent Coordinating Committee formed in 1960 by Ella Baker.

Sit-ins

The strategy whereby segregated areas, such as whites-only lunch counters, were occupied by protesters, refusing to move until the managers agreed to desegregation.

A principal method of the SNCC was the 'sit-in': the strategy whereby segregated areas, such as whites-only lunch counters, were occupied by protesters who refused to move until the managers agreed to desegregation. The craze for student **sit-ins** got underway after four students in February 1960 at Greensboro, North Carolina, requested meals at a whites-only counter in a Woolworths store. This was not the first sit-in by any means but it was spectacularly successful and received a good deal of media coverage. The students who refused to budge until they were served were soon joined by more and eventually 80 people were involved in the protest which lasted for three days before the shop was closed to all customers. Inspired by their example and the numerous sit-ins countrywide which followed, Ella Baker formed the SNCC at Shaw University in Raleigh, North Carolina in April 1960. Sit-ins could be as dangerous an activity for participants as marches; protestors were frequently abused and attacked while the police in many cases turned a blind eye. However such injustices provided useful propaganda for the movement whenever newspaper reporters, cameramen and TV crews were present.

Source 17

A sit-in at a Woolworth store lunch counter in Jackson, Mississippi, on 28 May 1963. The mob that opposed the sit-in was several hundred strong. The students, black and white, had sugar, mustard, salt and other foodstuffs poured over them. In the foreground is Hunter Gray, a young white teacher from Tougaloo College; he is covered in his own blood having been beaten with brass 'knuckle dusters' and a broken glass sugar container. A supposed FBI agent in dark glasses looks on while the local police stood outside the shop.

ACTIVITY

1   What does this photograph (Source 17) reveal regarding the nature and purpose of lunch-counter sit-ins?

2   What can be inferred from the age and sex of the people shown in this photograph?

3   What are the limitations of this photograph as evidence for sit-ins in the early 1960s?

In the following source a student, in March 1962, explains why he considers sit-ins such an important strategy.

Source 18 Desegregation

The masses of the Negroes are through putting up with segregation; they are tired of it. They are tired of being pushed around in a democracy which fails to practice what it preaches. The Negro students of the South who have read the Constitution, and studied it, have read the amendments to the Constitution, and know the rights that are supposed to be theirs – they are coming to the point where they themselves want to do something about achieving these rights, not depend on somebody else. The time has passed when we can look for pie in the sky, when we can depend upon someone else on high to solve the problem for us. The Negro students want to solve the problem themselves. Masses of older Negroes want to join them in that. We can't wait for the law. The Supreme Court decision in 1954 banning segregated schools has had almost eight years of existence, yet less than 8 per cent of the Negro kids are in integrated schools. That is far too slow. Now the people themselves want to get involved, and they are. I was talking with one of the student leaders of the South only last week; he said, 'I myself desegregated a lunch counter, not somebody else, not some big man, some powerful man, but me, little me. I walked the picket line and I sat in and the walls of segregation toppled. Now all people can eat there.'… So that's what's happening; you see, we are going to do something about freedom now, we are not waiting for other people to do it. The student sit-ins have shown it; we are winning. As a result of one year of the student sit-ins, the lunch counters were desegregated in more than 150 cities. The walls are tumbling down.

James Farmer from Haig and Hamida Bosmajian, *The Rhetoric of the Civil-Rights Movement*, published in 1969.

ACTIVITY

1 How does Source 18 reveal changes in the civil rights movement between the mid-1950s and the early 1960s?

2 How does the strategy described in Source 18 differ to that of Martin Luther King in the early 1960s? Explain your answer with reference to the source.

Sit-ins and similar protests such as read-ins in libraries and swim-ins in swimming pools proved to be very effective in leading to the desegregation of public places like eating areas and parks.

Janet McCloud, the NIYC and fish-ins

Young urban Native Americans in Albuquerque, New Mexico, established the National Indian Youth Council (**NIYC**), very much in the spirit of the SNCC. In the second half of the 1960s they supported **'fish-ins'**, initiated by Native American tribal peoples and the Survival of American Indians Association, to protect the livings of people who relied on fishing the Quillayute and Nisqually rivers in Washington State. These fish-ins were acts of civil disobedience since they violated state fishing laws. These laws, which contravened the terms of the treaties signed in the 1850s, were allegedly passed to protect dwindling salmon supplies. This action against over-fishing however did not prevent wealthy white game fisherman from continuing to enjoy their sport in these rivers. The fish-ins resulted in vicious white retaliation including beatings, some carried out by the police and game wardens, and shootings. Hundreds of fish-in protestors were arrested.

In the following source, the daughter of Janet McCloud, of the Tulalip tribe and a founder member of the Survival of American Indians Association, describes the trial in 1969 of those arrested for participating in a fish-in back in 1965.

NIYC

National Indian Youth Council

Fish-ins

Acts of civil disobedience in the later 1960s to protect the livings of Native-American people who relied on fishing the Quillayute and Nisqually rivers.

113

Source 19   The Nisqually River fish-in

On October 13, 1965, we held a 'fish-in' on the Nisqually River to try and bring a focus on our fishing fight with the State of Washington. The 'fish-in' started at 4.00 pm and was over at about 4.30 pm. It ended with six Indians in jail and dazed Indian kids wondering 'what happened?'... They were released after posting bail a few hours later.

... The trial was to begin on January 15, 1969, at 9.30 am. We went into the courthouse that Wednesday certain we would not receive justice as was proven to us in other trials... Many of us were dressed in our traditional way with headbands, leggings and necklaces. As we walked the length of the corridor to the courtroom, the game wardens looked us up and down, laughing at us.

... The first witness to our defence was Bob Johnson. At the time of the fish-in he was the editor of the 'Auburn Citizen' newspaper. He told of the tactics the game wardens used on us. Mr. Johnson also had evidence with him, pictures of game wardens, showing billie clubs and seven-celled flashlights.

... The next defence witness was Janet McCloud, Tulalip Indian. She told the facts about why the Indians had had the fish-in demonstration on that day... This was important because the State thought we were after blood that day. And we were not expecting any violence because all my brothers and sisters were there [Janet McCloud had eight children] and the youngest was four at that time. And if we had expected violence none of the children would have been there. She told how she felt the wardens were going to ram our boat and how she felt when she realized these men meant business with their seven-celled flashlights, billie clubs, and brass knuckles.

My two little brothers were in that boat when it was rammed, the youngest was seven and could not swim... the game wardens said that they did not ram the boat...

Laura McCloud, 'Tulalip', from P. Nabakov, *Native American Testimony: a Chronicle of Indian-White Relations from Prophecy to the Present, 1492–1992*, published in 1991.

THINK LIKE AN HISTORIAN

On the basis of the evidence in Source 19 and that for the sit-ins described in the previous section, comment on the points of similarity and difference between these two forms of protest.

The protestors, to their great surprise, were found not guilty of the charges they were facing. In a footnote to her report, Janet McCloud's daughter commented on how the news was received by the game wardens.

Source 20   Retaliation

The game wardens, incensed at the adverse verdict, left the Tyee Motel where they had been celebrating, prematurely, their victory and went down in large numbers to Frank's Landing. A sympathetic soul overheard the wardens and called the Landing to warn the Indians. Nevertheless the wardens caught a car load of Indians at the railroad trestle and surrounded them in their state game cars – they proceeded to hit the Indians' car with their nightsticks, cussing them and trying to provoke [them] to fight. It was obvious to the Indians that they had been drinking... So the war goes on – which goes to prove that the history books are wrong when they talk about 'the last Indian wars'. They have never stopped!

Laura McCloud, 'Tulalip', from P. Nabakov, *Native American Testimony: a Chronicle of Indian-White Relations from Prophecy to the Present, 1492–1992*, published in 1991.

Some progress in the 1970s was made regarding Native-American fishing rights, but these continued to be challenged throughout the 1980s.

James Farmer, CORE and the Freedom Rides

Sit-ins dated back at least as far as the establishment of the Congress of Racial Equality (CORE), set up by James Farmer in Chicago in 1942. In 1947 he organised the original Freedom Ride, a 'Journey of Reconciliation' through the upper southern states, in which a group of CORE activists exercised their civil right to sit where they liked on buses and were largely unmolested in doing so.

In 1961 Farmer revived the idea, this time with a group of seven black and six white activists aiming to test the extent to which desegregation at bus terminals, now required by law, was actually being practised. Assured of media coverage they hoped to expose southern racism and/or to persuade federal authorities to enforce desegregation by travelling the 1500 miles on two buses from Washington, DC to New Orleans, using bus station facilities as they travelled. The Freedom Riders included members of the SNCC, such as John Lewis, the national chairman of the SNCC from 1963 to 1966, and, after 1980, a leading African-American politician and campaigner for social justice. The SCLC and the NAACP branches en route promised their support in the form of meals and accommodation. The hostility the riders encountered was considerable and the Freedom Riders soon discovered they were as much at risk as those involved in other forms of non-violent protest.

At South Carolina they were attacked by a mob at the Greyhound bus station as they tried to use the whites-only facilities. On the Georgia-Alabama border the bus they were travelling in was surrounded by another crowd and burned out, its CORE passengers being savagely beaten as they tried to escape the burning bus; a lynching prevented at the last moment by the intervention of a plain-clothes armed Alabama policeman. Taking another bus they were next attacked at Anniston, Alabama, by a group of whites boarding the bus who targeted those black protesters sitting in the front of the bus. At Birmingham, Alabama, they were severely beaten, necessitating hospital treatment for some. One, a white academic, Dr Walter Bergman, suffered such serious head injuries that he suffered a stroke ten days later and spent the rest of life confined to a wheelchair. His wife, Frances, was also beaten in the assault. At this point, with no buses willing to carry them further, they abandoned the first Ride and flew the rest of the way to New Orleans. More Rides and more extreme white supremacist violence followed, later alleviated when the riders received some protection from the intervention of federal marshals on the instruction of President Kennedy, forced by the **Freedom Rides** to confront civil rights issues. Meanwhile, Freedom Riders arrested for disorderly conduct were treated with considerable barbarity in southern jails. Although Farmer became the reluctant participant in one Freedom Ride, other race leaders, including Martin Luther King, chose not to join the Freedom Rides, much to the dismay of others in the movement who derided King in particular for cowardice.

The following source summarises Farmer's objectives in launching his new Freedom Ride in 1961.

Freedom Rides

Well-publicised journeys by bus in which activists exercised their civil rights, and risked racist violence, by sitting where they liked on buses.

Source (21) The Freedom Ride

We planned the Freedom Ride with the specific intention of creating a crisis. We were counting on the bigots in the South to do our work for us. We figured that the government would have to respond if we created a situation that was headline news all over the world.

James Farmer quoted in B.J. Dierenfield, *The Civil Rights Movement*, published in 2008.

ACTIVITY

'Different methods, same purpose.' How far is this an accurate description of the various forms of non-violent protest explored in this chapter? Use quotations from the sources given to explain and justify your answer.

THINK LIKE AN HISTORIAN

Recognising developments over time.

The ability to recognise change and continuity in the historical record is a key exam skill. How do Sources 13–19 reveal ways in which the civil rights movement changed in the late 1950s and the early 1960s?

Chicano

People of Mexican origin living outside of Mexico. Originally a term of abuse, it came to be used by Mexican Americans with pride.

NFWU

The National Farm Workers' Union formed in 1962 by César Chávez.

César Chávez, the NFWA, strikes and hunger strikes

Hispanic-Americans ('**Chicanos**') were subjected to the same kind of racial discrimination as African Americans, including segregation, prejudicial treatment by the police and courts, and restricted political representation. Also, like black Americans, the average Hispanic-American standard of living was well below that of white Americans.

César Chávez founded the National Farm Workers' Union (**NFWU**) in 1962 to protect the interests of Hispanic-American agricultural labourers. Greatly influenced by the example of Martin Luther King, from the late 1960s he promoted a five-year-long boycott of grapes as a protest against the treatment of the people who picked them and the appalling poverty in which they were obliged to live. Millions of shoppers participated in the boycott. He also helped organise strikes in the Delano grape-growing region and secured particular media attention by staging his own 25-day-long hunger strike in 1968 as an alternative to the more militant actions, including the destruction of crops, that other union members were considering.

In the following source, Chávez, writing about the early days of the grape pickers' strike in 1965, explains the value of time-wasting as another effective non-violent strategy.

> **Source** (22) **Time-wasting as protest**
>
> *There was harassment on the picket lines. At one point, after we had been on strike for about five or six weeks, we were stopped constantly by deputies. Every striker was photographed, and a field-report card was filled in on each person. In some cases, it took as much as an hour and a half to go through this process. Then it was repeated every time we moved from one field to another. We have a man in Delano who was photographed, and the same report was filled in on him no less than twelve times.*
>
> *At first our tactic was total cooperation. Then we started taking their time. In my case, the officer took almost an hour because I went very slowly. I examined the card and the spelling, and I engaged him in conversation just to tie him up.*
>
> *Then we'd go on night picketing, get about thirty cars and go out at night, and they'd have to wake up the cops to follow us. We worked it so they had to have three shifts. If we'd go out of the office at 3.00 in the morning, they'd follow us.*
>
> *With us, it was a tactic to get them to spend as much money as possible. The county spent thousands of dollars on extra personnel. They'll never spend that much money again. Afterward there were a lot of complaints. A small group of liberals in Bakersfield checked up on the expense and found they had spent thousands of dollars.*
>
> *Finally we made up our minds we had been harassed enough. We refused to give them any information or to let them take our pictures. We told the enquiring officer from the Kern County Sheriff's Office that if he wanted to take our picture, he would first have to arrest us. And at that point we were able to gain some ground.*
>
> From J. Levy, *César Chávez: Autobiography of La Causa*, published in 1975.

EXAM TIP

When you are presented with sources in the exam that are extracts from the accounts of race activists, remember that they are likely to be biased even if they are factually true. Use a highlighter pen to identify words and phrases that reveal the 'tone' of the source. Consider not just what the source contains but also what it does not. Rarely will a single source provide the 'whole picture'.

ACTIVITY

1 According to Source 22, how did the strategies of the strikers change during the 1965 strike? How effective were they?

2 What did the strategies of Chávez have in common with other civil rights activists? In what ways were they different?

Although it took a long time, the strike action and the boycott of grapes proved effective and, by 1970, the Delano grape growers had all conceded to the workers' demands on pay and working conditions.

ACTIVITY Exam practice

Interpretation: The strategies of civil rights activists in the late 1950s and early 1960s were non-violent but catastrophist.

a   Explain how far the sources in this chapter support this interpretation. You may, if you wish, amend the interpretation or suggest a different interpretation. If you do this you must use the sources to support the changes you make.

Remember not to simply take the sources at face value. Use your knowledge of the period to interpret and evaluate them.

b   Explain how these sources are both useful and raise problems and issues for a historian using them.

Summary – what you have learned in Chapter 6

This chapter has introduced you to several of the most influential figures in the history of America's civil rights movement.

You have also learned about the importance of several civil rights organisations that worked in association with these individuals.

You have also been introduced to several of the non-violent strategies associated with these individuals and organisations.

By working through the various *Activity* and *Think like an historian* tasks you have practised and developed important skills for the examination:

- understanding the role of important individuals and the organisations with which they were associated
- understanding their different strategies in their common struggle for greater racial equality
- understanding why historians have arrived at different interpretations regarding their contributions
- understanding how and why segregation became the focus of the civil rights movement
- the analysis and evaluation of sources
- the comparison and contrast of sources such as eyewitness accounts of a single event
- recognising similarities and differences in the experiences and protests of different racial minorities
- using groups of sources to test hypotheses
- using groups of sources to form interpretations
- recognising the uniqueness of sources
- recognising continuity in history
- amending an interpretation
- cross-referencing sources
- assessing the value of oral history
- considering an interpretation.

Now take a look at the Exam Café at the back of the book for more advice and practice.

THINK LIKE AN HISTORIAN

1   On the basis of the evidence in this chapter, consider the reasons why some forms of non-violent protest were more effective than others. Identify the criteria you will you use to decide and then set the various protests out on a grid to map them against your chosen criteria.

2   Are the same criteria common to all the protests you classified as less effective? If some are not, what might this suggest?

7 The civil rights struggle: separatists, supremacists and terrorists

Overview

By the mid-1960s the broad coalition of civil rights groups had splintered. In the face of white resistance to change and disillusionment regarding the slow progress of non-violent methods many people were looking for alternatives. The civil rights movement was split along religious (e.g. Christian and Muslim) and political lines (e.g. Liberal and Communist), and also on ultimate objectives with some advocating racial integration and others separation. Most significantly many civil rights campaigners were no longer willing to follow Martin Luther King's 'turn the other cheek' policy, subscribing instead to the 'eye for an eye' outlook of new race leaders like Malcolm X.

Key Questions:

1   Why did African Americans in northern industrial cities become the focus of race-hate in the period after the Second World War?

2   How far was post-Second World War 'Black Power' a new concept?

3   To what extent and why were civil rights activists more prepared to resort to violence in the 1960s?

4   In what ways and why did the organisation of the civil rights 'movement' change in the 1960s?

White supremacists, the KKK and other organisations

African-American, Native-American and Hispanic-American civil rights activists in the 1960s embarked on a wide range of non-violent strategies to put pressure on society and those in authority to change. The methods they employed, such as sit-ins and marches, were designed to provoke a reaction, and in numerous instances protestors knowingly and willingly put themselves at great risk of racist violence. Much of this violence was spontaneous, sometimes it was coordinated by the KKK, possibly in collusion with the authorities. Other right-wing organisations, such as the Liberty League, the Black Legion, and the John Birch Society, played a part in trying to maintain the prejudiced racial *status quo* of old. Countless local associations and community groups were set up in northern towns and cities to 'protect' white interests, such as segregated residential areas, in the middle decades of the 20th century as more and more African Americans migrated from the South. In the following source, a modern historian describes one such action in Detroit in 1948:

Source (1) Racial tension in Detroit

The prevention of interracial residential and sexual contact was not just a masculine responsibility. Women also policed the boundaries of race and sex. The overlapping concerns of neighborhood integrity, racial purity, and domestic tranquillity gave particular urgency to demonstrations led by women against Edward Brock. Brock, the white owner of two houses on Detroit's lower west side, had sold them to Black families in 1948. Groups of ten to twenty-five women, many pushing baby strollers, gathered at Brock's workplace every day for a week, carrying hand-painted signs that read: 'My home is my castle, I will die defending it'; 'The Lord separated the races, why should Constable Brock mix them'; 'We don't want to mix'; and 'Ed Brock sold to colored in white neighborhood.' Passersby were taken aback by a picket line of white mothers and babies, an uncommon sight at a time when most demonstrations in Detroit were labor-oriented and male-led. Replete with the symbols of motherhood and family, these protests touched a deep, sympathetic nerve among onlookers, many of whom saw Black movement into a neighbourhood as a threat to virtuous womanhood, innocent childhood, and the sanctity of the home.

Thomas J. Sugrue (1995), 'Crabgrass-Roots Politics: Race, Rights, and the Reaction against Liberalism in the Urban North, 1940–1964', from J. E. Davis, *The Civil Rights Movement*, published in 2001.

ACTIVITY

1   Why are women often less prominent than men in the documentary evidence for the history of the civil rights movement?

2   Why would the position taken by the women in Source 1 have seemed hypocritical to recently demobbed black servicemen who had fought in the Second World War?

Just as the Second World War experience strengthened the determination of African Americans to fight 'fascism' at home, it also strengthened the resolve of white communities in the North to resist the migration of southern black families. Conveniently forgetting the very significant part played by non-white Americans in the war, one Detroit citizen, Michael J. Harbulak, in 1945 produced the following argument:

Source (2) Africans and Americans

Our boys are fighting in Europe, Asia, and Africa to keep those people off our soil. If when these boys return they should become refugees who have to give up their homes because their own neighbourhood with the help of our city fathers had been invade[d] and occupied by the Africans, it would be a shame which our city fathers could not outlive.

From J. E. Davis, *The Civil Rights Movement*, published in 2001.

THINK LIKE AN HISTORIAN

What does the term 'Africans', used here to describe black Americans, reveal about Michael J. Harbulak's prejudices?

The following source shows how right-wing white protestors endeavoured to further undermine the civil rights movement by associating it with communism. It is part of a letter sent to the Mississippi State Sovereignty Commission which was set up in 1956 to preserve segregation.

Source **Race and revolution**

Gentlemen:

The time is drawing near - soon, very soon, the forces of communism will make it's [sic] presence felt by every man, woman and school child in the State of Mississippi. It is a strange truth that if Russia marched an army of uniformed soldiers into Mississippi, the people of this State would fight with every means known to man but, of course, we've all been told many years ago that we would all be taken without firing a shot so no soldiers will be necessary - only orders from the communist infested federal government! All one can hear and see today is the negro - flaunting his arrogance from the mockery of a United Nations rostrum to the numberless demonstrations in the Congo. It is nauseatingly evident that the communist[s] are proving every day how weak and meaningless are our claims to our American heritage and Racial Integrity. Using the N.A.A.C.P. as a calling card, the communist[s] have bullied this entire nation into accepting an inferior race – demanding that they be allowed to intermingle in every way possible. They well know that enough amalgamation will follow which will lend strength, only, to the stupid and untrue words "all men are created equal"[sic]. This rotten untruth can be proven a million times over again and still some insipid nobody can stir the ignorant and [un]informed. Why is this true? What happens to the nation's morale? [...]

Yesterday, I heard that the Government had rehired hundreds of former employees who had been considered Security Risk[s] by the Committee on Un-American Activities. Will this go unchallenged? Oh yes, the man I heard it from was protesting but like the American Indian - who is he? Both political parties have questionable intentions with or without the knowledge of most of it's [sic] members - Tell me, Gentlemen, would we have the backing of the U.N. and maybe Russia if as Mississippians, we made a bid for freedom - Republic of Mississippi - would the federal government ply us with money or offers of same, if we made noises like the Congo? I've heard my grandfather tell of the arrogant and belligerent behavior of the negro during Reconstruction - just wait until the federal government gets through turning the country over to them! In time, this country will wind up just like the Congo - and eventually? Well, gentlemen, think it over.

Sincerely,

Mrs. Hugh Rodman, Jr.

From J. E. Davis, *The Civil Rights Movement*, published in 2001.

ACTIVITY

1   What does Source 3 reveal of white attitudes in the South in the later 1950s?

2   What are its limitations as a source of historical evidence?

3   Why might the readers of this letter be inclined to agree that supporters of the civil rights movement were likely to be communist sympathisers?

In a report from 1964, Benjamin Van Clark, the 20-year-old chairman of the Youth Division of Chatham County (Savannah) Crusade for Voters, described the nature of organised white resistance to the civil rights campaign.

Source 4 Violence in Savannah, 1964

I could cite many… cases of police brutality in recent months during our demonstrations. At first the police stood by, supposedly to protect the demonstrators. Then the white community, the White Citizens Council and the Ku Klux Klan elements, demanded that the Negro demonstrators be arrested. The police began to pick up Negro citizens and beat them on their heads with gun butts. One lady was hit in the stomach with a tear gas bomb. All this was done to nonviolent demonstrators. Jail cells that normally held ten persons were jammed with seventy-five.

… The community's reaction to these events is a very mixed one with one element saying 'be nonviolent' and the other saying 'you will get nothing without violence.' We tried to make them demonstrate non-violently and we finally convinced them that nonviolence would get them what they wanted, and they agreed… We have been blamed for the violence but everyone in Savannah knows that every act of violence has been perpetrated by the riot squad. The riot squad is trained to use police dogs and riot guns and the dogs are trained to attack only Negroes.

Quite recently the Cavalcade of White America was organized to try to frighten Negroes so they wouldn't demonstrate any more. Immediately after that, one of the local white businessmen and a former city detective came out advocating violence. The president of the White Citizens Council happens to be one of Savannah's most prominent attorneys.

The Cavalcade of White America advocates economic reprisals against the Negro community as a whole. This could not be a very successful venture because the white business community depends upon the Negro for its success..

Benjamin van Clark, 'Siege at Savannah' (1964), from J. E. Davis, *The Civil Rights Movement*, published in 2001.

ACTIVITY

1   To what extent does Source 4 reveal disunity within the civil rights movement? Explain your answer.

2   What does this source reveal about the nature of white opposition to the civil rights movement?

3   Were the tactics of the white opposition described here more likely to promote or prevent the campaign for civil rights? Explain your answer.

4   What are its limitations as evidence for the history of the civil rights movement?

THINK LIKE AN HISTORIAN

Why should historians pay careful attention to the provenance of Source 4 in evaluating its content?

Adam Clayton Powell and 'Black Power'

Adam Clayton Powell was a leading figure in the campaigns for desegregation and the ending of discriminatory employment in the immediate post-Second World War civil rights movement. In his youth he had been a member of Marcus Garvey's African Nationalist Pioneer Movement. Like several of his predecessors he is associated with a newspaper; the *People's Voice* which he established in 1942 to promote his views. He became an active New York politician, elected by the black voters of Harlem to the United States House of Representatives. Perhaps his most important contribution was in reinvigorating the struggle and, allegedly, coining the phrase '**Black Power**'. He was re-elected on 12 occasions between 1945 and 1969. In the following passage a modern historian, quoting the words of Powell, sums up his role in the civil rights movement.

Black Power

A term coined to describe the ideas and actions of African Americans that are based upon pride in their racial heritage and their determination to advance and/or assert their position in society.

Source 5 Adam Clayton Powell

In 1965 Adam Clayton Powell Jr. was one of Congress's most influential legislators. He'd been in the House of Representatives twenty years and, considering how he loved Harlem, it appeared he'd be there another twenty. In Chicago on March 28, 1965, he introduced a seventeen-point programme, 'My Black Position Paper for America's 20 Million Negroes', which was far from the assimilationist rhetoric of his peers. Powell spoke of blacks 'seeking audacious power – the kind of power which cradles your head amongst the stars' – and fused the ideas of Washington and Du Bois by demanding that the civil-rights movement 'shift its emphasis to the two-pronged thrust of the Black Revolution: economic self-sufficiency and political power.' He felt the legislation of Johnson, particularly the 1964 Civil Rights Act, meant nothing in the North without the economic component of 'black power' to support it. More than any other leader of his generation, Powell articulated the dissatisfaction of young blacks with the traditional integrationist views of the civil-rights movement and the rising currents of black nationalism it fuelled among activists.

Nelson George, 'Black Beauty, Black Confusion (1965–70)', in Floyd Windom Hayes, *A Turbulent Voyage: Readings in African American Studies,* published in 2000.

ACTIVITY

1   What is meant by the term 'assimilationist' (Source 5) and with which groups and individuals can it be associated?

2   What were the main ideas of Washington and Du Bois?

3   On the evidence of this source, comment on the extent to which Powell appears to have retained his youthful enthusiasm for the ideas of Marcus Garvey. Explain your answer.

4   Use the evidence of the source to explain why some, such as President Eisenhower, considered Powell a dangerous extremist.

One Harlem resident at the time when Powell was launching his spectacular political career in the early 1940s was the young Malcolm X, at this point in his career, a drug dealer and house-burglar. In his autobiography, Malcolm X recorded Powell's contributions at that time:

Source 6 Racial tension in Harlem

All through the war, the Harlem racial picture never was too bright. Tension built to a pretty high pitch. Old-timers told me that Harlem had never been the same since the 1935 riot, when millions of dollars worth of damage was done by thousands of Negroes, infuriated chiefly by the white merchants in Harlem refusing to hire a Negro even as their stores raked in Harlem's money.

During World War II, Mayor LaGuardia officially closed the Savoy Ballroom. Harlem said the real reason was to stop Negroes from dancing with white women. Harlem said that no one dragged the white women in there. Adam Clayton Powell made it a big fight. He had successfully fought Consolidated Edison and the New York Telephone Company until they had hired Negroes. Then he had helped to battle the U. S. Navy and the U. S. Army about their segregating of uniformed Negroes. But Powell couldn't win this battle. City Hall kept the Savoy closed for a long time. It was just another one of the 'liberal North' actions that didn't help Harlem to love the white man any.

From Malcolm X and Alex Hayes, *The Autobiography of Malcolm X,* published in 1965.

ACTIVITY

1. Who did Malcolm X refer to when he wrote 'Harlem said' (Source 6)?

2. What, according to Source 6, was the contribution of Powell to the civil rights movement?

3. Why did Malcolm X place the phrase 'liberal North' in inverted commas?

4. In his 300+ page autobiography, this is Malcolm X's only reference to Adam Clayton Powell. What can you infer from this information? What are the limitations of reliance upon a single source such as this?

THINK LIKE AN HISTORIAN

Comparing sources.

The ability to compare and contrast sources is an essential exam skill. How do the views of Stokeley Carmichael in Source 7 compare with those of Adam Clayton Powell in Source 5? Use quotations from both sources in answering this question.

The coalition into a single civil rights movement of various groups of protesters was covered in Chapter 6. It was fractured in the mid-1960s with the vigorous revival of the concept of Black Power and a growing frustration with the politics of non-violent protest. Meanwhile activists continued to be battered and beaten by mobs of white supremacists. Radicals and would-be revolutionaries began to infiltrate such organisations as the CORE and the SNCC. The views of Stokeley Carmichael, the new chairman of the SNCC, are evident in the following source:

Source 7 The views of Stokeley Carmichael

In an attempt to find a solution to our dilemma, we propose that our organization should be black-staffed, black-controlled, and black-financed. We do not want to fall into a similar dilemma that other civil rights organizations have fallen. If we continue to rely upon white financial support we will find ourselves entwined in the tentacles of the white power complex that controls this country. It is important that a black organization (devoid of cultism) be projected to our people so that it can be demonstrated that such organizations are viable.

More and more we see black people in this country being used as a tool of the white liberal establishment. Liberal whites have not begun to address themselves to the real problem of black people in this country; witness their bewilderment, fear, and anxiety when nationalism is mentioned concerning black people… Whites can only subvert our true search and struggle for self-determination, self-identification, and liberation in this country. Re-evaluation of the white and black roles must now take place

so that white people no longer designate roles that black people play but rather black people define white people's roles…

If we are to proceed toward true liberation, we must cut ourselves off from white people. We must form our own institutions, credit unions, co-ops, political parties, write our own histories.

These facts do not mean that whites cannot help. They can participate on a voluntary basis. We can contract work out to them, but in no way can they participate on a policy-making level.

The charge may be that we are 'racists', but whites who are sensitive to our problems will realise that we must determine our own destiny.

SNCC position paper, 5 August 1966, from B.J. Dierenfield, *The Civil Rights Movement*, published in 2004.

ACTIVITY

1. In what ways does the approach outlined in Source 7 differ from that of civil rights organisations in the earlier 1960s?

2. Why would 'assimilationists' have contested this approach?

3. Which civil rights leader's views does this approach have most in common with: Du Bois, Garvey, Washington, or King? Explain your selection and find a source to support your decision.

THINK LIKE AN HISTORIAN

Why should an historian be careful regarding the extent to which this 'position paper' (Source 7) reflects the views of all members of the SNCC?

While for many, Black Power represented confidence and pride in African-American communities others, including Roy Wilkins, the executive director of the NAACP from 1964, regarded it as a form of racial nationalism as bigoted and dangerous as that of the KKK. Furthermore, many advocates of Black Power were prepared to endorse violence as a legitimate approach to securing equality. They adopted a clenched fist salute and questioned King's role as the figurehead of the movement because of his alleged co-operation with whites.

Malcolm X, separatism and the NOI

That Malcolm X should live long enough to become the leading spokesperson for the Nation of Islam (NOI) was surprising given the nature of his earlier life on the streets of Harlem as a 'hustler' deeply involved in the underworld of drug dealing, prostitution and burglary, prior to his conversion to Islam in prison at the start of the 1950s. He routinely carried a gun, three guns for a time, and, according to his own account he came very close to being shot dead on the day of his arrest. In jail he was persuaded by his siblings on the outside to convert to the extraordinary faith of Elijah Mohammed's NOI. In his autobiography Malcolm X detailed the beliefs on which the cult was founded. According to Elijah, who had been the disciple of a messianic figure called Wallace Fard who he met in the early 1930s, all human beings originally were black, a 'fact' that seemed to be proven by the recent discoveries of the earliest human remains by the **Leakeys** in Africa. Eventually an evil scientist with an abnormally large head, Mr Yacub, used genetic modification to create a new race with devastating consequences:

The Leakeys

Louis Leakey and his wife Mary were archaeologists who played a pivotal role in developing the 'out of Africa' concept – the idea that all human beings can trace their ancestry back to the African continent.

> Source (8) Mr. Yacub
>
> *From his studies, the big-head scientist knew that black men contained two germs, black and brown. He knew that the brown germ stayed dormant as, being the lighter of the two germs, it was the weaker. Mr Yacub, to upset the law of nature, conceived the idea of employing what we today know as the recessive genes structure, to separate from each other the two germs, black and brown, and then grafting the brown germ to progressively lighter, weaker stages. The humans resulting, he knew, would be, as they became lighter, and weaker, progressively also more susceptible to wickedness and evil. And in this way finally he would achieve the intended bleached-out white race of devils.*
>
> From Malcolm X and Alex Haley, *The Autobiography of Malcolm X*, published in 1965.

EXAM TIP

Comparing ideas.

The ability to compare and contrast the ideas of racial leaders is likely to be a requirement of the exam. How do the ideas of the leaders of the NOI, as revealed in Source 8, compare with those of the KKK's Imperial Wizard expressed in Source 14 in Chapter 4? Note down the main points of similarity and difference.

ACTIVITY

On what grounds do you think Malcolm X rejected the Christianity of Martin Luther King and the SCLC as the 'white man's religion'?

Although it might read like the plot of a 1950s science fiction movie, Malcolm X was soon convinced by this alternative creation myth. From that point he considered white people, collectively, to be a race of devils, whose greatest atrocity was the enslavement of Africans. Malcolm X dropped his original surname Little since, as a black man with a slavery heritage, he knew the Little affix was of white origin and symbolic of his family's enslavement and, more particularly, the white grandfather he believed had raped his maternal grandmother and given him his unusual 'red' complexion.

Malcolm X advocated black unity in the struggle against this race of devils.

Source (9) Malcolm X's message

What you and I need to do is learn to forget our differences... we're all black people, so-called Negroes, second-class citizens, ex-slaves. You're nothing but an ex-slave. You don't like to be told that. But what else are you? You are ex-slaves. You didn't come here on the 'Mayflower'. You came here on a slave ship. In chains, like a horse, or a cow, or a chicken. And you were brought here by the people who came here on the 'Mayflower', you were brought here by the so-called Pilgrims, or Founding Fathers. They were the ones who brought you here.

We have a common enemy. We have this in common: We have a common oppressor, a common exploiter, and a common discriminator. But once we all realise we have a common enemy, then we unite – on the basis of what we have in common. And what we have in common is that enemy – the white man. He's an enemy to all of us. I know some of you all think that some of them aren't enemies. Time will tell.

'Message to the Grassroots', a speech delivered by Malcolm X at a large public rally in Detroit in 1963, from Carson C. et al, *The Eyes on the Prize Civil Rights Reader*, published in 1991.

THINK LIKE AN HISTORIAN

1   Why did this call for unity (Source 9) actually create divisions within the civil rights movement?
2   What are the implications of the statements Malcolm X makes in this passage?
3   What can you infer about the audience he was speaking to from the content of this source?
4   How might the nature of his audience have affected the content and tone of his speech?

In the same speech, Malcolm X argued that the civil rights revolution he campaigned for would come at a price.

Source (10) Malcolm X on violence and non-violence

You haven't got a revolution [in history] that doesn't involve bloodshed. And you're afraid to bleed. I said, you're afraid to bleed.

As long as the white man sent you to Korea, you bled. He sent you to Germany, you bled. He sent you to the South Pacific to fight the Japanese, you bled. You bleed for white people, but when it comes to seeing your own churches being bombed and little black girls murdered, you haven't got any blood... I hate to say this but it's true. How are you going to be nonviolent in Mississippi, as violent as you were in Korea? How can you justify being nonviolent in Mississippi and Alabama, when your churches are being bombed, and your little girls are being murdered... And if it is right for America to draft us, and teach us how to be violent in defense of her, then it is right for you and me to do whatever is necessary to defend our people right here in this country.

'Message to the Grassroots', a speech delivered by Malcolm X at a large public rally in Detroit in 1963, from Carson C. et al, *The Eyes on the Prize Civil Rights Reader*, published in 1991.

THINK LIKE AN HISTORIAN

What rhetorical methods does Malcolm X use in Source 10 to make an impact?

Malcolm X derided the work of the non-violent activists who were attempting to promote equality by other means:

Source 11 Malcolm X on non-violent revolution

There's no such thing as a nonviolent revolution. The only kind of revolution that is nonviolent is the Negro revolution. The only revolution in which the goal is loving your enemy is the Negro revolution. It's the only revolution in which the goal is a desegregated lunch counter, a desegregated theatre, a desegregated park, and a desegregated public toilet; you can sit down next to white folks – on the toilet. That's no revolution. Revolution is based on land… You don't know what a revolution is. If you did you wouldn't use that word.

'Message to the Grassroots', a speech delivered by Malcolm X at a large public rally in Detroit in 1963, from Carson C. et al, *The Eyes on the Prize Civil Rights Reader*, published in 1991.

ACTIVITY

1 How and why did Malcolm X differentiate between the 'Negro revolution' and the 'black revolution' (Source 11)?

2 Why, by this stage, had African Americans started to define themselves as 'black' and not 'Negro'?

3 Malcolm X did not actually engage in any form of violence during his time in the NOI. How far should the historian take the content of a political speech at face value? What purposes might such violent rhetoric have served other than persuading people to behave violently?

The land he believed should be the ultimate objective of the black revolution was unspecified and there is no evidence that he shared Marcus Garvey's 'Back to Africa' dream.

He saved his most damning criticism of the non-violent approach for the end of his speech. Here he portrayed the 1963 March on Washington, seen by many as the highpoint of the civil rights movement, as the work of northern liberals, the worst kind of 'white devils' in his opinion, trying to defuse the race time-bomb by infiltrating the movement.

Source 12 Malcolm X on the March on Washington

The same white element that put Kennedy into power - labor, the Catholics, the Jews, and liberal Protestants; the same clique that put Kennedy in power, joined the march on Washington.

It's just like when you've got some coffee that's too black, which means it's too strong. What do you do? You integrate it with cream, you make it weak. But if you pour too much cream in it you won't even know you ever had coffee. It used to be hot, it becomes cool. It used to be strong, it becomes weak. It used to wake you up, now it puts you to sleep. This is what they did with the march on Washington. They joined it. They didn't integrate it, they infiltrated it. They joined it, became a part of it, took it over. And as they took it over, it lost its militancy. It ceased to be angry, it ceased to be hot, it ceased to be uncompromising. Why, it even ceased to be a march. It became a picnic, a circus. Nothing but a circus, with clowns and all… I know you don't like what I'm saying,

but I'm going to tell you anyway. Because I can prove what I'm saying. If you think I'm telling you wrong, you bring me Martin Luther King and A. Philip Randolph and James Farmer… and see if they'll deny it over a microphone.

No, it was a sellout. It was a takeover. When James Baldwin [a black author] came in from Paris, they wouldn't let him talk, because they couldn't make him go by the script. Burt Lancaster [a white Hollywood actor] read the speech that Baldwin was supposed to make; they wouldn't let Baldwin get up there, because they know Baldwin is liable to say anything. They controlled it so tight, they told those Negroes what time to hit town, how to come, where to stop, what signs to carry, what song to sing, what speech they could make, and what speech they couldn't make; and then told them to get out of town by sundown. And every one of those Toms was out of town by sundown. Now I know you don't like my saying this. But I can back it up. It was a circus, a performance that beat anything Hollywood could ever do, the performance of the year. Reuther [Walter Reuther: a white trade union leader] and those other three devils should get an Academy Award for the best actors because they acted like they really loved Negroes and fooled a whole lot of

Negroes. And the six Negro leaders should get an award too, for the best supporting cast.

'Message to the Grassroots', a speech delivered by Malcolm X at a large public rally in Detroit in 1963, from Carson C. et al, *The Eyes on the Prize Civil Rights Reader*, published in 1991.

ACTIVITY

1   Who were the 'Toms' Malcolm X referred to (Source 12)? Why would this be regarded as a term of abuse by his African-American audience?

2   Why, on the evidence of this source, was Malcolm X so opposed to the white liberals who supported Martin Luther King?

Malcolm X began to become disillusioned with the NOI since it required him to refrain from making political speeches and because he discovered that Elijah Mohammed was not as 'clean-living' as he liked to make out. In 1964 he was thrown out of the NOI and he left America for a time to take a pilgrimage to Mecca. His experiences abroad, for example meeting white Muslims and observing white charity workers in Africa, caused him to readdress his own values and former intolerance of whites. He now believed that the best chance of gaining a solution for America's racial problems was through the intervention of the United Nations. Back in America, having converted to the orthodox Sunni Muslim faith, he was photographed in 1964 shaking hands with Dr King. Shortly afterwards, while delivering a speech in Harlem in February 1965, as he had predicted, he met a violent death, but not at the hands of white supremacists but of black supremacist NOI gunmen.

Stretch and challenge

Watch extracts from the 1959 television series *The Hate that Hate Produced* that raised white awareness of black Muslims and the NOI on the Internet.

How are African-American activists portrayed? How do you think white audiences might have reacted to this kind of film? How do you think African-American viewers might have regarded it?

Huey P. Newton, paramilitarism and the Black Panthers

The violence Malcolm X had once encouraged became a reality shortly after his death when, in the summers of 1965, 1966 and 1967, tens of thousands of black people rioted in Los Angeles and other cities. These riots are summed up, statistically, in the table below.

EXAM TIP

Recognising continuity in history.

In part **a** of the exam you should look out for opportunities to comment on how the sources provide evidence of both change and continuity in the historical record. Have another look at the sources in Chapter 5. To what extent did Malcolm X follow in the footsteps of either Marcus Garvey or W.E.B. Du Bois? Justify your argument with extracts from the sources in Chapter 5 and Chapter 7.

THINK LIKE AN HISTORIAN

In this book you will have come across the term 'the civil rights movement' on numerous occasions. It could be argued that, because this 'movement' was so fragmented, it never actually existed. Try thinking of a different, possibly more accurate way, in which the phenomenon could be described.

■ Table 7.1

Year	Riots	Killed	Injured	Arrested	Cost ($m)
1965	5	36	1206	10,245	40.1
1966	21	11	520	2298	10.2
1967	75	83	1827	16,389	664.5
Total	101	130	3553	28,932	714.8

Source: Paterson D.,et al, *Civil Rights in the USA, 1863–1980*, published in 2001.

ACTIVITY

1   How might these statistics have helped or hindered the civil rights movement?

2   What are the main limitations of statistics like these in explaining historical developments?

Some of those involved were encouraged to riot by Black Power activists such as H. Rap Brown, the new chairman of the SNCC. Amid the chaos and anarchy of the riots a new movement, the Black Panthers, emerged in Oakland, California, in 1966, founded by Huey P. Newton and Bobby Seale who had met at the San Francisco School of Law. The following source reveals the clear influence of Malcolm X in the thinking that led to the setting up of this movement.

Source 13 The Black Panthers

I would like to let the people here tonight know why we chose this black panther as our emblem. Many people have been asking this question for a long time. Our political group is open to whoever wants to come in, who would like to work with us. But we aren't begging anyone to come in. It's open, you come, at your own free will and accord.

But this black panther is a vicious animal as you know. He never bothers anything, but when you start pushing him, he moves backwards, backwards, and backwards into his corner, and then, he comes out to destroy everything that's before him.

Negroes in Lowndes County have been pushed back through the years. We have been deprived of our rights to speak, to move, and to do whatever we want to do at all times. And now we are going to start moving. On November 8 of this year, we plan to take over the courthouse in Hayneville. And whatever it takes do it, we're going to do it.

We've decided to stop begging. We've decided to stop asking for integration. Once we control the courthouse, once we

control the board of education, we can build our school system where boys and girls can get an education in Lowndes County. There are 89 prominent families in this county who own 90 per cent of the land. These people will be taxed. And we will collect the taxes. And if they don't pay them, we'll take their property and sell it to whoever wants to buy it. And we know there will be people who will buy land where at the present time they cannot buy it. This is what it's going to take.

We aren't asking any longer for protection - we won't need it - or for anyone to come from the outside to speak for us, because we're going to speak for ourselves now and from now on. And think not only in Lowndes County, not only in the state of Alabama, not only in the South, but in the North – I hope they too will start thinking for themselves. And that they will move and join us in this fight for freedom…

John Hulett, 'How the Black Panther Party was Organized', a speech given on May 22, 1966, at a meeting sponsored by anti-Vietnam War committees from Carson C. et al, *The Eyes on the Prize Civil Rights Reader*, published in 1991.

ACTIVITY

Compare this statement (Source 13) with Malcolm X's 'Message to the Grassroots' (Source 9). Select passages that reveal similarities between this source and Malcolm X's speech.

The Black Panthers' manifesto of October 1966 comprised a ten point programme:

Source (14) The manifesto of the Black Panthers

1. We want freedom. We want power to determine the destiny of Black Community…

2. We want full employment for our people…

3. We want an end to the robbery by the capitalists of our Black Community…

4. We want decent housing, fit for shelter of human beings…

5. We want education for our people that exposes the true nature of this decadent American society. We want education that teaches us our true history and our role in present-day society…

6. We want all Black men to be exempt from military service…

7. We want an immediate end to POLICE BRUTALITY and MURDER of Black people…

8. We want freedom for all Black men held in federal, state, county and city prisons and jails…

9. We want all Black people when brought to trial to be tried in court by a jury of their peer group or people from their Black communities, as defined by the Constitution of the United States…

10. We want land, bread, housing, education, clothing, justice, and peace. And as our major political objective, a United Nations-supervised plebiscite to be held throughout the Black colony in which only Black colonial subjects will be allowed to participate, for the purpose of determining the will of Black people as to their national destiny.

From Carson C. et al, *The Eyes on the Prize Civil Rights Reader*, published in 1991.

ACTIVITY

1 How 'revolutionary' is this programme (Source 14)? Explain your answer.

2 Which clauses can be defined as 'separatist'?

3 Which clause would be associated with communism by those in authority? Explain your decision.

4 How does this manifesto compare with the views of Malcolm X?

In line with the aim of point 7, the Black Panthers armed themselves, wore a uniform, and patrolled the streets of black communities in order, they claimed, to protect African Americans from police brutality. Huey P. Newton reported on the early success of these patrols:

Source (15) The strategies of the Black Panthers

At first, the patrols were a total success. Frightened and confused, the police did not know how to respond, because they had never encountered patrols like this before… With weapons in our hands, we were no longer their subjects but their equals.

Out on patrol, we stopped whenever we saw the police questioning a brother or a sister. We would walk over with our weapons and observe them from a 'safe' distance so that the police could not say we were interfering with the performance of their duty.

Huey P. Newton in Carson C. et al, *The Eyes on the Prize Civil Rights Reader*, published in 1991.

THINK LIKE AN HISTORIAN

What is significant about the terms 'brother' and 'sister', used in Source 15 to describe fellow African Americans?

The patrols were disciplined and careful to be seen to observe the law, although they did receive weapons and cash from the criminal fraternity in the black neighbourhoods they aimed to protect.

A proposal to ban the carrying of firearms in California prompted Newton, Seale and other Black Panthers to march on the building where the proposal was being discussed in May 1967. In the violence that followed, Newton was shot and wounded and two policemen were killed. Bobby Seale recorded his memories of these events in his history of the movement *Seize the Time* (1981). In the following extracts he outlines the Panthers objectives at the time:

ACTIVITY

To what extent does the strategy of the Black Panthers in 1967 have similarities with the strategies of both Malcolm X *and* Martin Luther King? Explain your answer with reference to these and other sources.

Source (16) Weapons and revolution

So Huey says, 'You know what we're going to do?... We're going to take the best Panthers we got and we're going to go to the Capitol steps with our guns and forces, loaded down to the gills. And we're going to read a message to the world, because all the press is going to be up there. They'll listen to the message, and they'll probably blast it across the country. I know, I know they'll blast it all the way across California. We've got to get the message over to the people.'

Huey understood a revolutionary culture, and Huey understood how arms and guns become a part of the culture of a people in the revolutionary struggle. And he knows that the best way to do it was to go forth, and those hungry newspaper reporters, who are shocked, who are going to be shook up, are going to be blasting that news faster than they could be stopped. I said, 'All right, brother, right on, I'm with you. We're going to the Capitol.'

Bobby Seale, *Seize the Time* (1981), from Carson C. et al, *The Eyes on the Prize Civil Rights Reader*, published in 1991.

Source (17) Weapons and publicity

On May 2, 1967, we went across the bridge to Sacramento with a caravan of cars. We wound up right in front of the Capitol building. There were thirty brothers and sisters. Six sisters and twenty-four brothers. Twenty of the brothers were armed.

... A lot of people were looking. A lot of white people were shocked, just looking at us. I know what they were saying: 'Who in the hell are those niggers with these guns? Who in the hell are those niggers with these guns? What are they doing?'

... I didn't pay a damn bit of attention to them because we knew our constitutional rights and all that stuff about the rights of citizens to have guns. The Second Amendment to the Constitution of the United States, and no police or militia force can infringe upon that right; it states that specifically.

... These brothers were off the block; righteous brothers off the block. From what they call the nitty gritty and the grass roots. You could look at their faces and see the turmoil they've lived through. Their ages ranged anywhere from sixteen, which was about the youngest we had there – that was Bobby Hutton – all the way down to myself, thirty-one. I guess I was about the oldest.

We righteously walked on up to the first stairs. Bobby Hutton was on my right side and Warren Tucker was on my left side. Bobby Hutton had a 12-gauge shotgun, a High Standard 12-gauge pump shotgun, that's what Bobby Hutton had. And Warren Tucker had a .357 Magnum.

... As we walked down the hall, cameramen were running from our left and from our right, around Bobby and around Tucker, jumping in front of us taking flicks and clicking flicks. Cameramen with movie cameras were shooting... Bulbs were flashing all over the place...

Bobby Seale, *Seize the Time* (1981), from Carson C. et al, *The Eyes on the Prize Civil Rights Reader*, published in 1991.

ACTIVITY

What does Source 17 reveal about the age, gender and background of the typical Black Panther?

In front of the cameras Seale read out a statement by Huey P. Newton, the Panthers' 'Minister of Defense'.

Source **18**   **Executive Mandate Number One**

The Black Panther Party for Self-Defense calls upon the American people in general and the black people in particular to take careful note of the racist California Legislature which is now considering legislation aimed at keeping black people disarmed and powerless at the very same time that racist police agencies throughout the country are intensifying the terror, brutality, murder, and repression of black people.

At the same time that the American government is waging a racist war of genocide in Vietnam, the concentration camps in which Japanese Americans were interned during World War II are being renovated and expanded. Since America has historically reserved the most barbaric treatment for non-white people, we are forced to conclude that these concentration camps are being prepared for black people who are determined to gain their freedom by any means necessary. The enslavement of black people from the very beginning of this country, the genocide practiced on the American Indians and the confining of the survivors on reservations, the savage lynching of thousands of black men and women, the dropping of atomic bombs on Hiroshima and Nagasaki, and now the cowardly massacre in Vietnam, all testify to the fact that toward people of color the racist power structure of America has but one policy: repressions, genocide, terror, and the big stick.

… We believe that the black communities of America must rise up as one man to halt the progression of a trend that leads inevitably to their total destruction.

Executive Mandate Number One, May 2, 1967, in Carson C. et al, *The Eyes on the Prize Civil Rights Reader*, published in 1991.

ACTIVITY

1   How does Source 18 reveal the breadth of the political agenda on which the Black Panther Party was based?

2   Why was a sense of history so important to civil rights leaders like Malcolm X and Huey P. Newton?

3   Why was the proposed gun legislation of such concern to the Black Panthers?

4   How does this statement differ from the views expressed by Malcolm X in his 'Message to the Grassroots'? How do you explain these differences?

The violence that occurred that day took place in the course of subsequent arrests following the Panthers' triumphant march on the Capitol building.

With its leaders in prison facing charges of causing violence and murder, the Black Panthers 'finest hour' had passed although they remained a threatening presence in some areas through the late sixties and into the seventies. In 1969, 27 Black Panthers were killed in gun battles with the police.

Clyde Bellecourt, 'Red Power' and the AIM

Native American activists, inspired by the 'Black Power' concept, championed '**Red Power**' in retaliation to attempts to move their people from the reservations and resettle them in cities. Furthermore, they were determined to try to improve the squalid living conditions endured by many Native Americans at a time when their life expectancy was just 40 years and their infant mortality rate was ten times greater than

Red Power

A term coined to describe the ideas and actions of Native Americans that are based upon pride in their racial heritage and their determination to advance and/or assert their position in society.

AIM

American Indian Movement formed in 1968.

the national average. The American Indian Movement (**AIM**) was established in Minneapolis in 1968. In the following source the brother of one of its founders, Clyde Bellecourt, describes its origins. Like Malcolm X, the Bellecourt brothers came from a deprived background, were subjected from an early age to various forms of racial abuse, and, as youths, migrated to lives of crime in the city.

> **Source 19 Clyde Bellecourt**
>
> *My brother Clyde was doing a tremendous amount of time in Stillwater State Prison in Minnesota, and he just gave up in despair and wouldn't eat. He went on a hunger strike and was going to stay on it until he died. He met a young Ojibwa [North American tribe] brother who was from a medicine family, a family of spiritual leaders, and this young man was also a spiritual leader.*
>
> *This young medicine man, Eddie Benton… he'd come by my brother's cell and try to talk to him and ask him to eat. But Clyde wouldn't eat… Then one day he started quoting literature, telling about the Ojibwas and our proud heritage. And finally one day, I guess just out of boredom, my brother finally picked up a piece of this literature and started reading about us. And he finally realised he wasn't the dirty Indian he'd been told he was by White students at school…*
>
> Vernon Bellecourt in P. Engelbert, *American Civil Rights: Primary Sources*, published in 1999.

ACTIVITY

What similarities are there between Bellecourt's and Malcolm X's prison experiences?

On leaving prison Bellecourt was inspired by this new-found pride in his heritage to act for the improvement of conditions for Native Americans.

> **Source 20 the American Indian Movement**
>
> *When Clyde got out of prison early in 1968, he went to work for a power company. He had one of the first organizational meetings, in mid-1968, with a group of people in Minneapolis, in the Indian ghetto community. Everything was deteriorating rather than getting better. There were police harassment and brutality, because of a complete breakdown of police-community relations.*
>
> *At the first meeting Clyde attended, they voted him the national director. There were twenty-seven or twenty-eight other Indian organisations in the Minneapolis community. Most of them were related to various churches – missionary work in disguise. For the most part, the boards of these organizations were White dominated. White do-gooders as consultants and advisers controlled them.*
>
> *… When AIM was forming, one of the first things they zeroed in on was police-community relations. Young men and women in the community formed the AIM patrol. They had red jackets with thunderbird emblems on the backs.*
>
> *… They got a small grant from the Urban League of Minneapolis to put two-way radios in their cars and to get tape recorders and cameras. They would listen to the police calls, and when they heard there was going to be an arrest or that police were being dispatched to a certain community or bar, they'd show up with cameras and take pictures of the police using more than normal restraint on people.*
>
> *They got evidence of beatings and of ripping people around with handcuffs too tight, ripping their wrists. It was very vicious. This sometimes becomes a way of life for the police. They just fall into it. They think that's the way Indians have to be treated. So AIM would show up and have attorneys ready. Often they would beat the police back to the station. They'd have a bondsman there and they'd start filing law suits against the police department…*
>
> Vernon Bellecourt in P. Engelbert, *American Civil Rights: Primary Sources*, published in 1999.

ACTIVITY

Which organisation did the AIM most closely resemble: the SCLC, the NOI, or the Black Panthers? Use Source 20 to explain your decision.

AIM, according to Vernon Bellecourt, also shared the separatist goal of race leaders like Marcus Garvey and Malcolm X.

> ### Source 'AIM for Sovereignty'
>
> *... We have the spirituality, yet we are warriors. We'll stand up and fight for our people... We put out a bumper sticker, 'AIM for Sovereignty'. Most of our people didn't even know what the word meant. Now they know.*
>
> Vernon Bellecourt in P. Engelbert, *American Civil Rights: Primary Sources*, published in 1999.

A main demand of AIM was the restoration of tribal lands that had been promised to Native Americans by treaties agreed 100 years earlier. Infiltrated by FBI agents, the movement weakened in the later 1970s and dozens of its members were shot dead in that period by police supervising the Pine Ridge reservation in the mid-1970s.

AIM remains an important Native American pressure group to this day and it continues to raise public awareness of Native American issues.

Reies López Tijerina, 'Brown Power' and the Brown Berets

Hispanic-American activists were also radicalised in the later 1960s, influenced, like Native Americans, by the example of 'Black Power'. In 1956 Reies López Tijerina, a pastor, together with 17 Chicano families, purchased 160 acres of land in the Southern Arizona desert to establish their own separate community in this 'Valley of Peace' that would not be tainted by the culture of white American society which, for example, promoted sex education in schools. By the 1960s however he was fully involved in politics and the complex business of communal land rights. Tijerina led the Alianza '**Brown Power**' movement and campaigned against the National Forest Service in New Mexico that had taken over land formerly used for grazing by Chicano farmers. By 1966 the Alianza had attracted 20,000 members. Alianza's strategies included 'camp-ins' on National Forest land and arson. Tijerina himself was charged with kidnapping and attacking the Tierra Amarilla courthouse in 1967 to release other Alianza activists. He was sent to prison in 1970 for convictions relating to this assault.

Meanwhile in Los Angeles in 1967, a Hispanic-American paramilitary group, the 'Brown Berets', was established. Like the Black Panthers and AIM, its objective was to protect Chicanos from prejudiced police. It was active until the early 1970s. In the following source a Los Angeles Chicano, Herman Baca of the Committee on Chicano Rights, recalls a mass demonstration, the 'Chicano Moratorium', organised by the Brown Berets on 29 August, 1970.

> ### Source The 'Chicano Moratorium'
>
> *Thirty-five years later, I still vividly remember what happened to me personally and politically in Los Angeles, California on August 29, 1970. Thirty thousand Chicanos from throughout the U.S. marched in the streets to protest and call for an end to the war in Vietnam. A war, much like Iraq today, that was destroying our most precious heritage... our youth. On that day, a police riot ensued and Los Angeles Times Reporter Ruben Salazar, along with citizens Angel Diaz and Lynn Ward were killed. Numerous persons were wounded and hundreds were jailed by the L.A. Police and*
>
> *Sheriff's Department, including national Chicano leader, Rodolfo "Corky" Gonzales.*
>
> *... While many young white males received college deferments, white controlled draft boards systematically recruited poor people, blacks and especially Chicanos, in record numbers to fight the war in Vietnam. At the time, Chicanos comprised 6% of the nation's population, but were 20% of the war's casualities. Many of my own friends served and died in Vietnam.*

ACTIVITY

Why was separatism a more realistic objective for Native Americans than African Americans?

Brown Power

A term coined to describe the ideas and actions of Hispanic Americans that are based upon pride in their racial heritage and their determination to advance and/or assert their position in society.

After five years of this war, reality finally hit the Chicano community. Young Chicanos were dying in obscene numbers and 'body bags' were being returned to the homes of grieving families throughout the U.S.

The Chicano Movement recoiled in anger and called for protests against the government's policy of sending its young people to die in foreign wars. The movement's political position had always been that the white, racist system had made Chicanos strangers in their own land by placing them last in jobs, education and rights, while placing them first to die in its wars.

In the early stages of organizing the Moratorium, a 'generational' divide arose within our community over the movement's anti-war position.

Bitter discussions and arguments occurred even within our own families. Strong opposition to the anti-war position came mainly from the men we admired and looked up to most; our grandfathers, fathers, uncles and older brothers... The older generation could not understand why, if we were men, we did not want to enlist or serve in Vietnam. However, as the war and casualties wore on, many of the same veterans began to understand and support our anti-war position.

At its onset, the moratorium demonstration was planned as a peaceful protest seeking redress from the U.S. Government based on rights supposedly protected and guaranteed under the U.S. Constitution and Bill of Rights.

...The moratorium demonstration turned out to be the largest protest organized by Chicanos in their 130 years history as a conquered people in the U.S.

When the march started, people rallied behind banners of the Virgin De Guadalupe, MAPA, Brown Berets, MEChA, Crusade for Justice, UFW.

Along the route, people yelled words of encouragement. Many joined the procession. After five long miles, we finally arrived at Laguna Park (now Salazar Park).

Sitting down in the park, we heard a commotion and saw police coming from the direction that we had just left... As the police advanced, I witnessed scenes that I will never forget; hundreds of our people (children, women, young, and old) all being beaten, tear gassed, maimed, and arrested.

The police and sheriff deputies appeared to be totally out of control. They seemed crazed with a desire to hurt, maim and kill Chicanos.

Chicanos witnessing the attack stood up in self-defense and fought back. I remember at one point, the bright August sky turned black because of the large number of objects being thrown back at the police. People protected themselves by throwing bottles, cans, sticks, dirt; any object they could get their hands on.

... we saw undercover police coming out from the sides of the streets with guns drawn and shooting into the sky, and then at the crowd...

Around 6:30 P.M. we finally departed to San Diego. I remember looking back, seeing East Los Angeles burning!

Herman Baca, 'The Day the Police Rioted!' from *La Prensa San Diego*, August 26, 2005.

THINK LIKE AN HISTORIAN

Comparing sources.

Practise your skill in comparing sources by looking for points of similarity and difference beween the Black, Red and Brown Power movements. Make reference to Sources 13–22.

ACTIVITY

1   In what ways does Source 22 reveal changing attitudes towards race issues in the United States?

2   How far does this evidence and your own knowledge support the interpretation that civil rights related violence was the result of police brutality? Explain your answer with reference to sources. If you disagree, amend this interpretation or offer an alternative one and explain why it fits the evidence more accurately.

EXAM TIP

Understanding patterns of change and continuity is a key criterion against which you will be assessed in the exam. You will be provided with sources which, when compared, should provide you with plenty to discuss in relation to these central concepts. Sometimes, as in Source 22, you will find evidence for change and continuity within a single extract. Now that you have completed this chapter you can start trying to map out change and continuity for the whole of this Study Topic. Try using devices like charts to summarise how the historical 'landscape' changed between 1865 and the 1970s.

Source 23

Brown Berets c. 1970

ACTIVITY

Why did civil rights protesters resort to paramilitary approaches in the late 1960s and early 1970s?

ACTIVITY

Exam practice

Interpretation: By the late 1960s the civil rights movement had been taken over by violent supremacists and separatists.

a   Explain how far the sources in this chapter support this interpretation. You may, if you wish, amend the interpretation or suggest a different interpretation. If you do this you must use the sources to support the changes you make.

Remember not to simply take the sources at face value. Use your knowledge of the period to interpret and evaluate them.

b   Explain how these sources are both useful and raise problems and issues for a historian using them.

Summary – what you have learned in Chapter 7

This chapter has highlighted similarities and differences, tensions and rivalries among civil rights leaders and movements. You have been introduced to several of the most influential figures in the history of America's civil rights movement.

You have learned about the methods and aims of several civil rights organisations that worked in association with these individuals.

You have also been introduced to the key concepts associated with these individuals and organisations.

You have been able to think about the relative importance of different leaders and organisations in the struggle for change. You have also been given a range of evidence from which to weigh up whether individuals or organisations were more significant in bringing about effective change.

By working through the various *Activity* and *Think like an historian* tasks you have practised and developed your skills in the analysis and evaluation of sources, and in the forming and testing of hypotheses. You have also practised the following skills:

- recognising bias
- recognising change and continuity in history
- comparing sources and ideas
- recognising continuity in history
- recognising developments in history.

Now take a look at the Exam Café at the back of the book for more advice and practice.

8 And finally...

> **Key Question:**
>
> To what extent had the objectives of civil rights campaigners been achieved since 1865?

This book has examined a wealth of historical evidence to explore the ways in which attitudes in America towards racial minorities changed between 1865 and the 1970s, to understand why the pace of change was far from constant over time, and to consider how individuals, groups, and those in authority both helped and hindered these changes. This evidence has shown us that the pattern of change was unpredictable and this closing section addresses the extent to which the objectives of civil rights campaigners had been achieved by the 1970s, and how far race relations remained a problem in American society.

Change and continuity

ACTIVITY

Read through this conclusion. Use the information and your own knowledge to assess the validity of the following interpretations:

1   'The objectives of those seeking racial equality in America had been achieved by the 1970s.'
2   'Despite years of campaigning those seeking racial equality in America had not yet achieved this objective by the 1970s.'

Which of these interpretations do you find the most convincing and why?

On the basis of the evidence below and your own knowledge how would you modify this interpretation?

In the immediate aftermath of the American Civil War, African Americans achieved:

■ Emancipation from slavery
■ Full American citizenship
■ The vote.

Although it took a long time, and state legislation was frequently ignored at a local level, by the 1970s racial minorities benefited from laws that, in principle, forbade all forms of racial discrimination.

Where once the struggle for racial equality was very much a 'Southern' issue in America, the migration of African Americans throughout the 20th century helped shift the focus to the North, especially the ghettoes of the northern cities in which the race riots of the 1960s and early 1970s erupted.

Through the course of the 20th century many organisations were established to promote racial equality. Some were dissolved while others have survived to the present day. In the early 1970s there was a handful of significant groups that continued to champion the cause of African Americans. These included:

■ CORE (founded 1942)
■ NAACP (founded 1909)

- SCLC (founded 1958)
- SNCC (founded 1960).

Throughout the history of the civil rights struggle, charismatic leaders had acted as the spokesmen and women of the eras in which they lived. All had some kind of association with a particular organisation that promoted the rights of the racial group with which they were identified. In many cases they were the founders of organisations.

Although the civil rights movement for a short time in the late 1950s and early 1960s appeared to bring diverse groups of people, white and non-white, together in a common cause, the history of the struggle is mostly one of competing organisations and the clash of philosophies. In much the same way as Marcus Garvey divided opinion by his criticism of the methods and motives of W.E.B. Du Bois in the early 1920s, Malcolm X played a role in breaking the unity of 'the movement' through his hostile attacks on Martin Luther King in the early 1960s. The highpoint of King's career, the March on Washington in 1963, Malcolm X ridiculed as 'the Farce on Washington'. In both cases the argument revolved, in part, around the issue of integration. Du Bois and King were dedicated integrationists and welcomed the support of white people in their campaigns, whereas Garvey and Malcolm X were driven by forms of African nationalism, perceiving whites as oppressive colonists and demonised by Malcolm X as 'white devils'. Organisations that hitherto had been multiracial in principle began to distance themselves from white involvement. In 1966 whites were excluded from membership of the SNCC and from CORE in 1968. Such actions as this that alienated white liberals ultimately undermined the Black Power movement by estranging a crucial source of financial support. By the later 1960s assertive, sometimes aggressive, Black, Brown and Red Power organisations undermined the non-violent principles of other activists. In 1968 the SNCC allied itself with the revolutionary Black Panthers. By 1970, however, the organisation had been crushed by the combined endeavours of the police and FBI which resulted in hundreds of arrests, and shootings. In just one year, 1969, 27 Panthers were killed in shoot-outs with the police.

Ultimately the success of campaigns for racial equality would be determined by the attitudes and actions of the white majority. These were influenced by the activities of minority race organisations and individuals, sometimes inspiring reform but frequently prompting reactive behaviour and legislation. King and the SCLC doubtless helped pave the way for the Civil Rights Act of 1964, but the work of Du Bois and the NAACP half a century earlier probably stiffened the resolve of white supremacists to suppress racial minorities through 'Jim Crow' legislation and KKK intimidation. How far individuals or organisations actually had an impact is something that cannot be quantified. Changing circumstances and the actions of others always played a significant part in the history of race in America from 1865 to the 1970s.

Opportunities for raising public awareness of organisations, ideas and individuals developed throughout the 20th century. The birth of cinema had the effect of focussing attention through the production of the controversial film *The Birth of a Nation* (1915), while recorded music, notably Billie Holiday's *Strange Fruit*, could make equally dramatic and affecting statements. Photographs of lynchings in southern states must have shocked many northern newspaper readers while improving levels of literacy enabled more people to read the articles that accompanied them. Television became a particularly important medium: a documentary series called *The Hate that Hate produced* (1959), created widespread awareness of the NOI. Television also helped make Martin Luther King's 1964 'I have a dream' speech one of the best known of the 20th century.

The triumph of the 1964 Civil Rights Act did not mark the end of the troubled history of race relations in the United States. Having raised hopes of fundamental change, the reality of life for those living in the black ghettoes of northern cities remained that of deprivation, exacerbated by very high rates of unemployment. This was the inequality that spurred the anger of Malcolm X, the Black Power activists and the urban rioters. In the last year of his life King launched the SCLC's 'Poor People's Campaign', leading to several ineffectual multiracial rallies in Washington in 1968. Such organisations as the SCLC became less focussed on the race issue as they became involved in a range of other contemporary concerns including anti-Vietnam War protests. Some organisations in the late 1960s, such as the Black Panthers, advocated the politics of proletarian revolution which was class, as opposed to race, based. In so doing they distanced themselves from other Black Power activists, including Stokeley Carmichael, the leader of the SNCC, who had black-nationalist objectives. Unions of African-American car plant workers merged in 1969 to form the League of Revolutionary Workers (LRW).

Black Power advocates, such as Malcolm X, were very much concerned with appearances. In his autobiography he described the laborious and painful process by which, as a fashionable young hustler in the Harlem ghetto, he would flatten his hair so that it resembled that of someone of white European descent. Later in life he came to regard such practices as a symbol of the subjugation of African Americans. In the 1960s many African Americans adopted, with pride, Afro hairstyles and African modes of clothing. Meanwhile Black Studies courses became available at universities and a greater emphasis in such subjects as English Literature, History and Art, moved away from the traditional 'white' curriculum. The increased public demand for such initiatives was also reflected in the demand for records of African-American artists who had a high profile in the pop music revolution of the late 1950s and the 1960s. Bob Dylan and other 'protest singers' participated in the civil rights movement in the early 1960s, while white rock and roll musicians played a form of music derived from African-American blues. On occasion the rock stars themselves were black: the success of guitarist Jimi Hendrix for example, though bigger in the UK than the US, was emblematic of the fact that skin colour did not necessarily bar the possibility of winning white fans. The same could be said of other famous African-American stars in different fields such as the Olympic athlete Jesse Owens in the 1930s and the post-war Hollywood actor, Sidney Poitier.

However, the possibility of the American people electing a non-white President was inconceivable in the 1970s. Although new charismatic civil rights leaders had emerged, notably Jesse Jackson, and new organisations, such as the one he founded in 1971, People United to Save Humanity (PUSH), the civil rights movement had lost much of the momentum that had enabled it to have such an impact upon American society in the late 1950s and throughout the 1960s. Black Power remained a powerful idea but as a 'movement' it had largely disintegrated. The necessary legislative foundations had been laid for the elimination of racial inequality but discriminatory attitudes and economic deprivation were problems that were far from resolved. In a multiracial society, like that of America between 1865 and the 1970s, race relations are the most fundamental of all social issues; racial *conflict* is the antithesis of multiracial *society*. How far, by the 1970s, America had moved along the path towards becoming a successful multiracial society is the question that this book, in part, has been designed to help you to answer.

ACTIVITY

Exam practice

Interpretation: In terms of race relations, American society in the late 1960s had nothing in common with that of America at the start of the century.

a Choose any seven sources in this book and explain how far they support this interpretation. You may, if you wish, amend the interpretation or suggest a different interpretation. If you do this you must use the sources to support the changes you make.

Remember not to simply take the sources at face value. Use your knowledge of the period to interpret and evaluate them.

b Explain how these sources are both useful and raise problems and issues for a historian using them.

EXAM TIP

The sources you will have to analyse in the actual exam will, by definition, provide a partial picture of the past. It is likely that, when you consider them as a set (and you must), they will clearly lean towards either supporting or challenging the interpretation you have been asked to evaluate. Don't let this be the main consideration in arriving at your own conclusion; remember that your knowledge of the period should be employed to determine how complete they are as a set. Almost certainly the examiners will have left out something important when choosing which sources to include.

ExamCafé
Relax, refresh, result!

Relax and prepare

GETTING STARTED...

Tom

I did well at GCSE without really pushing myself or doing much revision so I guess I was a little overconfident about how I'd do at AS-level. I didn't think it would be so different and I was totally unprepared for how much I was expected to do by myself. I skipped some of the research homeworks we were set, wrote stuff at the last minute and managed to get by in lessons but when I came to start revising I couldn't avoid the mess that my notes were in. There were gaps and half-finished bits and pieces all over the place. My advice would be to remember this: it isn't your teacher who's taking the exam – it's YOU! Unless you're prepared to make the extra effort, you aren't going to do brilliantly.

Rhiannon

The best piece of advice I'd give myself looking back at the start of the year? Easy – get a folder and get organised! The notes come really thick and fast and you need to collect them together properly. Just stuffing them in your bag or starting a new page of your refill pad every lesson won't do. They end up looking like scrap and they're useless for revision. I also wish I'd checked my notes over more outside of lessons and maybe rewritten some of them to make them clearer while the topic was still fresh in my mind.

READING SOURCES...

Dave

I found it hard to concentrate on what a source was saying. My mind would wander off and I'd end up reading and re-reading the same bit without getting anywhere. So I found ways to keep my mind focused and my eyes on the text. I use a ruler and put it under the first line of the source then move it down to the next line and so on. That way, I only look at one part at a time. I also stop after every sentence and repeat back to myself what I have just read. I know some people use a highlighter as well, but I was highlighting everything! So I tend to write a running summary in the margin or on a piece of paper.

Ali

My teacher said that I was losing marks because I wasn't reading sources carefully enough. What she meant was that I was reading too quickly and missing useful information or ideas. I had to learn to slow down! What I do now is read the source through once at my usual speed without writing anything down. That gives me a general picture of what the source is about. Then I read it twice more – the first time I use a highlighter to pick out all the relevant points. Then – and here's the thing that really made a difference for me – I read it again but only the bits I haven't highlighted. That way, I can ask myself if I have missed anything out.

USING THE INTERNET...

Mark

The Internet is a great resource but watch out for dodgy websites. You have to ask yourself who is putting this information onto the web and why – so that you can avoid sites that are obviously biased. I used what looked like great websites but I found out that some of them were written by amateurs who knew even less than me! Also watch out for how long the information has been there – it could be stuff that's out of date.

Sunita

I printed loads of stuff off the internet to put in my file. Just one problem – I didn't actually read any of it! Using the internet was really just a way of avoiding making proper notes. Cutting and pasting stuff into a Word document made me feel I was motoring through the research, but I ended up binning most of it and starting again when I revised.

Jamie

I always used a textbook to make my notes from. The trouble was I wasn't really learning how to research. It took a bit of effort to go into the library and find out what was there – not just the books but magazine articles and online information – but it was worth it because that's what you'll have to do if you go to university. Things aren't always packaged for you.

GETTING DOWN TO STUDY...

Sufia

I found it hard to settle down to study – there was always something more interesting that I could be doing. My teacher suggested using a ritual to get me started. Now what I do is make myself a cuppa when I want to start working. As the kettle is boiling I start thinking about what I need to do so if it's an essay, I start thinking about what I'm going to write. By the time the drink's ready I've already started work and I can sit down and put pen to paper.

Jeff

I'm a morning person. I know that I can get up and start work straight away for a few hours. Then my interest starts flagging. At night I'm too tired or distracted to work for very long. So I plan my study around how I am – essays and big tasks in the morning, finishing off and small tasks at night.

Asif

Break everything down into small tasks if you find it hard to get started. You aren't writing an essay, you're writing one paragraph. Get that done, congratulate yourself then write another paragraph! Keep taking short breaks – get up and walk about – and have a treat ready for when you've finished to motivate yourself to get through the work.

MAKING NOTES...

Phil

I used to write notes that were basically just copies of the chapter I was reading! As soon as I started reading I just started writing and writing and writing – I might as well have just put a photocopy of the book in my file! I learned that the best way to make notes was not to have a pen in my hand – read everything first, think about what seems important to keep a record of, THEN write it down!

Catherine

I have some really colourful notes – I took a highlighter and marked all the important things. Unfortunately, nearly everything has ended up being highlighted! I'm going to use colour more sparingly from now on – maybe just for key words or quotes.

Jas

A good piece of advice is to write notes on one side of paper and leave the reverse blank. That way, when the pages are in your file there's always a blank sheet on the left hand side that you can use to add extra stuff later.

STRUCTURING ANSWERS...

Jane

Everyone sort of expects you to know this but I was really stuck about how to put paragraphs in my answers. This is the advice I got – each paragraph is for a new idea in your answer (like a different factor or a different argument). The first sentence should set out what this idea is, then other sentences either explain and develop the point further or give an example or evidence. It's also a good idea to finish with a sentence recapping the main point you have been trying to make.

Senka

Putting in supporting evidence is really important because the exam is all about using sources as evidence! Make sure that every time you introduce an idea into your answer you can back it up with a short quote from the sources or some extra knowledge that you have revised.

Marcus

You need an introduction and conclusion because these are the places where you can set out your overall ideas about the question – in the introduction, what you think the question means, definitions of key words and a summary of your argument. The conclusion summarises your main argument and is a place where you can spend time improving the interpretation you have been given.

REVISION...

Harry

I took a 50/50 approach to revision. I spent half the time learning all the key information – the usual stuff – so I knew my facts in the exam. The other half of my revision concentrated on skills because I knew that I was going to be assessed on how good my ability to work with sources was. I practised reading sources, writing paragraphs about their strengths and weaknesses, devising my own hypotheses. I made sure I knew how I needed to approach the questions as well as background information

Hayley

I wanted to make sure that I knew exactly what the exam was going to be like. My teacher made sure we had a copy of the syllabus so we could see what topics might come up. I checked the OCR website and there was some good stuff on there – like markschemes and examiners' reports that gave me more clues about what I needed to do to get a good mark. I also got copies of past papers and checked the timing and then practised like mad!

Ammar

I got really, really bored just reading my notes over and over again, so I decided to put everything onto my PC. Then I made some powerpoints about each topic. Typing it all out, deciding what to put in and what I could safely leave out, and setting up all the pages with layouts, animations and so on actually made the facts start to stick. When my friends found out what I had done they actually offered to buy the powerpoints off me! When I revise for next year's exams I might check out podcasts so I can carry my notes round with me on my iPod!

Alex

I like to make mind maps of the topics we have covered, the more colourful the better. I can remember the shape of the mind maps and that helps me to recall the information I've written on them. Using lots of colours, sketches and doodles helps as well. I can visualise the mind-map better if I've take trouble to design it.

Jo

I get into a panic if I leave revision to the last minute, I like to draw up a plan so that I can cover all the topics in good time. I don't go as far as to set out what to do each day because I can never stick to that, but I do set myself a target for each week. I set small targets because I really feel I've achieved something when I've completed them.

Get the result!

Writing an effective introduction

Getting started on writing an answer is often the hardest part. Some students miss out introductions altogether and just get straight on into their answer, but that's a bad idea. Introductions are useful because they allow you to:

▷ explain to an examiner what you think the question means

▷ show what your thinking about the answer to the question is. That way the examiner can follow your argument in the rest of the answer.

So a good introduction to a Race and American Society answer will contain the following features:

▷ a clear understanding of what the interpretation deals with

▷ an unpacking of the interpretation – what the key words and ideas are

▷ comments about the weaknesses of the interpretation that you have spotted which could form the basis for an improvement.

Exam question

Question 1

Interpretation: Civil rights leaders played the most important part in promoting racial equality in America between 1865 and the 1970s.

Explain how far Sources 1–7 support this interpretation. You may if you wish, amend the interpretation or suggest a different interpretation. If you do this you must use the sources to support the changes you make.

Model answer

A clear opening statement. The student has unpacked the interpretation confidently and shown that there are a number of issues that can be picked up in the answer.

To improve, it might be worth explaining more fully what an amended interpretation might contain. Some comment could have been made on how individuals both helped and hindered progress.

Introduction

This interpretation deals with influential individuals who played a part in the struggle for racial equality in America. It suggests that they played the most important part in the struggle. There are two issues implicit in the hypothesis that need to be considered: the role of individuals and the role of the organisations and institutions with which they were associated. The hypothesis is not suggesting that individuals were entirely responsible for the history of the civil rights struggle but it does maintain they were the most important element. Several of the sources highlight the importance of other factors and the issues they raise might form the basis for amending the interpretation being suggested.

Using sources as evidence

To be successful in the exam you will need to read the sources carefully and extract as much relevant information and as many ideas from them as you can. When you read a source ask yourself three questions:

▷ What facts does the source contain that are relevant to the question?

▷ What opinions does the source contain that are relevant to the question?

▷ Does the source hint at anything else?

Exam question

Question 1

Interpretation: Civil rights leaders played the most important part in promoting racial equality in America between 1865 and the 1970s.

Explain how far Sources 1 and 2 support this interpretation. You may if you wish, amend the interpretation or suggest a different interpretation. If you do this you must use the sources to support the changes you make.

Source 1   An obituary for a 'race leader'

Booker T. Washington was the greatest Negro leader since Frederick Douglass, and the most distinguished man, white or black who has come out of the South since the Civil war. On the other hand, in stern justice, we must lay on the soul of this man, a heavy responsibility for the consummation of Negro disenfranchisement, the decline of the Negro college and the firmer establishment of color caste in this land.

W.E.B. Du Bois' verdict on Booker T. Washington following the latter's death in 1915, quoted in D.Paterson et al, *Civil Rights in the USA, 1863–1980*, published in 2001.

Source 2   An African American criticises the failure of blacks to organise themselves in the struggle for racial equality

A handful of men, with no report of work accomplished, no one in the field to spread it, no plan of work laid out – no intelligent direction – meet and by their child's play illustrate in their own doings the truth of the saying that Negroes have no capacity for organisation. Meanwhile a whole race is lynched, proscribed, intimidated, deprived of its political and civil rights, herded into boxes (by courtesy called separate cars)… and we sit tamely by without using the only means – that of thorough organisation and earnest work to prevent it. No wonder the world at large spits upon us with impunity.

Ida B. Wells, quoted in V. Saunders, *Race Relations in the USA 1863–1980*, published in 2006.

Model answer

The opening sentence links directly to the question, keeping the answer relevant.

Good use of short quotations.

Evidence of contextual knowledge.

Using the sources as evidence

Source 1 does not entirely confirm this interpretation. It acknowledges that Booker T. Washington was an inspirational figure, 'The greatest Negro leader... who has come out of the South since the Civil War' but it also stresses the limitations of his achievements. The writer goes on to blame Washington for being too ready to compromise with the white majority and for actually hindering progress towards equality by failing to resist 'Negro disenfranchisement'. This refers to how African Americans were deprived of the opportunity to use their right to vote by 'Jim Crow' legislation that imposed certain qualifications on this right.

Source 2 is one spokesperson's comments on the consequences of poor leadership. Without 'intelligent direction' she believes the African-American people will continue to be 'proscribed'. However it is clear from this source that she believes 'organisation' is the way forwards and that organisations, as opposed to individuals, are the means by which to prevent the world spitting 'upon us with impunity'. Thus this source does not entirely support the interpretation.

The closing sentence also links directly to the question and directs the reader towards an alternative interpretation.

Opportunities for cross-referencing were missed in this answer.

Examiner's tips

Cross-referencing

This is an important skill to demonstrate in the examination as it is one of the criteria that marks out a higher level answer.

Weaker candidates tend to approach sources one at a time, examining each carefully in turn then putting it down and moving on to the next, completely forgetting what they have just been looking at. This means that they lose any sense of development, similarities or difference between the sources they have been given.

A much more effective approach is to keep thinking about links between the sources you are reading – how does something in one source compare with information or opinions in another?

Exam question

Question 1

Interpretation: Civil rights leaders played the most important part in promoting racial equality in America between 1865 and the 1970s.

Explain how far Sources 3 and 4 support this interpretation. You may if you wish, amend the interpretation or suggest a different interpretation. If you do this you must use the sources to support the changes you make.

Source ③ An African American addresses the white elite in the South

There is no defense or security for any of us except in the highest intelligence and development of all. If anywhere there are efforts tending to curtail the fullest growth of the Negro, let these efforts be turned into stimulating, encouraging, and making him the most useful and intelligent citizen.

… nothing in thirty years has given us more hope and encouragement, and drawn us so near to you of the white race, as this opportunity offered by the Exposition… I pledge that in your effort to work out the great and intricate problem which God has laid at the doors of the South, you shall have at all times the patient, sympathetic help of my race; only let this he constantly in mind, that, while from representations in these buildings of the product of field, of forest, of mine, of factory, letters, and art, much good will come, yet far above and beyond material benefits will be that higher good, that, let us pray God, will come, in a blotting out of sectional differences and racial animosities and suspicions, in a determination to administer absolute justice, in a willing obedience among all classes to the mandates of law. This, coupled with our material prosperity, will bring into our beloved South a new heaven and a new earth.

Booker T. Washington, The Atlanta Exposition Address, 1895.

Source ④ An African American activist for racial equality comments on 'leaders' of the movement

The essence of the present situation lies in the fact that the people whom our white masters have "recognized" as our leaders (without taking the trouble to consult us) and those who, by our own selection, has actually attained to leadership among us are being revaluated and, in most cases, rejected. The most striking instance from the latter class is Dr W.E.B. Du Bois, the editor of the Crisis. Du Bois's case is the more significant because his former services to his race have been undoubtedly of a high and courageous sort.

Dr Du Bois first palpably sinned in his editorial, "Close Ranks". But this offense lies in a single sentence: "Let, us, while this war lasts, forget our special grievances and close our ranks." It is felt by all his critics that Du Bois, of all Negroes, knows best that our "special grievances", which the War Department Bulletin describes as justifiable, consists of lynching, segregation and disfranchisement and that the Negroes of America cannot preserve either their lives, their manhood or their vote (which is their political lives and liberties) with these things in existence.

Hubert Harrison, *The Voice*, published in 1918.

Model answer

Cross-referencing means drawing out points of similarity or difference between sources and the candidate has noticed two things here: the similarity of topic and difference of tone.

Additional knowledge is used to set the sources in their historical context. However, some comment could have been made on the provenance of the sources, such as the fact that Booker T. Washington's conciliatory remarks were presented to a white audience whereas Hubert Harrison was addressing the African-American readership of *The Voice* newspaper.

Cross-referencing

Both Sources 3 and 4 highlight the role of African-American leaders in the struggle for racial equality. However, only one, Source 4, suggests that they could have done more. Indeed Source 4 suggests one leader, W.E.B. Du Bois, actually threatened to hold the movement back by urging African Americans to 'forget our special grievances'. The writer of Source 4 would probably have been equally hostile to the 'gradualist' approach of Booker T. Washington who stressed co-operation rather than confrontation with the white people of America: 'you shall have at all times the patient, sympathetic help of my race'. These sources, taken together, help us to understand how some African-American civil rights activists, especially black nationalists, would have felt that both Washington and Du Bois did not go far enough in asserting the rights of their people. The sources help to explain why many African Americans found the proposals of Marcus Garvey after the First World War much more appealing. Hubert Harrison in Source 4 comments that people like Du Bois in any case are merely the people 'whom our white masters have "recognized" as our leaders', probably because, as revealed in Source 3, Du Bois and Washington were so eager to co-operate with the 'white masters'. The implication of Source 4, is that, because of the ineffectiveness of the strategy outlined in Source 3, people were looking to different leaders with different methods by the end of the First World War; people like Marcus Garvey.

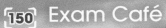

Exam question

Question 1

Interpretation: Civil rights leaders played the most important part in promoting racial equality in America between 1865 and the 1970s.

Explain how far Sources 1–7 support this interpretation. You may if you wish, amend the interpretation or suggest a different interpretation. If you do this you must use the sources to support the changes you make.

Source 5 A statement signed by W.E.B. Du Bois and 22 other African Americans in 1910

The undersigned Negro-Americans have heard, with great regret, the recent attempt to assure England and Europe that their condition in America is satisfactory. They sincerely wish that such were the case, but it becomes their plain duty to say that Mr. Booker T. Washington, or any other person, is giving the impression abroad that the Negro problem in America is in process of satisfactory solution, he is giving an impression which is not true.

We say this without personal bitterness toward Mr. Washington. He is a distinguished American and has a perfect right to his opinions. But we are compelled to point out that Mr. Washington's large financial responsibilities have made him dependent on the rich charitable public and that, for this reason, he has for years been compelled to tell, not the whole truth, but that part of it which certain powerful interests in America wish to appear as the whole truth.

Today in eight states where the bulk of the Negroes live, black men of property and university training can be, and usually are, by law denied the ballot, while the most ignorant white man votes. This attempt to put the personal and property rights of the best of the blacks at the absolute political mercy of the worst of the whites is spreading each day.

From a statement signed by W.E.B. Du Bois and 22 others, 1910.

Source 6 A speech by the leader of the UNIA facing trial for corruption

My case… is the biggest case that is to be tried in the United States Court, not only in New York, but all over the country. It is a case that involves not Marcus Garvey but the existence of the Universal Negro Improvement Association.

… Now understand that Marcus Garvey is not concerned a bit about the trial. As far as I am concerned it does not affect me as far as my work goes… my work cannot be destroyed; my work will live through the ages. (Applause.) Those who think that they can destroy Marcus Garvey are making a tremendous mistake… Let me say this: that Marcus Garvey is not afraid of hell itself, because Marcus Garvey has one conviction, and that is: until the Negro lays a foundation for his own freedom he will never have it and that there is only one way that it can be laid, and it must be laid through sacrifice, through death, through suffering (applause) and Marcus Garvey is prepared to go the whole length… when Garvey dies a million other Garveys will rise up… Marcus Garvey is satisfied that he has stirred Africa from corner to corner and Africa will take care of herself. (Applause.)

… Marcus Garvey has been the target, believing that they can destroy Garvey they can subsequently destroy the Universal Negro Improvement Association… If Garvey should die or if Garvey should be imprisoned, let them know it will be only the beginning of the work in Africa. The Negro is in no mood to be tampered with now. The Negro who died on Flanders field.

Marcus Garvey, speech at Liberty Hall, New York, 1923.

Source ⑦ Memoirs of Malcolm X

Over the ensuing years, I'd had various kinds of evidence that a high percentage of New York City's black people responded to what I said, including a great many who would not publically say so. For instance, time and again when I spoke at street rallies, I would draw ten and twelve times as many people as most other so-called 'Negro leaders'... I knew that the great lack of most of the big-named 'Negro leaders' was their lack of any true rapport with the ghetto Negroes. How could they have rapport when they spent their time 'integrating' with white people?

From Malcolm X, *The Autobiography of Malcolm X*, first published in 1965.

Model answer

Shows a clear line of thinking at the start.

Good demonstration of the scope of the hypothesis.

Re-visits earlier discussion to draw out key findings to justify conclusion.

Uses criticisms as a way of moving on to an improvement of the interpretation by reference to sources and own knowledge.

Improving an interpretation

Although there is much evidence to support the interpretation that civil rights leaders were crucial in the history of the civil rights movement, the interpretation that they were the 'most' important factor is problematic. One problem, highlighted by Sources 4, 5 and 7, is to do with definitions and the extent to which African Americans identified the same people as their leaders as white Americans. Several of the sources show how differences of opinion between the so-called leaders divided and weakened the movement. Sources 1, 4 and 7 support the view that the policy of certain leaders of co-operation and gradual integration was inappropriate and ineffective throughout the period. However, all of the sources, in one way or another, do commemorate the impact that leaders must have had. Many though are not mentioned, such as the most famous of them all, Dr Martin Luther King, and so this collection of sources, is far from complete. Other factors are revealed as important — even Marcus Garvey, in Source 6, seemed to have recognised that the organisation he led, the UNIA, was of more importance than himself. Other organisations are alluded to but many, including those of racial minorities other than the African Americans, are not. Furthermore there is no mention whatsoever in these sources of the role of presidents, politicians and judges in promoting and hindering the civil rights' struggle. This is a serious omission. Consequently it can be concluded that, as a set, the sources do broadly support the interpretation but, because this collection of sources is so incomplete, this does not prove the validity of the interpretation. The evidence in fact points to the interpretation that civil rights leaders played <u>an</u> important part in promoting racial equality in America between 1865 and the 1970s, but not necessarily the 'most' important part.

Assessing usefulness

The part (b) question in the exam will ask you to discuss the usefulness to an historian of the sources you have been given. It is very important not to produce a pre-learned answer to this question but to apply your understanding of the value of the sources to the specific ones on the exam paper. Also, think about the sources as a set as well as looking at them individually. Ask yourself the question: if these were all the sources we had on this topic, what uses could they be put to?

Among the issues you could discuss are the following.

How the sources reveal information and opinions about:

The different experiences of people in the North and South of America

▷ Changes over time

▷ Different perceptions of the 'race' issue

▷ Different ways of tackling the 'race' issue

▷ The involvement of different groups of people in the civil rights movement.

You could also comment on:

▷ the variety of viewpoints contained in the set of sources

▷ the ways in which the sources can be used to support different interpretations

▷ the ways in which the sources can be used to answer different questions.

Merging usefulness and problems

As well as considering ways in which the set of sources can be useful to an historian, you will also be asked to consider what problems and issues they raise.

Once again, beware of producing a pre-prepared answer because what you say MUST be directly related to the sources you are given in the exam.

Among the issues you could discuss are the following:

Gaps and omissions in the set of sources – are any of the main people and organisations in the history of race and American society missing? Does it make a difference if they are?

Typicality – how representative are the sources of the range available on this topic? Would there have been any better types of sources to have chosen?

Reliability – based on the content and provenance of the sources, are there any issues of reliability to be considered (remember not simply to dismiss a source as 'biased')?

Exam question

Question 1

(b) Explain how these sources are both useful and raise problems and issues for an historian using them.

Merging usefulness and problems

An historian would find these sources useful for many reasons including the range of coverage, the variety of viewpoints, the different interpretations they offer and questions they can answer. However, although they are all relevant to the issue of leadership, the sources also raise problems. In particular, they are incomplete, they are not representative of all of the leaders involved in the civil rights struggle and they do not cover all of the elements that determined the history of race and American society between 1865 and the 1970s.

They represent a range of different viewpoints including those of civil rights leaders themselves as well as their critics. This provides some useful opportunities to compare and contrast different points of view: Malcolm X in Source 7, for example, had much in common with the views of Hubert Harrison in Source 4, even though these sources were forty years apart. Comparisons can be made between the strategies of leaders and their effectiveness – the integration policy of Booker T. Washington (Source 1), for example, and the non-integration policy of Malcolm X (Source 7). Although they are mostly concerned with the issue of leadership some of the sources, such as Source 6, provide information about the organisations, the UNIA, that the leaders represented.

This set of sources is also a diverse one in terms of type of source. It includes extracts from an autobiography (Source 7), speeches (e.g. Source 1) and newspaper articles (Source 4). It is useful to read the opinions of the leaders themselves (e.g. Sources 6 and 7). However, most of the sources could be described as 'propaganda' and as such the historian needs to recognise the possibility of exaggeration and exclusion of information in their analysis. For example, it would be foolish to assume that Malcolm X was so much more popular than other leaders in Harlem simply because he said so in Source 7. Furthermore, the apparent confidence of Marcus Garvey and his claim that 'The Negro is in no mood to be tampered with now', in

Side annotations:

- Sets an agenda of points.
- Introduces balance in the answer from the start.
- Uses evidence from the sources to support claims. Specific sources used are identified as they are used.
- Avoids a source by source approach – focuses on issues instead and so pulls together related material from various sources.
- Good awareness of both usefulness and inherent problems.

Source 6, is surprising and misleading since when he made this statement he was on the brink of imprisonment for corruption and his movement, the UNIA, was going into a rapid decline.

The set of sources spans much of the period although it does not cover the late 19th century and there is only one source from the period after the Second World War. The most serious omission is that one type of leader – the President – is not mentioned at all. Furthermore there is little direct comment on the big issues that helped determine the history of race and American society in the period, such as the Great Migration, the Depression, and the two World Wars. Also some of the most influential civil rights leaders, such as Bobby Seale and Dr Martin Luther King, are not mentioned by name. Furthermore there is no mention of several of the important organisations that such people represented, such as the NAACP and the Black Panthers. This is important since, as Garvey implies in Source 6 and Malcolm X made clear in his autobiography (Source 7), some leaders were eager to tell their supporters that the organisation was more important than its individual leaders. Equally there is no mention of the brave individuals, such as Rosa Parks and James Meredith, who were not leaders as such, but made a significant contribution nevertheless. Another problem is that all of the sources are concerned with the African-American struggle for civil rights; there is no mention of the other racial communities that were discriminated against such as Asian Americans, Hispanic Americans, and Native Americans.

Recognises gaps and omissions.

Relates the problem to the wider historical context and reveals sound knowledge of the subject.

Good consideration of reliability without slipping into common mistakes about 'bias'.

More direct quotation from the sources would have been useful.

Writing about bias

This can be a significant learning trouble spot for students. There are two common mistakes.

▷ *The knee-jerk response* – the moment a student comes across bias in a source, a reflex reaction kicks in. The reaction goes something like this – because there is bias in the source, that must be a bad thing which means that the source is useless because what it says can't be trusted.

▷ *The skimmer's response* – this is the other extreme; the student doesn't question sources at all, but just sails along taking everything at face value and seeing the point of the exercise as only to go looking for facts in the sources.

Instead, treat sources more subtly by understanding that BIAS ISN'T NECESSARILY BAD. When you're dealing with sources, think critically about them – but that doesn't mean just thinking negatively. Bias in a source will give you valuable evidence about ideas and attitudes.

Ignoring key terms

Make sure that you spend time finding and defining the key terms in the interpretation. Defining terms is a good way to get at the heart of an answer. Don't leave words like 'success' hanging. Make sure you explain what you think they mean, then use your definition as a focus for your analysis.

Refresh your memory

Revision techniques

According to books on study skills, there is an ideal approach to revising that involves devising a schedule so that everything is covered in good time to avoid cramming, breaking work down into small chunks of learning and revising in an active way by producing summaries, planning answers and self-testing rather than just reading and re-reading your notes. However, revision is a personal thing and you should not get depressed if you can't follow all the advice you're given. What's important is to develop good habits and not to fool yourself into thinking that last minute cramming will get you that brilliant grade you're after.

Exam technique

With all the pressure of taking an exam, it can be easy to forget some of the basic things that you should be doing in your answers.

Bring highlighters with you so that you can mark up the sources: one colour for evidence in support of the interpretation; one for the evidence against. Don't be afraid to write all over the exam paper while you are reading the sources –

putting ideas, extra information and summaries in the margins really can help.

This unit assesses the nature and status of historical evidence and its use in testing interpretations. It focuses on historical enquiry of a topic over a period of approximately 100 years.

The examination you will take for this unit is 1 hour 30 minutes long, It consists of an interpretation and a set of 5–7 sources (which could be written, statistical and/or visual).You will be asked two questions:

Question (a) will ask you to judge the validity of the interpretation using the sources and your own knowledge to guide your comments. To achieve higher marks you will be encouraged to think of ways of amending and improving the interpretation you have been given. This question is marked out of a maximum of 35 (so is worth 70 per cent of the total mark for this exam).

Question (b) will ask you to analyse the source material you have been given. Examiners will expect you to comment on the usefulness of the sources and any problems using them might create. This question is marked out of a maximum of 15 (so is worth 30 per cent of the total mark for this exam).

Keep an eye on the time – you have two questions to answer in this exam, one worth 35 marks, the other 15. Make sure that you divide your time appropriately – perhaps spend 15 minutes reading the sources and planning your answers, then 50 minutes on part (a) and 25 minutes on part (b).

It's probably best to stick to the order that questions appear on the paper rather than beginning with (b).This is because the (a) question is all about debating what can be learned from the sources, so it will provide some of the ideas you need for (b). As a planning tip, keep thinking about (b) as you are working on (a) and jot down any issues about the sources that you want to come back to in that answer.

Make sure that you present evidence FOR and AGAINST the interpretation offered in the question. Don't just stick to the side you think is best. You need to really explore the strengths and limitations of the interpretation you have been given.

Try to use ALL the available evidence, not just a few sources. If you find that the interpretation works best for a particular group of sources, say so! That might be a way into refining the interpretation later.

Don't use the sources one at a time. The worst answers start with source 1, then move on to source 2 and so on. It's far better to treat the sources in groups. Where two or more sources agree about something, point it out. Where there is a contradiction between several sources, point it out. Keep moving between the sources in your answer to show that you can cross-reference them. Use the sources as a set, to be analysed together.

Revision checklist

The most important skills you have developed through the study of this unit are:

▷ the analysis and evaluation of sources

▷ the forming and testing of hypotheses

Historians analyse a range of sources, all of which have value *and* present problems to the historian. These include:

▷ The evidence of official documents

▷ The evidence of newspapers

▷ The evidence of political cartoons

▷ The evidence of statistics and distribution maps

▷ The evidence of personal accounts

▷ The evidence of novels

▷ The evidence of films

▷ The evidence of photographs

▷ The evidence of popular music

The struggle for and against civil rights in America involved:

▷ Federal legislation

▷ State legislation

▷ Violent forms of protest

▷ Peaceful forms of protest

Historians, for convenience, divide the history of race and society in America between 1865 and the 1970s into periods defined by what are perceived to be the prevailing attitudes of the time. These include:

▷ The Reconstruction era

▷ The 'Jim Crow' years

▷ The era of the New Deal

▷ The post-war Civil Rights Movement

Key pieces of federal legislation in the struggle for civil rights in America include:

▷ the 13th, 14th and 15th Amendments to the American Constitution

▷ the Civil Rights Act of 1875

▷ the Dawes Act of 1887

▷ the Civil Rights Act of 1957

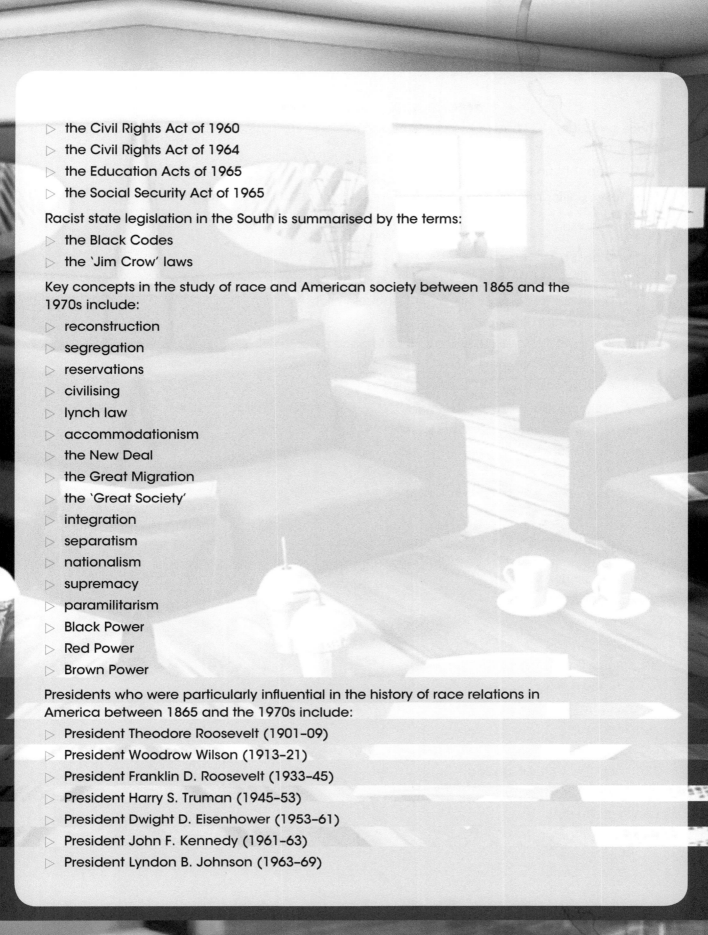

> the Civil Rights Act of 1960
> the Civil Rights Act of 1964
> the Education Acts of 1965
> the Social Security Act of 1965

Racist state legislation in the South is summarised by the terms:

> the Black Codes
> the 'Jim Crow' laws

Key concepts in the study of race and American society between 1865 and the 1970s include:

> reconstruction
> segregation
> reservations
> civilising
> lynch law
> accommodationism
> the New Deal
> the Great Migration
> the 'Great Society'
> integration
> separatism
> nationalism
> supremacy
> paramilitarism
> Black Power
> Red Power
> Brown Power

Presidents who were particularly influential in the history of race relations in America between 1865 and the 1970s include:

> President Theodore Roosevelt (1901–09)
> President Woodrow Wilson (1913–21)
> President Franklin D. Roosevelt (1933–45)
> President Harry S. Truman (1945–53)
> President Dwight D. Eisenhower (1953–61)
> President John F. Kennedy (1961–63)
> President Lyndon B. Johnson (1963–69)

These presidents led one of two political parties:

▷ The Democrat Party
▷ The Republican Party

The most significant organisations in the history of race and American society include:

▷ the National Association of Colored Women (NACW)
▷ the Niagara Movement
▷ the National Association for the Advancement of Colored People (NAACP)
▷ the Universal Negro Improvement Association (UNIA)
▷ the Ku Klux Klan (KKK)
▷ the Southern Christian Leadership Conference (SCLC)
▷ the Student Non-violent Coordinating Committee (SNCC)
▷ the Congress of Racial Equality (CORE)
▷ the National Indian Youth Council (NIYC)
▷ the National Farm Workers' Union (NFWA)
▷ the Nation of Islam (NOI)
▷ the Black Panthers
▷ the American Indian Movement (AIM)
▷ the Alianza
▷ the Brown Berets

The strategies adopted by organisations associated with the struggle for civil rights included:

▷ education
▷ charity
▷ propaganda
▷ intimidation
▷ violence
▷ boycotts
▷ strikes

Important 'race leaders' and other racial equality activists in America between 1865 and the 1970s included:

▷ Booker T. Washington
▷ W.E.B. Du Bois
▷ Marcus Garvey
▷ Oliver Brown

- ▷ Kenneth B. Clark
- ▷ The Little Rock Nine
- ▷ Daisy Bates
- ▷ Rosa Parks
- ▷ Martin Luther King
- ▷ Ella Baker
- ▷ Janet McCloud
- ▷ James Farmer
- ▷ César Chávez
- ▷ Adam Clayton Powell
- ▷ Malcolm X
- ▷ Huey Newton
- ▷ Clyde Bellecourt
- ▷ Reies López Tijerina

Historians ask questions of the evidence they have. When considering the role of 'race leaders', these include:

- ▷ What motivated this individual?
- ▷ What impact did this individual have upon other people?
- ▷ Would the history of race relations have been significantly different without this individual's involvement?
- ▷ How reliant upon these individuals were the organisations with which they were associated?

Non-violent strategies associated with civil rights protests include:

- ▷ Campaigns against school segregation
- ▷ Bus boycotts
- ▷ Civil rights marches
- ▷ Sit-ins
- ▷ Fish-ins
- ▷ Freedom Rides
- ▷ Strikes
- ▷ Hunger-strikes

Examiner's tips

It is important to remember that OCR History B is a **skills-based** course and examination. As well as demonstrating a sound level of knowledge, examiners will expect you to understand and make use of a series of skills including source evaluation. Students often find this a difficult balancing act. To achieve your best, remember that the topic knowledge you have built up is there to act as the context for your work on the sources in the examination.

The following shows the general mark-scheme for Levels 4 and 5 of Question (a) in the examination.

	AO 1: Knowledge and understanding	AO 2a: Interpretation of sources	AO 2b: Historical interpretations
Level 5	Uses sound knowledge and understanding of changes and developments across the period to evaluate sources. Uses appropriate historical terminology accurately. Structure of argument is coherent. Writing is legible. **13–15**	Evaluates sources of evidence in their historical context: makes sophisticated inferences from the sources, makes an informed use of the provenance of the sources and cross-references the sources to reach a reasoned and supported conclusion. **9–10**	Shows a sound understanding that interpretations are dependant on the available evidence and how it is interpreted. Suggests and justifies, through a sophisticated use of sources and knowledge, an amended or alternative interpretation. **9–10**
Level 4	Uses knowledge and understanding of changes and developments across the period to make inferences from sources. Uses historical terminology accurately. Structure of argument is clear. Writing is legible. **10–12**	Evaluates evidence from sources in their historical context: makes inferences from the sources, makes an informed use of the provenance of the sources or cross-references the sources to reach a supported conclusion. **7–8**	Shows an understanding that interpretations are dependant on the evidence that is inferred from sources. Uses interpretations of the sources to support and challenge the interpretation and reaches an overall conclusion. **7–8**

Think about the following.

1. In AO 1 there is a difference between drawing inferences from sources and evaluating them. What does each term mean?

2. In AO 1 there is a reference to accurate use of 'historical terminology' – can you give examples of specialised terms used in this unit that an examiner would expect you to be confident at using?

3. In AO 2a both levels talk about evaluating sources in context – what is 'context'?

4. In AO 2a there is an additional element at Level 5 – 'informed use of the provenance of the sources' – what does this mean?

5. What additional steps are needed at Level 5 in AO 2b?

One way of meeting the criteria in AO 2b is to find the key that unlocks the interpretation. It is impossible to find a fool-proof method for doing this, but generally speaking, you will need to look for and make something of:

▷ a worrying word in the interpretation

▷ a source that doesn't fit

▷ something missing from the sources.

The following shows the general mark-scheme for Levels 4 and 5 of Question (b) in the examination.

	AO 1: Knowledge and understanding	AO 2a: Analysis of sources
Level 5	Good and detailed knowledge and understanding of the characteristics of the period and changes and developments across the period, used to support analysis of sources. 5	Explains, with examples from most of the sources, that the value of sources depends on the purpose of the historian, the questions being asked, different interpretations of the sources and judgements about the typicality, purpose and reliability of the sources. Candidates will explain both the value and the problems associated with using these sources. Candidates will also show knowledge of the range of sources used for studying this period. 9–10
Level 4	Reasonable knowledge and understanding of the main characteristics of the period and the main changes and developments across the period used to support analysis of the sources. 4	Explains, with examples from some of the sources, that the value of sources depends on most of the following issues: the purpose of the historian, the questions being asked, different interpretations of the sources and judgements about the typicality, purpose and reliability of the sources. Candidates will explain both the value and the problems associated with using these sources even if one side of the explanation is stronger than the other. Candidates will show awareness of some of the types of sources used for studying this period. 7–8

Again, notice the differences, especially in AO 2a.

1. You are given a list of possible elements that could show whether you understand what controls the value that historians place on sources. What is the difference in how the list is presented between levels 4 and 5?

2. The level 5 statement for AO 2 makes a stronger point of two other features of top-scoring answers. What are these?

Glossary

Accommodationism – a word, often used derisively, to describe a willingness to compromise the struggle for political and legal racial equality in order to achieve economic advances for minority races.

African Americans – formerly known by such problematic terms as 'Negro Americans' or 'Black Americans', this term is accepted, presently, as the best way to describe American citizens who are identified as, or identify themselves as, having ancestors who originated in the African continent.

American Constitution – this is the list of 'rules' according to which America is governed.

AIM – American Indian Movement formed in 1968.

Black Codes – legislation in the Southern states, evolving into the 'Jim Crow' laws, that undermined endeavours in the post-Civil War 'Reconstruction' era to promote racial equality.

Black Panthers – paramilitary Black Power movement formed in 1966.

Black Power – a term coined to describe the ideas and actions of African Americans that are based upon pride in their racial heritage and their determination to advance and/or assert their position in society.

Brown Berets – paramilitary Brown Power movement formed in the later 1960s.

Brown Power – a term coined to describe the ideas and actions of Hispanic Americans that are based upon pride in their racial heritage and their determination to advance and/or assert their position in society.

BSCP – the Brotherhood of Sleeping Car Porters, a trade union for black railway workers formed in 1925.

BSL – The Black Star Line steamship company set up by Marcus Garvey in 1919 to promote international commerce and unity among black people.

Chicano – people of Mexican origin living outside of Mexico. Originally a term of abuse, it came to be used by Mexican Americans with pride.

Chinatowns – ghettos in American cities inhabited mainly by people of Chinese origin.

Civil Rights Movement – term usually used to describe the struggle for equality in post-Second World War America.

Confederate – the Confederate states were those that broke away from the United States and fought against the North in the Civil War.

CORE – the Congress of Racial Equality established in 1942 by James Farmer.

CPUSA – the Communist Party of the United States of America.

Disenfranchised – to be deprived of the right to vote.

Federation – the Federal Government serves a 'federation' (grouping) of the 50 separate states that form the USA.

Fish-ins – acts of civil disobedience in the later 1960s to protect the livings of Native-American people who relied on fishing the Quillayute and Nisqually rivers.

Freedom Marchers – civil rights activists who joined protest marches.

Freedom Rides – well-publicised journeys by bus in which activists exercised their civil rights, and risked racist violence, by sitting where they liked on buses.

Garveyist – Attitudes in line with the views of Marcus Garvey.

Ghettoes – communities based upon common ethnic backgrounds and cultures and living in a closely-defined area.

Gilded Age – a phase of unprecedented industrial growth in late 19th century America.

the 'Great Migration' – internal migration, particularly in the inter-war years, in which large numbers of people, including a high proportion of African Americans moved from the rural South to industrial cities, particularly in the North.

the 'Great Society' – President Johnson's vision for America in the 1960s.

Hispanic Americans – American citizens with Spanish American origins.

Integrationist – the concept of people of different racial origins mixing in the workplace and in public spaces.

'Jim Crow' – laws passed in the southern states of America from the later 19th century legalising the segregation of African Americans and white Americans.

KKK (The Ku Klux Klan) – a white-supremacist organisation founded in the South in the late 1860s.

the Leakeys – Louis Leakey and his wife Mary were archaeologists who played a pivotal role in developing the 'out of Africa' concept – the idea that all human beings can trace their ancestry back to the African continent.

Lynch mob – a crowd of people intent on punishing without a fair trial, usually by hanging, an individual accused of a serious misdemeanour.

MIA – the Montgomery Improvement Association, led by Martin Luther King, was established in 1956 to co-ordinate the Montgomery bus boycott campaign.

Miscegenation – inter-racial marriages.

NAACP – the National Association for the Advancement of Colored People formed in 1909.

NACW – The National Association of Colored Women formed in 1896.

'Native Americans' – term now used to describe the aboriginals of the northern part of the American continent, once known as 'Red Indians'. In the first half of the 20th century, it denoted those of descent from the first British settlers.

New Deal – series of economic initiatives to combat America's economic depression taken by the administration of President Roosevelt from 1933.

NFWU – the National Farm Workers' Union formed in 1962 by César Chávez.

the Niagara Movement – founded by a group of 32 African-American intellectuals in 1905 at a location near Niagara Falls.

NIYC – the National Indian Youth Council.

the Panic – a period of economic depression lasting from 1893 until 1896.

the Plains Wars – series of conflicts between the US Army and Native Americans in the 1860s.

Provenance – where something, e.g. a piece of historical evidence, comes from.

Ratify – ratification is the process by which proposed constitutional changes receive approval from the peoples' representatives in Congress and become law.

Reconstruction – the decade of reform and reconstruction after the American Civil War that promoted racial equality, primarily, through three amendments to the Constitution.

Red Power – a term coined to describe the ideas and actions of Native Americans that are based upon pride in their racial heritage and their determination to advance and/or assert their position in society.

Rhetoric – language, such as that of presidential election campaign speeches, that is designed to persuade.

SCLC – Southern Christian Leadership Conference formed in 1958 by Martin Luther King.

Separation of powers – Federal government in America is divided into the Presidency, the Congress, and the Courts. Each has specific powers and responsibilities. This 'separation of powers' is replicated in each state.

Separatists: – term used to describe any white and non-white Americans who believed that the integration of the races was either wrong or impractical.

Sit-ins – the strategy whereby segregated areas, such as whites-only lunch counters, were occupied by protesters, refusing to move until the managers agreed to desegregation.

SNCC – Student Nonviolent Coordinating Committee formed in 1960 by Ella Baker.

Uncle Toms – term used in the 1960s as a term of derision for African Americans prepared to make compromises in the struggle for equal rights.

UNIA – Marcus Garvey's Universal Negro Improvement Association established in 1914 by Marcus Garvey.

WASPs – 'White Anglo-Saxon Protestants'.

White supremacists – those who believe that people of Caucasian ethnic origin are superior, for example, intellectually, to the other races.

Bibliography

Bates, D. (1962), *The Long Shadow of Little Rock: a Memoir*, David Mackay Company

Bosmajian, H. and Bosmajian, H. (1969), *The Rhetoric of the Civil-Rights Movement*, Random House

Carson C., Garrow D.J., Gill G., Harding V., Hine D.K. (1991), *The Eyes on the Prize Civil Rights Reader*, Penguin

Davis, J.E. (2001), *The Civil Rights Movement*, Blackwell

Dierenfield, B.J. (2004), *The Civil Rights Movement*, Longman

Engelbert, P. (1999), *American Civil Rights: Primary Sources*, U.X.L.

Franklin, J.R. and Starr, I. (eds) (1967), *The Negro in Twentieth Century America*, Random House

George, N, 'Black Beauty, Black Confusion (1965–70)'. In Floyd Windom Hayes (2000), *A Turbulent Voyage: Readings in African American Studies*, Rowman & Littlefield

King, M.L. (ed.) (1964), *Why We Can't Wait*, Signet

Levy, J. (1975), *César Chávez: Autobiography of La Causa*, W. W. Norton

Malcolm X. and Haley, A. (1965, 2001), *The Autobiography of Malcolm X*, Penguin

Nabakov, P. (1991), *Native American Testimony: a Chronicle of Indian-White Relations from Prophecy to the Present, 1492–1992*, Viking

Paterson, D., Willoughby, D., Willoughby, S. (2001), *Civil Rights in the USA, 1863–1980*, Heinemann

Saunders, V. (2006), *Race Relations in the USA 1863–1980*, Hodder Murray

Thompson, P. (1988), *The Voice of the Past*, Oxford University Press

Verney, K. (2000), *Black Civil Rights in America*, Routledge

Index

Index